America's
Library

1800–2000

Foreword *by James H. Billington*
Introduction *by Edmund Morris*

Yale University Press, New Haven and London
in association with The Library of Congress, Washington, D.C.

America's Library

The Story of the Library of Congress

1800–2000

James Conaway

Designed by Mary M. Mayer
Set in Bembo type by Amy Storm
Printed in Singapore by CS Graphics

Library of Congress Cataloging-in-Publication Data
Conaway, James.
    America's library: the story of the Library of Congress,
    1800–2000/James Conaway; foreword by James H. Billington;
    introduction by Edmund Morris.
        p. cm.
    Includes bibliographical references (p.) and index.
    ISBN 0-300-08308-4
    1. Library of Congress—History. 2. National libraries—
    Washington (D.C.)—History—19th century. 3. National
    libraries—Washington (D.C.)—History—20th century.
    I. Library of Congress. II. Title.
Z733.U6 C595 2000
027.573—dc21   99-058751 (alk. paper)

A catalogue record for this book is available from the British
Library.

10 9 8 7 6 5 4 3 2 1

Title page illustration: U.S. Capitol by John Rubens Smith,
ca. 1829 (see p. 37).

Contents

Foreword

Two hundred years ago, the United States was taking its first shaky steps toward becoming a great democratic nation. Born out of revolution and defined by an independent spirit, the new country was guided by extraordinary people whose ideals had been shaped by the precepts and attitudes of the Enlightenment—among them reliance on reason, belief in progress, and a profound appreciation for the importance of knowledge in an ever-changing world. "Knowledge will forever govern ignorance," James Madison wrote in 1822. "And a people who mean to be their own governours, must arm themselves with the power which knowledge brings."

In 1800, the Congress of the United States established a Congressional Library to help provide it with the information required to make laws for this boisterous and expanding country. Under a series of devoted Librarians of Congress and a Library staff that grew as the institution did, the Library expanded and changed to meet the challenges inherent in being not only a resource for Congress but also, increasingly, the national library of the United States and one of the world's great intellectual and cultural resources. The initial collection of a few hundred books and three maps has grown into diverse collections numbering over 115 million items—and we continue to acquire many thousands of items each year.

Treasures both humble and sublime are housed within the Library's three buildings: four-thousand-year-old clay tablets providing information on Sumeria's economy are cared for here, as are sixteenth-century holograph music scores, seventeenth-century scientific treatises, eighteenth-century fine prints and political cartoons, photographs and dime novels from the nineteenth century, and twentieth-century motion pictures, television shows, and CD-ROMs. Reflecting America's history, as well as this country's membership in the community of nations, our collections come from around the world.

Researchers from other nations are made welcome here along with the hundreds of thousands of Americans who visit our buildings—their buildings, and their collections—each year. Around the globe, many millions more visit us on the Internet. As the twenty-first century begins, we have made more than five million items from our collections accessible on our Web pages, and this will increase. Entering our third century of service to Congress, the nation, and the international community, the Library of Congress continues to be guided by the belief in the power of knowledge that inspired its creation.

In *America's Library*, James Conaway invites you to learn the story of this great and complex institution, from its creation through the first two centuries of its development, as the men and women within its walls worked to collect, preserve, and make useful the heritage it holds. Its collections represent and celebrate the many and varied ways that one generation has informed another. We invite you to visit us—through this book and our other publications, in person, or by means of the Internet. In all these ways, we hope you will share this priceless legacy.

James H. Billington
Librarian of Congress

Author's Note

Many people at the Library of Congress assisted me in the completion of this book and I would like to thank them all. The Librarian, James H. Billington, was forthcoming with his views and assessments. John Y. Cole, Director of the Center for the Book, offered early encouragement and critical information and guidance throughout. Ralph Eubanks, Director of Publishing, strongly supported and shepherded the project. A special debt of gratitude is owed to my editor, Evelyn Sinclair, for her tireless research and crucial advice in all stages of the book's development. Thanks also to Blaine Marshall for diligently seeking out the best illustrations for this unique, invaluable American story.

At Yale University Press, where the publishing of this book was carried forward, I want to thank Judy Metro, who managed the project, Dakota Shepard, Jeffrey Schier, and, above all, Mary Mayer, who is responsible for the design and production of the book. Thanks to Alexa Selph for indexing it. The cover design is by Lance Hidy, who gave us the gift of his imagination, enthusiasm, and artistic talent. We are grateful that he joined in the endeavor.

One Writer's Library

To work in the circular, central reading room of the Library of Congress is to get the surreal impression that one is inside Thomas Jefferson's cerebellum. This vast yet intimate space literally was designed, a century ago, around our third president's book collection, which he conveyed to the nation under circumstances that will be related in the following pages. Brain-like, it silently throbs with knowledge. Invisible connections—fact to fact, thought to thought, thesis to antithesis—flash back and forth at who knows how many million times a minute, whenever we lesser scholars (mere cell clusters in comparison!) puzzle out our own connections below.

One also has the notion, after the skylights have darkened and that spell-breaking call, "The Library is now closed" has echoed through the room, that—just as Jefferson's brain presumably never stopped while he slept—the silent intellectual exchange will continue all the night. For books do talk to books, in an osmotic sort of way, at least when they are juxtaposed in the Library of Congress's unique groupings—subjects thematically sequential, authors deliberately dissociated in alphabetical order. Else why, under this dome as no other, does one return to one's seat for another day of research with a sense of new possibilities opening up, fresh ideas proliferating even before one cracks the first volume on overnight hold?

Thirty-three years ago I came to the Library of Congress as a young, would-be biographer anxious to learn as much as could be learned about Theodore Roosevelt (after Jefferson, without question the most cerebral of our presidents, and himself an avid patron). The Manuscript Division then occupied a pleasant room in the Adams Building, with big lockers outside ample for the storage of my suitcase. I lived in New York on the usual scribe's pittance, and research time was so precious that I habitually did without lunch, and drank as little water as possible from the corridor fountain. The documents emerging sheet by sheet from "pulled" boxes (this was before the age of mass microfilming) were so fascinating to read, and so tactile in their perfect state of preservation, that I felt myself to be living all day long in the nineteenth century—a state of "time out of mind" familiar to most biographers.

For some reason I recall as a particularly evocative discovery, not an item that tumbled out of a Roosevelt box but an envelope in the collection of William McKinley. (Already the osmotic impulse was at work, and my researches were leading from one collection to the next.) The envelope contained nothing but a swatch of white silk strips, still lustrous after seventy-eight years, each carefully signed "Wm. McKinley." They were probably presidential keepsakes, handed out to important White House visitors, much as ballpoint pens are today. But their cool lightness in my hand, and the slight bleed of those repetitive signatures, made me feel I was back in "the days of McKinley"—to borrow the title of Margaret Leech's great biography, also researched here.

I remember marveling, as I slipped the swatch back into its envelope, that the privilege of being able to find it and touch it and think about it, and maybe make literary use of it some day, was free, a gift of Congress to me as an American citizen. Minor as the find was, it might just as easily have been major, as when Daniel J. Boorstin, appointed Librarian of Congress in 1975, opened a little safe in the Jefferson Building and discovered the last contents of Abraham Lincoln's pockets, forgotten for more than a century. We were both of us—Librarian and lowly scribe—beneficiaries of the world's most generous cornucopia of cultural and historical riches.

The Manuscript Division has long since moved out of Adams, to new quarters in the Madison Building—third and largest (so far) of the Library's ever-growing complex. Dr. Boorstin has been succeeded by James Billington, as Dr. Billington will himself one day give way to another in the long line of Librarians of Congress. Every time I wander back into the Main Reading Room (and I have been doing so, now, practically once a week, often every day, for two decades), I am enriched. A textbook of metallurgy lying open beside a copying machine will hypnotize me with the cold precision of its language, yielding a phrase or two which may come in for metaphorical use some day. A poster by an elevator will direct me to a lecture on repetitive stress syndrome, or a seminar on medieval cartography. A display cabinet of French daguerreotypes will remind me that Cléo de Mérode was the most beautiful woman who has ever lived.

But such encounters are mere serendipity. Perhaps I can best convey the Library's limitless powers to inform, inspire, and stretch the mind by citing some of the intellectual journeys it has sent me on as a freelance writer. The reader should bear in mind that I am but one of uncounted millions of scholar gypsies, all with their own travel stories to tell.

There were, to begin with, the private diaries of Theodore Roosevelt, which he kept almost daily as a college student and young New York State assembly-man from 1876 to 1884. I had seen extracts from them in the writings of many Roosevelt scholars, but nothing in biographical research compares with the actual perusal of words written, long ago, by a living hand on paper which physically responded to it (the pages tending to buckle on days when either he or the weather was hot). I read them through, day by day and year by year, and in the process developed an almost physical intimacy with my subject: looking over his shoulder, as it were, and sharing the thoughts that spilled out of his pen. Thus, when he curtly addressed posterity on his honeymoon night with beau-tiful Alice Hathaway Lee ("our happiness is too sacred to be written about"), I felt myself reprimanded for being a voyeur—which is indeed what every biographer is at heart. And when he later drew a huge cross from corner to corner of the page dated February 14, 1884, those two despairing slashes spoke more eloquently of bereavement (Alice had just died of Bright's disease) than his additional scrawled notation: "The light has gone out of my life."

Just as eloquent, if less consciously autobiographical, was the extraordinary archive of receipts amassed some fourteen years later when TR, as assistant sec-retary of the navy, was a member of a luncheon group trying to overcome the McKinley administration's resistance to a war with Spain over Cuba. Every one of these almost daily receipts was for "double lamb chops." Unremarkable in themselves, they together painted a portrait of a man so obsessed with politi-cal intrigue that he regarded food as mere fuel.

The contemporary policy of the Library of Congress is no longer to accept such ephemera in collections. No doubt this makes storage sense, in an age when public figures are accumulating more and more pieces of paper (and writing less and less on them), but future biographers will be the poorer.

Eighteen years ago my wife embarked on a biography of Clare Boothe Luce, whose manuscript collection (larger than those of many presidents) is one of the Library's most important twentieth-century archives. Massive as it is, it has the lacunae that always seem to frustrate biographers, no matter how many other papers spill out of boxes. A 1928 obituary of Mrs. Luce's father—a bril-liant musician who spent much of his life as a traveling salesman—mentioned that at the time of his death in Los Angeles, he had been working on a series of transcendental exercises for the violin, playable only by performers of Paganini-like technique. There was no indication in the obituary, nor indeed anywhere else in the Luce collection, as to what had happened to this improb-able-sounding manuscript.

My wife mentioned it to me one day in the Madison Building cafeteria. Acting on what I can only describe as a scholarly whim, I dropped into the

Music Division, six floors down, riffled through a card catalog, and in less than a minute found the entry, "BOOTHE, William Franklin—Fingered Octaves and Primary Extension Exercises. Unpublished pencil and ink ms., 18 pp., 1931. Gift of Ruth Paddock Hutchinson, December, 1931." Fifteen minutes later—about as long as it took for me to summon my wife from the nearby Manuscript Division—the precious artifact was in her hands. Meanwhile, a new avenue of research was opening up: who was the mysterious Mrs. Hutchinson, and why should she have chosen to deposit these eighteen fly-specked sheets here, unaware that William Boothe's daughter would also enrich the Library of Congress one day?

Thus go the endless byways of biography.

When the Madison Building was first opened in 1980, one of its most tempting new features was an array of "reading rooms" in the Music Division, equipped with Steinway pianos and massively soundproofed walls. Lacking an instrument at home, I became a habitué of these rooms, rejoicing particularly in the big grand in no. 11. Library regulations grant free access to such instruments, providing they are used for serious study of materials in the Music Division's holdings. Thus, when researching an essay on the Romantic Piano for the *New Yorker*, I was able to explore the works of Ferrucio Busoni *seriatim*, and write about them from the perspective of a piano player who had literally "felt" his way through that strange composer's harmonies.

While serving as a freelance music critic for the *Washington Post*, I used the Music Division to prepare for assigned concerts. I have held in my hands—even furtively sniffed—the speckled manuscript of Anton von Webern's 1938 String Quartet. To see the precision with which Webern inked every note with its attendant accidental (like the scintilla of a sparklet), and then to hear those notes materialize as music five hours later (skittering and whispering in the Kennedy Center's Terrace Theater) is to experience the miracle of musical creation, from mind to hand to paper to bow to string to sound.

This essay, I notice, constantly evokes tactile values, nothing being more "primary" in archival research than contact between source and scholar. The microfilm machine and the computer screen, not to mention *fin de siècle* needs for security and preservation, are making such moments of total empathy less and less attainable. More's the pity. But the Library of Congress, through the sheer quantity of its holdings, still offers abundant opportunities to "only connect."

I recall, for example, the timbre of Justice Oliver Wendell Holmes's ninety-year-old voice reverberating in my earphones, on a morning in the Recorded Sound Section when I also listened to a recording of Rosa Ponselle singing

Verdi in 1933, and Ronald Reagan breathily informing the National Press Club in 1971 that Washington was a nice place, "but I wouldn't want to live here."

Each of these auditory experiences gave life to sentences or phrases in literary projects I was working on at the time. On other occasions, I have pored over fire insurance maps of midwestern villages, so minutely detailed that one can count the windows of every house and tell whether they were glazed or screened; the purplish pages of a run of the London *Daily Mirror*, published at the height of the Blitz and remarkable for the size of its laxative advertisements; boxes of Depression-era glossies by the great WPA photographer Marion Post Wolcott, some so freshly preserved they still give off a faint reek of the darkroom; obscene, uproarious, feverishly inventive counterculture "comix" from the radical sixties; politico-satirical poems from the age of Samuel Johnson; and a complete sequence of translations of Wolfram von Eschenbach's *Parzival*, which the Main Reading Room's uniquely long reading surfaces enabled me to lay out chronologically from left to right, so that I could (as it were) perambulate, page by page, through a hundred years of changing semantics and sensibilities.

I have sat at a Moviola machine playing with a pristine print of Michelangelo Antonioni's movie *Zabriskie Point*, manually shifting a few frames back and forth and watching its famous sabotaged mansion exploding and imploding in the dry desert sky. I have seen Jorge Bolet, at a master class on Liszt playing in the Coolidge Auditorium, advise young pianists to perform single-octave passages with the left hand alone, "because it looks better." In the Mary Pickford Theater, I have attended a screening of *Destination Moon* (1950), not, I confess, for any intellectual purpose, but out of a sense of debt to a ten-year-old Kenya boy who once cried bitterly at being kept from from this camp classic. I have attended biographical symposia, presidential dinners, folk festivals, cartoon exhibitions, academic councils, poet laureate recitations, and a sublime, evening-length traversal of Bach's Art of the Fugue, arranged for the Library's resident string quartet. And times without number, I have stood at sunset on the fifth floor of Adams watching the great copper dome opposite turning rose, then violet as the lights beneath twinkle on.

Those lights, those glowing rectangles and portholes, are windows into the central repository of our nation's cultural intelligence: a cerebellum, a sanctum of free thought forever energized by the spirit of Thomas Jefferson.

Edmund Morris

America's
Library

1800–2000

Prologue

On a cold day in December 1800, in the north Atlantic, a dozen trunks toss in the hold of a vessel named for the country toward which it sails. In the trunks are books, according to the document accompanying them, sent "by the Grace of God, in good Order and well-conditioned . . . upon the good Ship called the American" and protected against all but "the Act of God, the King's Enemies, Fire, and all and every other Dangers and Accidents of the Seas, Rivers, and Navigation, of whatever Nature and Kind."

The 740 uneasy volumes include Adam Smith's *Wealth of Nations*, the works of Francis Bacon and those of 150 other authors, some charts, and "Arrowsmith's two Maps of America, on Canvas and Rollers." They cost 475 pounds sterling, owed by the struggling, impecunious young nation awaiting them.

Its newly elected representatives authorized the purchase but were at odds about the wisdom of doing so; their books, if they reach Baltimore, are to continue south to eventually find their way onto shelves in a dim room in the new Capitol, where they will fuel oratory and other aspects of political persuasion.

This nucleus will burgeon into something impossible to foresee in the first year of the century, not by virtue of its name, not by chance, but by the determination of a relatively few people. Their collective effort will transcend the notion of mere printed works "for the use of Congress in the said city of Washington" to become the substance of the American imagination.

I

Such Books As May Be Necessary ————————

(1800–1814)

> *In the full tide of successful experiment.*
>
> Thomas Jefferson

The coach trundling south from Washington to Richmond in the spring of 1800 carried a Supreme Court justice named Samuel Chase, the self-appointed Federalist interrogator of all who opposed the regime of President John Adams. As he traveled, Chase read *The Prospect before Us*, a political tract whose publication had been timed to coincide with the opening of the current presidential campaign, said to be the dirtiest in American history and possibly the most important.

Vice President Thomas Jefferson was opposing Adams, and Jefferson's newly conceived Democratic-Republicans had been prevented by the Sedition Act from speaking out against the president and his policies. The Alien and the Sedition Acts were, in Jefferson's opinion, repressive, and he had encouraged the author of the book in Chase's hands, James Thomson Callender, a propagandist, to put forth arguments against Federalist policies that Jefferson and his supporters could not lawfully oppose in public. These included pro-British sentiments as well as the encouragement of commerce conducted at the expense of agrarian interests and the common man.

Already the justice, Chase had brought about the imprisonment of Republicans in Delaware and Philadelphia, and shortly after arriving in Richmond he sentenced Callender to nine months in jail and fined him $400, an enormous sum. While in jail, Callender was visited by prominent Republicans, among them the governor of Virginia, James Monroe, the chancellor, George Wythe, and Jefferson himself. The vice president believed in free discourse and considered the Federalists the antithesis of intellectual freedom and a threat to the liberty of all Americans.

During the eighteen months the Sedition Act was in force, twenty-five writers, editors, and printers were tried and ten imprisoned. Meanwhile Jefferson's enemies attacked him directly for his religious views, his scholarship, and his devotion to unalloyed democracy; they seized on his writing as evidence of subversion and apostasy. Jefferson became a social outcast of sorts. "Happily for truth and for us," wrote a Reverend John M. Mason, a Federalist who had found evidence that Jefferson doubted the reality of the biblical Flood, "Mr. Jefferson has *written*; he has *printed*."

Ideas and free expression—and by implication, books—stood at the center of what has been referred to as the second American revolution, the outcome of which was only months away and utterly unpredictable.

The year before, Jefferson had written to a student at the College of William and Mary, his alma mater: "I join you therefore in branding as cowardly the idea that the human mind is incapable of further advances. This is precisely the doctrine which the present despots of the earth are inculcating & their friends here re-echoing; & applying especially to religion & politics. While the art of printing is left to us, science can never be retrograde. As long as we may think as we will, & speak as we think, the condition of man will proceed in improvement."

Jefferson's regard for books was passionate and long-standing. The son of a civil engineer who had married into a prominent Virginia family, he was raised in privilege and instilled with an almost messianic belief in the value of knowledge, freedom, and the agrarian ideal. His authorship of the Declaration of Independence—no secret to Americans in 1800—emerged from a lifetime of scholarship going back to his own student days in Williamsburg.

He later described it as "the finest school of manners and morals that ever existed in America." His mentors and companions there—George Wythe, lawyer, William Small, professor of law, and Francis Fauquier, the royal governor of Virginia—were all products of the Enlightenment. Jefferson's subsequent service as a member of the Virginia House of Burgesses exposed him to the indignities of monarchical rule, and as a delegate to Congress from Virginia he put forward a constitution proposing complete political freedom, backed by a knowledge of classical law and literature.

In Virginia, Jefferson sought land reform and to overturn laws prohibiting the freeing of slaves. His tenure as governor of Virginia during the American Revolution exposed him to the harshness of Tory military forays and further hardened him against British colonialism; in Congress after the Revolution, Jefferson became the voice of the common man against various mercantile and planter schemes.

Jefferson continued pursuit of his wide-ranging scholarship—in architecture, classical history, horticulture—during his sojourn in France as America's representative. He agreed to be secretary of state in Washington's administra-

1743 *Th Jefferson.* 1826
from the original portrait by Gilbert Stuart in possession of Bowdoin College-Brunswick, Maine

Thomas Jefferson, who considered books as crucial to his existence as air or water, was the principal visionary of a congressional library whose holdings would encompass not only statecraft but all fields of knowledge.

After a portrait by Gilbert Stuart. Prints and Photographs Division, Library of Congress. LC-USZC4-2283

tion, then himself ran for president in the election of 1796, losing to Adams and assuming the post of vice president with little influence on the Federalist policies he abhorred.

Throughout his lifetime he spent hours of every day reading, and had amassed one of the most impressive private libraries in America, at Monticello. He would say unequivocally, "I cannot live without books."

Those books ordered by Congress from England in early 1800 had been approved in principle during the U.S. Congress's first session in 1789, held in New York. The impulse went back several years, to 1774, when the directors of the Library Company of Philadelphia offered the use of its books to the prospective Congress. In 1782, Theodorick Bland, Jr., a delegate from Virginia, suggested that Congress import books from Europe, and the following year a committee chaired by James Madison approved Bland's motion.

The first U.S. Congress met in New York's Federal Hall in 1789 and had access to the New York Society Library in the same building. The representative from Massachusetts, Elbridge Gerry, proposed "that a committee be appointed to report a catalogue of books necessary for the use of Congress, with an estimate of the expense, and the best mode of procuring them."

During the second session, in 1790, the motion was adopted and Gerry, a signer of the Declaration of Independence, headed the committee. He was joined on it by Aedanus Burke of South Carolina and Alexander White of Virginia. The following year, Gerry reported to the House that the committee was confining itself "to books necessary for the use of the legislative and executive departments, and not often found in private or circulating libraries."

Such libraries were still rare in America. Benjamin Franklin had started the first lending library in 1731, in Philadelphia, with fifty subscribers, an example emulated elsewhere in the colonies. Subscription libraries with fewer than a hundred volumes were scattered around the country by the late eighteenth century, but the total of their holdings and those of society libraries and private collections was probably fewer than fifty thousand volumes, a third of those theological in nature.

President John Adams, who in 1800 signed the first appropriation to include books for the use of Congress "and a suitable apartment for containing them."

Lithograph by Pendleton, after a portrait by Gilbert Stuart. Prints and Photographs Division, Library of Congress. LC-USZ62-3992

Gerry's report had continued: "The committee are therefore of the opinion that a sum, not exceeding 1,000 dollars, be appropriated in the present session, and that the sum of 500 dollars be hereafter annually appropriated to the purchase of books for a public library, and be applied to the purpose by the Vice-President, Chief Justice, and Secretary of State of the United States, without confining them to the catalogue reported, until, in the opinion of Congress, the books provided shall be adequate to the purpose."

The first formal proposal for a library for Congress clearly stipulated a permanent collection not limited by local needs, one that would be national in character and would serve all branches of government; its initial purchase suggested its international character.

Far-sighted, profound, the idea of the library still had its detractors, like the reader of the *Independent Chronicle* of Boston, who asked in May 1790, "What connection has a Library with the public? With our Commerce; or with any other national concern?—How absurd to squander away money for a parcel of Books, when every shilling of the Revenue is wanted for supporting our government and paying our debts?"

The First Congress moved to Philadelphia and was granted library privileges by the Library Company. In 1794, Washington's secretary, Tobias Lear, was instructed by the Senate to purchase its own copies of Blackstone's *Commentaries* and Vattel's *Law of Nations*. Other volumes had accumulated, among them one of poems by Robert Burns, Dr. Benjamin Rush's *Yellow Fever*, a history of England by Hume, Morse's *American Geography*, and some periodicals. As the eighteenth century drew to a close Congress owned all of 243 volumes.

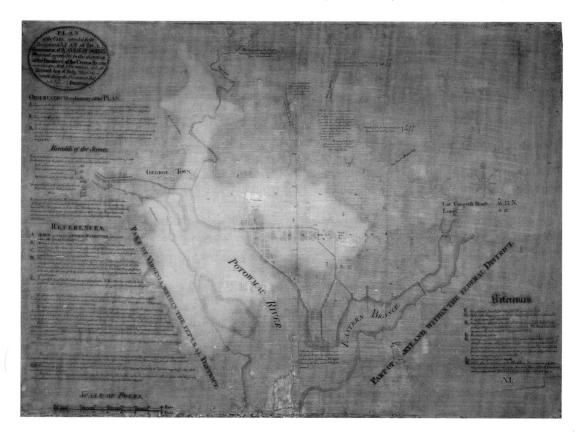

On April 24, 1800, President Adams signed a bill for outfitting the Executive Mansion and Congress in the District of Columbia. Congress had realized that no library existed there, and the bill included a section providing "for the purchase of such books as may be necessary for the use of Congress at the said city of Washington, and for fitting up a suitable apartment for containing them, and for placing them therein the sum of five thousand dollars shall be, and hereby is, appropriated." The catalog was to be furnished "by a joint committee of both Houses of Congress to be appointed for that purpose."

Pierre-Charles L'Enfant's *Plan of the city intended for the permanent seat of the government of t[he] United States . . .* (1791). The federal government's move to Washington, D.C., took place in the fall of 1800.

Geography and Map Division, Library of Congress. G3850 1791.L4

In the fall, the presidential campaign in full swing, Congress moved from Philadelphia to Washington, from the country's most sophisticated city to the least so. There had been two possible sites for the new capital, the more generally favored on the Delaware River near Philadelphia, the other along this miasmal shore of the Potomac. The latter was chosen by Congress as a concession to the southerners whose votes were needed for the federal government to assume the debts incurred by the states during the Revolution.

Instrumental in the decision was Jefferson, then secretary of state, and his

The new U.S. Capitol building as it looked in 1800, with only the north wing completed. The Congress, Supreme Court, and Library of Congress all shared the crowded space within.

Watercolor by William Birch, 1800. Prints and Photographs Division, Library of Congress. LC-USZC4-247

fellow Virginian, George Washington, who had set a cornerstone at Jones Point, in Alexandria, on April 15, 1791, a few miles from his home at Mount Vernon. This formally initiated the rise of an audacious, much dreamed-of federal city.

The District of Columbia was to embody the ideals and governance of a new nation still in the process, like its capital, of inventing itself, and Washington had encouraged a young French engineer, Pierre L'Enfant, to design it. L'Enfant set upon its uncertain terrain a plan more suitable to his continent, as large as Paris, with broad avenues and grand roundabouts all trending toward what was known as Jenkins Hill, eighty-eight feet above the height of the river, calling it "the Capitoline."

In keeping with democracy, an open competition had been launched for a Capitol building, and Jefferson, an ardent amateur architect, entered his own plan anonymously. The one chosen was that of another amateur, from Philadelphia, Dr. William Thornton, and Washington praised the proposed building for its "grandeur, simplicity and convenience." Washington ceremoniously placed that cornerstone in 1793, but Dr. Thornton's classical vision had a painfully slow realization.

The arriving congressmen saw only two wings, with nothing in between, and only the north wing ready for use. But even the unfinished Capitol made its point. "The conception proved that the United States understood the vastness of their task," Henry Adams later wrote in his history of the period, "and were willing to stake something on their faith in it."

The city itself was a collection of rough byways and low, rudimentary houses of brick and clapboard scattered in the shadow of "the Hill," as remote from L'Enfant's vision as a frontier outpost from the palaces of imperial Europe. Pennsylvania Avenue, leading from the Capitol to the President's House, was boggy for almost its entire length, and that house, too, still under construction: just six rooms had been completed when Adams and his wife, Abigail, arrived.

Jefferson, a widower by then, lodged at a boardinghouse within walking distance of the Capitol, as did many congressmen—"like a convent of monks," as Henry Adams surmised, although some boardinghouses provided free alcohol—"with no other amusement or occupation than that of going from their lodgings to the Chambers and back again." There was a paucity of shops and markets. Some congressmen lived in the somewhat more agreeable environs of Alexandria or Georgetown and journeyed to the Capitol each day over roads plagued with dust, or mud. A visitor from abroad, Thomas Moore, would write of Washington just a few years later:

> This fam'd metropolis, where fancy sees
> Squares in morasses, obelisks in trees;
> Which second sighted seers e'en now adorn
> With shrines unbuilt and heroes yet unborn.

With Congress in session, the city had only thirty-six hundred inhabitants, but the population of the entire country was then only about 5.3 million. This was a third of Great Britain's and less than a fifth of France's total populace. Twenty percent of the people living in America were slaves. In many ways Washington, not Philadelphia or even Baltimore, more accurately reflected the country as a whole, which was developing and dauntingly rural.

Two-thirds of Americans lived within fifty miles of the Atlantic coast. Roughly half the houses further inland were made of logs, many without windows. Clothing, working materials, and methods of agriculture were decidedly those of the previous century; currency used to pay debts or to purchase supplies was usually European—shillings or pistareens—the American copper cent being the only commonly used indigenous coin. Disease and illiteracy proliferated. Salt pork was common daily fare, whiskey the common dram.

There was one general mail route in 1800, from Portland, Maine, to Louisville, Georgia, a trip requiring weeks; branch routes extended to Canandaigua, New York; Lexington, Kentucky; and Nashville, Tennessee; but revenue from the entire national postal system was negligible. Three rough wagon roads may have penetrated the western wilderness, but they provided struggling settlements beyond the Alleghenies with little real contact with the outside world.

The best road ran from Boston to New York, and a stagecoach with passengers required three days to make the trip. New York to Philadelphia required two days. No stagecoach ran to the new capital city. Travel anywhere in America usually involved horses, or flat-bottomed boats, and great stamina; arduous river crossings were common (of the eight rivers between the District of Columbia and Monticello, Jefferson's home in Albemarle County, Virginia, five had neither bridges nor ferries).

Way stations on the roads leading to Washington were dirty and crowded, some with as many as eight beds to a room, and they were expensive. Arriving Congressmen had been allowed six dollars reimbursement for every twenty miles they covered, an amount insufficient to meet expenses.

The congressmen who came to reside in the new capital in 1800 had an election on their minds. The previous spring in New York, Republican Aaron Burr had packed the state legislature with presidential electors committed to Jefferson. Alexander Hamilton, the former treasury secretary, attempted to undercut the process by asking the governor, John Jay, to call a special session, change the rules by which electors were chosen, and thus frustrate the Republicans.

Jay, a Federalist, was the architect of the controversial 1794 treaty with Great Britain that failed to address Republican concerns, among them impressment of American seamen. Hamilton had reason to think Jay might comply with his request, but Jay refused. Jefferson won the vote in the New York assembly, and Aaron Burr was chosen as the Republicans' candidate for vice president.

In Congress, the Federalists voted to support Adams and Charles Cotesworth Pinckney of South Carolina equally, an indication that the incumbent president faced trouble within his own party. Pinckney was a former delegate to the Constitutional Convention and a member of the disastrous diplomatic mission to France, known as the XYZ Affair. It, like the Jay Treaty, had fueled the national debate over demands of foreign governments and America's proper place in the world.

Three American envoys to France charged with peace-making—Pinckney, Elbridge Gerry, and John Marshall—had been opportuned by their three French counterparts, referred to as X, Y, and Z, who demanded that the United States assume claims in America against France, finance a loan at double the usual rate, and pay a bribe of 50,000 pounds. Despite the resulting outcry, Pinckney remained the choice of most Federalist leaders, including Hamilton.

President Adams addressed the first joint session of Congress in November 1800, and spoke of "the prospect of a residence not to be changed," meaning that the federal government was forever fixed in Washington, D.C. The 134 elected officials were committed to an unfinished Capitol in an unfinished city and faced with the prospect of a new chief executive who just might be a Republican.

The president and the Federalists had not done well in other state assemblies, with Adams carrying only his home region of New England, New Jersey, and Delaware. Jefferson and Aaron Burr emerged from the overall voting with seventy-three electoral votes apiece, and the election was thrown into the House of Representatives. In February 1801, after weeks of political maneuvering, the deciding vote went to Jefferson on the thirty-sixth ballot; power shifted from the party of Washington and the Founding Fathers, and a bitter Adams left the city before his rival's inauguration.

The Federalists would not recover from their defeat, but the two-party principle had been established through what Jefferson called "as real a revolution in the principles of our government as that of 1776 . . . by the rational and peaceful instrument of reform, the suffrage of the people."

On April 1, 1801, Congress's books ordered from England and sitting in the Baltimore harbor were placed on a packet and shipped to Georgetown. A month later the secretary of the Senate, Samuel A. Otis, wrote to President Jefferson that the packages had arrived "perfectly dry." The books were sent up to the office of the clerk of the Senate.

The following January, Jefferson signed a bill entitled "An Act Concerning the Library for the Use of Both Houses of Congress." All books belonging to the Senate and the House were combined in a room on the west side of the north wing of the Capitol. The room was eighty-six feet long and thirty-five feet wide and had thirty-six-foot ceilings, galleries, and two ranges of windows for natural lighting—a proper setting for statesmen perusing the works of scholars and scientists with bearing on future acts of Congress.

This act gave the president of the Senate and the Speaker of the House the power to regulate the Library. Borrowers of books and maps were limited to the president, the vice president, and members of Congress; appropriations for new books were to be handled by a joint committee of three senators and three representatives. The act stipulated that a librarian be "appointed by the President of the United States solely," a job that was to pay "a sum not exceeding two dollars per diem."

Jefferson appointed his friend and fellow Virginian John James Beckley, a colorful, highly partisan political operative who had played an important role in Jefferson's election but so far had not fared well in Jefferson's parsimonious use of patronage. Beckley, an Englishman by birth, had served over the years in various administrative positions: secretary to the Phi Beta Kappa Society at the College of William and Mary, clerk of the Virginia House of Burgesses, Clerk of the House of Representatives during the first Congress, friend of the powerful, and himself an influential if outspoken Republican.

Beckley had aided James Madison in his opposition to the policies of Alexander Hamilton and written often and effectively, if pseudonymously, to discredit the Federalists. Well-read, gregarious, sickly, he had a talent for speechmaking and enunciation and a natural bent for behind-the-scenes maneuvering.

He had turned against Washington when he signed the Jay Treaty. While Congress was in Philadelphia, Beckley served as unofficial chairman of the Republican party, and his cajoling was crucial in delivering Pennsylvania for Jefferson during the presidential campaign of 1800. He encouraged the propagandist Callender to publish a report about Hamilton's affair with the wife of James Reynolds that thoroughly discredited Hamilton, and he defended Jefferson against attacks from the clergy.

Beckley lost his clerkship of the House, and only loans from friends— among them Jefferson and Dr. Benjamin Rush—saved him from debtors' prison. After the move to Washington, however, he won back the clerkship of the House (he would have preferred clerk of the Senate, which was less demanding and more prestigious), a job that made considerable demands on a man in poor health. He hoped in vain for an early political plum from President Jefferson and was finally made Librarian.

Now Beckley the political strategist had to attend lengthy meetings of congressional committees and comply with requests from members of Congress, including the determination of how much of the original appropriation for books remained. He discovered that there was no statement of account rendered for those first books ordered from England, and so he had to piece the record together.

Early in 1802 the head of the Joint Committee on the Library, Abraham Baldwin, senator from Georgia and former chaplain in the Revolutionary Army, appealed to President Jefferson for guidance in the new, vaguely defined Library of Congress. Jefferson replied to Baldwin on April 14, "I have prepared a catalogue for the Library of Congress in conformity with your ideas that books of entertainment are not within the scope of it, and that books in other languages, where there are not translations of them, are to be admitted freely."

"I have confined the catalogue to those branches of science which belong to the deliberations of the members as statesmen," Jefferson continued, "and in

these have omitted those desirable books, ancient and modern, which gentlemen generally have in their private libraries, but which cannot properly claim
a place in a collection made merely for the purposes of reference."

In the realm of "law of nature and nations," Jefferson "put down everything" he thought worthy because "this is a branch of science often under the
discussion of Congress." Likewise were included books on parliamentary procedures, to protect against "caprice and despotism from the chair." He recommended two encyclopedias and "a set of dictionaries in the different languages,
which may be often wanting."

History was represented, and some philosophy, but no theology, pedagogy,
technology, art, or music—a library, "in other words," David C. Mearns remarked
in his history of the Library, *The Story Up to Now,* "very practical and very dull."

Beckley saw to it that Jefferson's catalog was printed. It included a number
assigned to each book, the title, the number of volumes, and the estimated
value of the 212 folios, 164 quartos, 581 octavos and 7 duodecimos. There were
964 volumes in all, plus 9 maps and charts.

Jefferson instructed the U.S. consul in London to look for more books from
a different supplier, thinking that the original supplier, Cadell & Davies, had
charged too much for the first shipment. In practical fashion, Jefferson further
instructed that the consul look for books with "neat bindings, not splendid
ones," and small "good editions, not pompous ones."

This was not to be Jefferson's ultimate contribution to the Library which,
like his vision of the American landscape, would prove to be both daring
and inspirational.

In July 1802, Beckley put together a statement of remaining funds—
$2,480.83—and sent it to Congress and to the president, with a suggestion
of his own for books by the naturalists Georges Buffon and Mark Catesby.
Beckley spent two months in the fall at Berkeley Springs, in Virginia, recovering his health, still in debt and responsible for a large extended family, and
returned to his duties in the Capitol.

There he asked Benjamin Rush to send copies of all his publications to the
Library and was soon encouraging other authors to make such donations. His
friend and editor of the *National Intelligencer,* Samuel Harrison Smith, wrote
approvingly in 1803 that the Library "already embraces near fifteen hundred
volumes of the most rare and valuable works in different languages. We observe
with pleasure that authors and editors of books, maps, and charts begin to find
that, by placing a copy of their works on the shelves of this institution, they do
more to diffuse a knowledge of them than is generally accomplished by catalogues and advertisements."

Early in his first term Jefferson appointed his young secretary, Meriwether Lewis, to undertake an unprecedented exploration of the vast trans-Mississippi region known roughly as Louisiana. The territory had not yet been purchased from France but was considered by Jefferson a logical, and crucial, extension of the American nation. The expedition was inspired in part by Jefferson's curiosity about natural phenomena, in part by his belief in the continental destiny of his country.

Lewis chose as his subaltern an army friend, William Clark. What became known as the Lewis and Clark expedition could be seen as a material exploration equivalent to the intellectual notion of a national library: inchoate, unlimited, lastingly significant.

Packing sextant, chronometer, spirit level, and other vital tools, the party traveled to a winter camp outside St. Louis in 1804. In the spring the thirty-four soldiers and ten civilians proceeded up the Missouri River by boat to winter in Mandan and Arikara villages. The following spring, in the foothills of the Rocky Mountains, they acquired the crucial Shoshone guide, Sacajawea, who helped them procure horses and other support. They crossed the Continental Divide, moved north through the Bitterroot valley, followed the Clearwater, Snake, and Columbia rivers, and reached the shore of the Pacific Ocean in November 1805.

The following spring the party began the eastward journey, dividing after re-crossing the Rockies. Lewis retraced the former route while Clark dipped south to the Yellowstone River; they were reunited at Fort Union, near the junction of the Missouri. They arrived in Washington laden with botanical and geological specimens and recorded observations of peoples, climate, flora, and fauna. The four-thousand-mile journey—accomplished with no hostile encounter between explorers and native peoples—was a tribute both to Jefferson's foresight and to the explorers' stamina and ingenuity.

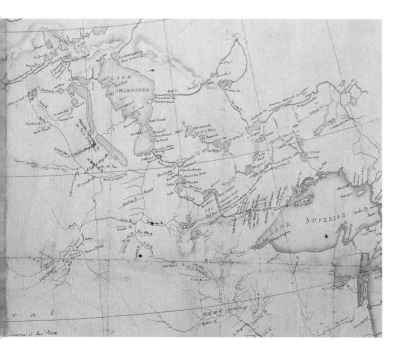

The Lewis and Clark expedition (1803–6) owed its success in part to meticulous cartographic research on the northwest regions. This map, prepared by a War Department draftsman, is believed to have been carried and annotated by Meriwether Lewis during the journey.

Manuscript map by Nicholas King, 1803. Geography and Map Division, Library of Congress.

(opposite) American Indians—the Mandan, the Arikara, the Shoshone—aided Lewis and Clark in their journey across the continent. An early account of the expedition illustrated this collaboration.

Engraving from Patrick Gass, *A Journal of the Voyages and Travels of a Corps of Discovery under the Command of Capt. Lewis and Capt. Clark* (Philadelphia: Matthew Carey, 1812). Rare Book and Special Collections Division, Library of Congress.

William Clark was chosen by Meriwether Lewis to help him lead the expedition that set off from St. Louis for the Pacific Ocean in 1804, returning to Missouri in 1806. Clark became governor of the Missouri Territory in 1813.

Oil painting by Charles Willson Peale. Courtesy of Independence National Historical Park.

President Jefferson chose the man who had been his private secretary since 1801 to lead the expedition to explore the territory west of the Mississippi River purchased from France in 1803.

Captain Meriwether Lewis by Charles B. J. F. Saint-Mémin. Watercolor, 1807. From the collection of the New-York Historical Society.

Beckley acted as willing host for the new Library and Congress, providing informal tours to dignitaries and other visitors increasingly attracted to the Capitol in 1804. The famous German naturalist Baron Alexander von Humboldt arrived accompanied by the noted American artist Charles Willson Peale. "Mr. Beckley received us with politeness," Peale wrote in his diary, ". . . the Library is a spacious and handsome Room, and although lately organized, already contained a number of valuable books in the best taste of binding."

The internal politics of Congress and the Library were anything but ceremonious for Beckley. He had given a Federalist clerk, Josias King, a position in the Library despite the fact that King had wanted the job of Librarian himself and harbored resentment. Beckley fired him in 1805, and King charged Beckley with failing to divide the Librarian's pay with him and preventing King from obtaining extra compensation for services rendered.

The House investigated the charges and found that King had no claim, but the incident exacerbated Beckley's already stressful life and introduced the element of controversy to the Librarian's post.

Congress took back the quarters occupied by the Library at the beginning of Jefferson's second term and provided a less impressive committee room in a wing of the Capitol. The room was too small for the ever-increasing collection of books, the roof leaked, and the floor shook.

Congress still expected the Library to serve its needs, though all the Library's funds had been spent. The Senate appointed a committee "to inquire into the expediency of purchasing maps and books for the library," chaired by Samuel Latham Mitchill of New York, known to colleagues as the "Stalking Library" and the "Chaos of Knowledge" because of his erudition. Mitchill conducted a study and in early 1806 judged the Library lacking in works of literature, science, geography, history, and politics.

Mitchill asked for a new appropriation, as the 1806 report stated, "to furnish the library with such materials as will enable statesmen to be correct in their investigations, and by becoming a display of erudition and research, give a higher dignity and a brighter lustre to truth." A symbolic role for the Library, in addition to its practical one, was envisioned.

Three members of the committee—John Quincy Adams, Joseph Clay, and Mitchill—were each authorized to draw as much as $494 from the Library's financial agent for buying books in Boston, New York, and Philadelphia, for the first time bestowing congressional favor on the American book trade.

Beckley feuded with another political adversary, Federalist senator William Plumer of New Hampshire, over the availability and choice of books in the Library. He involved himself in the city government of the District of Columbia, as he had earlier in Richmond and Philadelphia. In addition to these distractions, he fought legal battles related to tracts of valuable but largely unsalable lands he had earlier obtained in western Virginia.

Short of cash and in increasingly poor health, Beckley died on April 8, 1807, bringing to a close a highly varied career of a learned man whose impulses were primarily political and whose fondness was for Republican goals. He left the Library well organized and—fittingly—well defended against the encroachments both of politics and anti-intellectualism that remained an undercurrent in American public life.

President Jefferson had more important considerations in mind than the succession at the Library of Congress. Among them were the trial in Richmond of Aaron Burr, charged with treason, and continuing problems with the British. That country's sea captains continued to impress American seamen, and the British warship H.M.S. *Leopard* had launched an unprovoked attack on the U.S. frigate *Chesapeake*. There was talk of another war.

There were many applicants for the job of Librarian, and even more for the clerkship of the House. One of the latter, Patrick Magruder, the son of a Montgomery County, Maryland, justice, had attended Princeton University, had served as an associate judge in the circuit county court, and had been elected a Republican member of the U.S. House of Representatives in the Ninth Congress. He had lately lost his seat to the uncle of Francis Scott Key after a bitter campaign in which he painted his opponent as a Tory and a local Federalist newspaper opined that "rudeness and insolence will always meet with their proper reward, contempt and defeat."

There were no fewer than eight candidates for the clerkship. Magruder was elected after several ballots, with the fortuitous support of Congressman John Randolph of Roanoke, and three congressmen then recommended Magruder to Jefferson for the additional post of Librarian, seen as a customary adjunct to the clerkship. The president had doubts about automatically putting the clerk of the House in charge of the Library, and there was the question of other petitioners, some loyal Republicans like Beckley's chief clerk in the Library, Nicholas Van Zandt, who also wanted the job.

Never comfortable with decisions involving patronage, Jefferson put off the decision for half a year, fortunately for Magruder, who did not formally apply until Congress reconvened in October. Finally, on November 6, Jefferson wrote him a brief note, affirming that Magruder had been selected. "Mr. Van Zandt having been charged pro tem with the care of the books since the death of Mr. Beckley, you will be pleased to receive that charge from him."

In 1807 the Library committee placed Representative Samuel W. Dana in charge of "the making and printing of a new list of books." The new forty-page

James Madison, who took office as the fourth U.S. president in 1809. During Madison's tenure, long-simmering conflicts with England escalated into open warfare, with dire consequences for the fledgling Library of Congress.

Portrait by Charles Willson Peale, 1783. Rare Book and Special Collections Division, Library of Congress.

First Lady Dolley Madison, whose legendary charm and verve as a Washington hostess did much to transform the new capital city's social image. Her courage and quick thinking during the 1814 attack on Washington also saved crucial state documents and works of art from British torches.

Painting by Gilbert Stuart, ca. 1800–1812. Pennsylvania Academy of Fine Arts, Philadelphia. Photograph, Prints and Photographs Division, Library of Congress. LC-USZ62-24859

catalog that appeared tripled the size of the previous one. It set forth a new set of rules for routine operations and for circulating, labeling, shelving, and cataloging the books. Expenses were carefully recorded, as now required by law. Complete sets of laws and various journals were deposited at the Library as the House and Senate required, and the practice of fining members for overdue books was instituted.

Beckley had left the day-to-day operation of the Library to his assistants, a practice Magruder willingly continued. The second Librarian did find time to petition the president on behalf of friends from Montgomery County and Georgetown seeking political appointments. Magruder, again like his predecessor, Beckley, suffered from poor health and yet found time to participate in local politics, but he played no decisive role in Library affairs beyond the duties required by Congress. The laxness of his record-keeping would come back to haunt him.

Jefferson left office in 1809 and was replaced by his old friend and supporter James Madison, former secretary of state and a fellow founder of the Republicans.

Madison was more schooled in political science than his predecessor but lacked Jefferson's imagination and his imposing bearing. Slight, a bit dour, perpetually dressed in black, Madison provided a sharp contrast to Jefferson's disheveled enthusiasm and intellectual fervor. But Madison had been a persistent and effective force in Congress, battling the Federalists' money-making schemes and championing farmers and patriots against what he saw as British encroachment and "monocrats" at home; Jefferson valued and respected Madison, describing him as "the greatest man in the world."

Madison's wife, Dolley, was a lively, sympathetic figure. She had served occasionally as the unofficial hostess for the widower president, Jefferson. Now, for the first time in eight years, the Executive Mansion had an official First Lady in residence.

Her husband's early negotiations with the British over nonintervention in American trade were successful, but the agreement soon broke down. Impressment of American seamen continued. In the western reaches of the continent, frontiersmen pushed to acquire land that belonged either to the Indians or to the British. The so-called "war hawk" Congress led by Henry Clay and John Calhoun clamored for expansion.

Madison signed an act of Congress in 1811 renewing the Library's annual $1,000 appropriation for five years. Magruder had been retained as Librarian. He was married in May to Martha Goodwyn, the daughter of a Democrat in the House, and that November won reelection as clerk of the House without opposition. He remained active in local Masonic affairs, and he and his wife participated in modest social functions relating to the Library.

In 1812, the Library issued its first classified catalog, but Magruder's role in its preparation is not clear. It listed 3,076 volumes and 53 maps, charts, and plans. The same year, members of Congress, who had never been happy with the penalties for overdue books, exempted themselves from such fines and authorized Supreme Court justices to use the Library.

Meanwhile, Madison's presidency was dominated by the prospect of open conflict with England. For years he had opposed its incursions and discriminatory trade policies, and on June 12, 1812, he sent a message to Congress recommending the use of force. On June 18 war was declared by a narrow vote; so uncertain was the mood of the country that a fourth of the Republicans in Congress abstained from voting. Federalists labeled it "Mr. Madison's War," criticizing his dealings with Britain, and managed to double their numbers in the congressional elections of 1812, but Madison was elected to a second term.

He became preoccupied with the fighting, which was limited to the coast and the border with Canada and did not go well for the country. An American force invaded Canada and captured York (now Toronto) in 1813; the Americans burned the Parliament buildings, including the library of the legislature—a bad precedent.

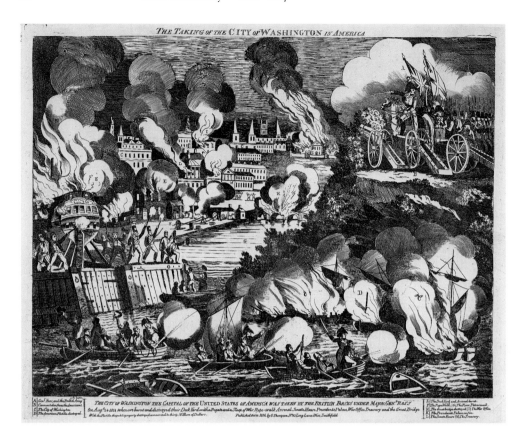

THE TAKING OF THE CITY OF WASHINGTON IN AMERICA

"The Taking of the City of Washington in America," dramatizing the August 1814 British attack on the capital city, in which "the public property destroyed amounted to Thirty million of [sic] Dollars."

Wood engraving by G. Thompson (London), 1814. Prints and Photographs Division, Library of Congress. LC-USZC4-4555 (color); LC-USZ62-1939 (black and white)

Magruder became ill in December 1813, and had to be replaced as clerk by his brother, George. The following July he took sick leave from all duties and traveled to Virginia to recuperate. The British naval blockade of American ports had proved highly effective, but there seemed to be no imminent danger to the capital city.

Then in August 1814 an expeditionary British force came ashore from the Chesapeake Bay. The local militia was called up to oppose it, draining the Capitol and other public buildings of protective forces. The only person on duty in the Library was an over-age clerk named J. T. Frost, left in charge by George Magruder, who was serving as a colonel. Frost was later joined by a furloughed clerk, Samuel Burch.

On August 22, Frost began to pack the Library files after sending Burch in search of transportation. Most wagons in Washington had been commandeered as other government workers fled; Burch returned with only a cart and four oxen. The two men managed to evacuate most, but not all, of the Library records.

The British troops had advanced to within ten miles of Washington. On the morning of August 24, President Madison met with his cabinet at the Navy Yard to devise a plan of defense. The American force was more numerous than

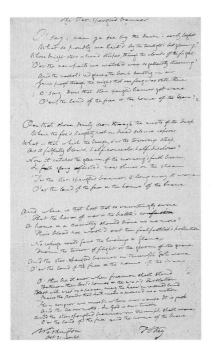

FRANCIS SCOTT KEY · 1780–1843

the British one, but poorly trained; some seventeen hundred British soldiers assembled at Bladensburg, in nearby Maryland, routed several thousand Americans, and prepared to march on Washington.

Madison returned to the Executive Mansion to discover that Dolley had already left with the presidential plate and other valuables. He and his Cabinet fled west out of the city. The British advanced virtually unopposed and that night and the following morning set fire to the most symbolic structures in the city: the War Office, the Treasury, the Executive Mansion, the offices of the *National Intelligencer*, a bridge over the Potomac, and the Capitol.

The glow of the flames could be seen as far away as Baltimore. Included in the general conflagration was the Library of Congress. Books were used to kindle the fire, burned in retaliation for the earlier burning of the legislative library in York by American troops. The invaders were charged with barbarity by witnesses and by commentators all over America, their action compared to the burning of the great Alexandrine library in classical times.

The records of Congress pertaining to the Library were lost, as were those of expenditures made during Patrick Magruder's term. This was to have unhappy consequences for the sickly second Librarian.

The 1814 British offensive was finally routed at Baltimore, in the battle for Fort McHenry. Francis Scott Key, serving as an emissary to the British, watched the night's battle from an enemy ship. At daybreak, on seeing the American flag still atop the fort, he excitedly penned his impressions in verses that would become the basis of a patriotic song. (It was not officially designated the U.S. national anthem, however, until 1931.)

Autograph lyric in ink, 1814. Music Division, Library of Congress.

The British went on to Baltimore, where they unsuccessfully bombarded Fort McHenry, a dubious victory for the Americans that inspired Francis Scott Key to write "The Star Spangled Banner." The war would grind on without an apparent winner, and, finally, Congress voted to end the hostilities in early 1815. Two weeks before that, in New Orleans, General Andrew Jackson had resoundingly defeated the British force there, his victory essentially ending two centuries of European involvement in America.

The Library of Congress, unlike the temporarily dispersed but still extant government of the United States, had ceased to exist. Gone were all the books originally ordered from England, as well as the valuable acquisitions made since the Library's founding fourteen years before, precious volumes all, envisioned by learned men as beacons to the new nation. Gone also was much of the resolve for a great national library as a weakened citizenry and a contentious Congress sought order after chaos.

Jefferson and Monticello

One hundred miles southwest of Washington, on the "little mountain" in Albemarle County, Jefferson had retired from politics to devote himself to reading, farming, and completing his ideal Palladian home. Monticello's various renovations and additions, years in progress, had become a life's work, one that engaged Jefferson's genius for architectural adaptation and practical invention and, in the process, drained his resources.

Jefferson had never lived within his means, receiving as he did, wherever he found himself, a constant stream of humanity for conversation and political cajoling, all in the interests of the country and an informed society. His dealings in land, crops—and slaves—had left him deeply in debt at the age of seventy-one. The author of the Declaration of Independence, former president, and the most revered living American was faced with financial ruin.

One of the centerpieces of Monticello—and one of his chief consolations—was his library,

probably the most extensive private one in the land. It occupied a suite near the east portico that could be entered by way of a passageway from the hall, through the south piazza (also the greenhouse), and from the aviary. Its owner was in the habit of locking the library so that his browsing would not be interrupted by his many guests.

Jefferson's bookish reveries had been going on since he was fourteen, when his father had left him about forty books. He had added to the collection while in Williamsburg, acquiring Francis Bacon's *Philosophy* and other volumes, some from abroad; he studied and collected other philosophical works, including those of John Locke, Montesquieu, and Burlamaqui, but his bibliophilia was not limited.

The library he had earlier assembled at the family home at Shadwell was destroyed by fire in 1770, prompting what might be characterized as a book-buying obsession that lasted a lifetime. By 1773, Jefferson's books at Monticello numbered 1,256 books and included the complete libraries of

By the time Jefferson retired from public service, he had amassed considerable personal debt from a lifetime's pursuit of a vast range of interests and projects—most notable among them the planning, construction, and furnishing of his beloved home Monticello.

Engraving by Charles Balthazar Julien Fevret de Saint-Mémin, ca. 1804. Prints and Photographs Division, Library of Congress. LC-USZC4-5179 (color); LC-USZ62-200 (black and white)

Richard Bland and Peyton Randolph. In Philadelphia, and anywhere he traveled, he searched for more books.

He had collected about two hundred books a year and by 1814 owned between six and seven thousand. Those volumes relating to North and South America probably comprised the best such collection anywhere. All the books were arranged in the library at Monticello in custom-made pine boxes constructed in Jefferson's cabinet shop under the supervision of carpenter John Hemings, Jefferson's talented slave. The boxes varied in dimensions and were stacked according to size—folios on the bottom and above them quartos, octavos, duodecimos, and smaller books on top.

In addition, there were the large and expensive volumes of finely detailed architectural engravings of classical antiquities, precursors of the coffee table book. These included Robert Wood's *The Ruins of Balbec*, Antoine Desgodets's *Edifices Antiques de Rome*, Charles-Louis Clerisseau's *Antiques de la France*—Clerisseau was chosen by Jefferson as a collaborator on the design of the capitol at Richmond—and works by Palladio.

Literally stuffed with books, the library was ill-designed for such a purpose: a pair of semi-octagons with doors, windows, an alcove bed, and a fireplace that consumed valuable space. Nowhere was there more than seven feet of exposed wall available for shelves. The suite probably contained, in addition, a tall reading desk with Chinese fretwork made by a Virginia cabinetmaker, an octagonal filing table inlaid with the letters of the alphabet, another desk, and several chairs.

To Jefferson, books were finite components in the infinite puzzle of learning, through which he constructed his personal universe. By extension, a national library might be expected to exert a similar informing and civilizing influence on the nation as a whole.

Jefferson wanted to be able to locate quickly any single book he desired. Instead of using the common classification system based on broad categories like natural philosophy, history, politics, and literature, he devised one based on Baconian principles, with forty-four categories of knowledge. It would prove to be another lasting Jeffersonian legacy, the intellectual touchstone of an enlightened man who found solace and meaning within the bounds of human knowledge and imagination.

News of the burning of the Capitol by the British caused Jefferson to despair, in part because of the loss of so many books so painstakingly assembled. He quickly saw a way to raise the Library from the ashes, however, and to ease his own perilous finances in the process, if only his friends—and his enemies—could see the wisdom of it.

Exterior and interior views of Monticello. Its unparalleled library, painstakingly assembled by Jefferson over many years, would form the nucleus of the Library of Congress's book collection following the Library's devastation during the War of 1812.

Photographs by Robert C. Lautman/Monticello.

2

The Source

What spectacle can be more edifying or more seasonable, than that of Liberty & Learning, each leaning on the other.

James Madison

News of the destruction of the Capitol traveled outward along the rough roads of America, inspiring disbelief and despair. At Monticello, Thomas Jefferson was dismayed, but the reclusive former president soon conceived of a way whereby Congress might quickly restore some of what had been lost to the depredations of the British. At the same time, Jefferson might relieve his own relentless burden of debt.

On September 21, 1814, Jefferson sat down at his desk and began a long letter to an old friend, Samuel Harrison Smith, publisher of the *National Intelligencer*, long a supporter of the Library of Congress. The subject of the letter was the precious assembly of books surrounding Jefferson; the tone of the letter was both ardent and beseeching.

"You know my collection," Jefferson wrote, "its condition and extent. I have been fifty years making it, and have spared no pains, opportunity or expense . . . While residing in Paris, I devoted every afternoon I was disengaged, for a summer or two, in examining all the principal bookstores, turning over every book with my own hand, and putting by everything which related to America, and indeed whatever was rare and valuable in every science."

He had also ordered books continually from dealers in Amsterdam, Frankfurt, Madrid, and London that pertained to America. "[S]uch a collection was made as probably can never again be effected, because it is hardly probable that the same opportunities, the same time, industry, perseverance, and expence . . . would again happen to be in concurrence." He had continued to augment the collection after returning home, so that his library, while including "what is chiefly valuable in science and literature generally, extends more particularly to whatever belongs to the American statesman."

27

Jefferson estimated that his library contained between nine thousand and ten thousand books. He included this prescient idea: "I do not know that it contains any branch of science which Congress would wish to exclude from their collection; there is in fact no subject to which a member of Congress may not have occasion to refer."

Smith was asked to forward Jefferson's offer to Congress, along with an incomplete catalog Jefferson had prepared. He suggested that members of Congress determine the library's value, and offered to accept payment by annual installment "so as to spare the present calls of our country, and await it's days of peace and prosperity." He added that eighteen or twenty wagons "would place it in Washington in a single trip of a fortnight."

Congress had been called into special session a few days before, and one of the items dealt with early on by the angry lawmakers was the absence of their Library. Senator Robert Henry Goldsborough, of Maryland, had put forward a request for the appointment of a joint committee "to have the direction of the money appropriated to the purchase of books and maps for the use of the two Houses of Congress." The resolution was quickly approved, but no one knew at the time where such a large collection of necessary books might be found.

Meanwhile Congress was denouncing the destruction of the Capitol by the British and, in an ugly mood, seeking to assign blame. A resolution was introduced to appoint a committee to look into "the causes of the capture of this city by the enemy; also into the manner in which the public buildings and property were destroyed."

The Speaker put before the House a letter from the sickly clerk of the House and second Librarian of Congress, Patrick Magruder, "detailing the circumstances attending the destruction of his office by the enemy" and asking for an investigation to clear up the matter. But Magruder's presence at a spa in Virginia, where he was recuperating from an "alleged" disposition at the time of the attack, instead of at the Capitol, did not sit well with the congressmen.

A selection of books from Thomas Jefferson's library, which in 1815 he called "the choicest collection" in the United States. The open volume of Cicero's letters in the foreground, featuring dual-language text and a handwritten emendation by Jefferson, reveals both the state of the art of bookmaking in the eighteenth century and its intimate relation to Jefferson's erudite, exacting mind.

Rare Book and Special Collections Division, Library of Congress.

No doubt to his surprise, an investigation was launched. Congress subsequently ruled that Magruder had made no preparations for possible hostilities "to secure the library and papers appertaining to the office of the House of Representatives."

Books had not been the only loss suffered during the fire; records pertaining to the Library, and to the House of Representatives, had also gone up in smoke, including those of expenditures made during Magruder's term. He was held responsible—rightly or wrongly—for $18,167.09 in funds from the United States Treasury. He could not adequately account for this staggering sum.

Magruder's lax system of payments for services rendered to Congress and to the Library and his inability to document the expenditures were not necessarily proof of malfeasance. As likely, he was a scapegoat in a time of remonstrance and national self-doubt, dismissed as Librarian and forced to resign his clerkship of the House the following January.

This permitted, wrote the hapless Magruder, "those by whom I am persecuted to attain, with greater ease, an object to which they have been willing to sacrifice not only my family but my reputation." He retired to his wife's home in rural Virginia, and had suit filed against him by the federal government for the money; there is no record of the case ever coming to trial.

Jefferson's offer of a library was seized upon by his supporters and his detractors. A bill authorizing the purchase of the library was passed by the Senate, but the House was another matter. The debate was affected, as usual, by partisan politics and soon took on the anti-intellectual sheen that had characterized the election of 1800.

Those in favor of the acquisition included such respected Democrats in the House as Jefferson's supporter Robert Wright, of Maryland, formerly the governor; Adam Seybert, of Pennsylvania, who had studied abroad and was a member of the American Philosophical Society; Thomas Bolling Robertson, of Louisiana, alumnus of William and Mary known for his use of strong language in debate; and even a Federalist, Joseph H. Hawkins, of Kentucky.

These men, according to the official record, argued that such a collection of books as Jefferson had offered, "one so admirably calculated . . . was not to be obtained in the United States" anywhere other than at Monticello. "[A]lthough there might be some works to which gentlemen might take exception, there were others of very opposite character; that this, besides, was no reason against the purchase."

Those members of the House taking exception were Federalists like the orotund Thomas Jackson Oakley, an outspoken critic of the Madison administration, and Thomas Peabody Grosvenor, both New Yorkers and both graduates of Yale, and John Reed, of Massachusetts, a graduate of Brown. Their fine educations notwithstanding, these men objected to the size of Jefferson's library, its presumed cost, and "the nature of the selection, embracing too many works in foreign languages, some of too philosophical a character, and some otherwise objectionable."

The sort of book whose nature was objectionable used imagination and satire and was typified by the works of Voltaire. The questionable political writings included James Thomson Callender's *The Prospect before Us*, which had caused such controversy fourteen years earlier.

Cyrus King, Federalist of Massachusetts and half-brother, ironically, of the noted bibliophile Rufus King, opposed the purchase on grounds that the library would help his political enemy, Jefferson, and spread Jefferson's "infidel philosophy." The books, King said, were "good, bad, and indifferent, old, new, and worthless, in languages which many can not read, and most ought not."

Another opponent proposed buying part of the library, knowing that Jefferson had stipulated that it must not be divided and would never agree.

The joint committee reported that the library contained 6,487 volumes and, in the winter of 1814, authorized their purchase for $23,950. But the wrangling continued into the new year. King proposed removing from Jefferson's library, after it arrived in Washington, "all books of an atheistical, irreligious, and immoral tendency."

He, Grosvenor, and a large contingent that included some Democrats—and Daniel Webster—opposed the funding "on account of the scarcity, and the necessity of appropriating it to purposes more indispensable than the purchase of a library; the probable insecurity of such a library . . . its miscellaneous and almost exclusive literary (instead of legal and historical) character, &c."

Proponents now included James Fisk, of Vermont, a minister of the Universalist church, and John Whitefield Hulbert, a Federalist of Massachusetts. In concert, they answered the opponents "with fact, wit, and argument, to show that the purchase . . . could not affect the present resources of the United States; that the price was moderate, the library more valuable from the scarcity of many of its books, and altogether a most admirable substratum for a National Library."

The bill finally passed in the House by a margin of only ten votes, the most unified support coming from the South, and was signed into law by President James Madison on January 30, 1815. The desirability of a highly diverse library for the use of Congress had been thoroughly debated and acceded to by men of reputation. The library's considerable cost was recognized as a necessary expense of the struggling nation.

As yet, there was no official building to receive the books. Mindful of this,

George Watterston, the third Librarian of Congress (1815–29), was the first to hold the post on a full-time basis. An eclectic-minded bookman and writer, Watterston envisioned a Library of Congress with a broad scope of acquisition and use comparable to the great national libraries of Europe.

Watercolor portrait attributed to Thomas Birch of Philadelphia, 1811. Rare Book and Special Collections Division, Library of Congress.

Congress passed, and the president signed, a bill "to cause a proper apartment to be immediately selected and prepared for a library room" in a refurbished building serving at the temporary Capitol, to contain "the library lately purchased from Thomas Jefferson."

Madison and others recognized—owing in part to Patrick Magruder's botched record keeping—that the Library's management required the attention of a person devoted to books and undistracted by the daily operations of Congress. The practice of combining the jobs of clerk of the House and Librarian of Congress was therefore done away with in the appointment of the third Librarian, the first to serve full time.

He was George Watterston, a lifelong resident of Washington and a minor literary celebrity: intermittent journalist, pamphleteer, poet, and novelist. Born on shipboard in the New York harbor in 1783, the son of a Scottish master builder attracted to Washington by the public building projects, Watterston had enjoyed a classical education at Charlotte Hall School in Maryland. He went on to study law and to practice it, but disparaged the profession in print.

An inheritance had enabled him to travel, and to write. As a young man he published the novel *Glencarn; or, The Disappointments of Youth* and a play and a poem, both heavily sentimental. Another of his poems, "The Wanderer in Jamaica," was dedicated to Dolley Madison: "Madame, I have presumed to address this poetical effusion to you, from the reputation you have acquired of being desirous to promote the cause of general literature."

Speculation had it that he had received his appointment because of this, although the fact that he had served as editor of *Washington City Gazette*, started two years earlier to support the Republicans, seems more likely. In addition, he was a recognized writer, had fought at Bladensburg—his house had been one of many pillaged by the British—and had earlier appealed to Madison for a political appointment. So his name was presumably known to the president.

Thin-skinned, afflicted with a sense of superiority, and intensely political, Watterston had an appealing side. A social commentator, Anne Royal, wrote in her Sketches that he had "a fine figure, and possessed of some personal beauty . . . shows genius and deep penetration, marked with gravity." She added that "a sweet serenity diffuses itself over his countenance, which no accident can ruffle." Clearly the third Librarian could charm.

Watterston promptly wrote to Jefferson and requested that the present arrangement of Jefferson's books, according to Baconian notions of order, be maintained. He added, "I have long thought the arrangement of the old Library was incorrect and injudicious."

The more utilitarian method of arranging books generally by title and broad subject matter might better please members of Congress, but it didn't please their new Librarian. Watterston began by retrieving what he could from the ruins of the existing Library, and rounded up those books that had been on loan during the invasion of Washington. He placed them all in the sizable building at Seventh and E Streets, known as Blodget's Hotel. It had been designed by James Hoban, architect of the White House, and erected by an early real estate speculator, Samuel Blodget; it had served as a theater but never as a hotel and had been occupied by squatters before being taken over by the government.

Now it contained the Patent Office, the General and City Post Offices, Congress, and, on the third floor, Congress's Library. Carpentry, painting, and furnishings to improve the room were paid for from $1,520.77 provided by Congress. Watterston acquired various items for the Library's operation— wood for the fireplace, candles, a broom, shears, ink, stationery—and 1,100 labels and bookplates.

Damaged books sent out for repairs were added to the collection, and bookplates installed; the Library of Congress was back in business.

Watterston's ideas were loftier than the mere provision of source material for elected officials. He saw the Library as a repository of the nation's literature and had a notice printed in the *National Intelligencer* asking writers, artists, and engravers to send to the Library works that might be made available to the public.

At Monticello, Jefferson's precious books were protected by sheets of paper and by boards nailed across the fronts of the cases; each case was wrapped in oil-cloth and loaded onto a wagon. On May 10, 1815, Jefferson wrote to a friend, "Our tenth and last wagon load of books goes off today. . . . It is the choicest collection of books in the United States, and I hope it will not be without some general effect on the literature of the country."

Clearly the enlightenment of Congress was not envisioned by Jefferson as the only objective of his personal library.

As the cases arrived, Watterston had them set up just as they had been shipped. He began work on a new version of Jefferson's catalog in which books were still listed within each of the forty-four divisions of Francis Bacon's classification of knowledge, but Watterston alphabetized the books within the divisions instead of using Jefferson's various subdivisions.

Jefferson didn't care for the altered version but admitted to a friend, "I think it possible the alphabetical arrangement may be more convenient to readers generally."

Congress liked it less, not because of the alphabetizing but because it seemed unscientific and so strongly resembled Jefferson's original system. When the *Catalogue of the Library of the United States*—Watterston's title—appeared in the autumn, it clearly bore the stamp of the third president, taken as an indication that Watterston had done little to make it more intelligible to members. The term, "the Library of the United States," suggested a national role for the inchoate institution that some members thought too grand.

The Joint Committee on the Library's report was issued in early 1816. It stated that "however ingenious, scientific, philosophical, and useful such a catalogue may be in the possession of a gentleman who, as was the case with the former proprietor of this, now the Library of Congress, has classed his books himself, who alone has access to them, and has become from long habit and experience as perfectly familiar with every book in his library . . . still this form of catalogue is much less useful" than the catalog of the old Library. That had not been arranged according to the Baconian system.

The lawmakers also deplored the expense of the catalog—$1,356.50. This amounted to more than the entire annual appropriation. "The Library Committee are dissatisfied with me," Watterston wrote to Jefferson, "for having the catalogue printed without having waited to consult their *superior judgement*." His added emphasis suggests that the Librarian had a jaundiced view of his employers' intellectual capabilities.

Watterston seems to have been little affected by Congress's disapproval or by the fact that he was denied compensation for the workers he hired to assist him. His salary was raised to $1,000 a year, however, and he continued to advo-

James Monroe, who assumed the presidency in 1816, resisted efforts to replace Watterston, whose political outspokenness and personal irascibility gave fuel to detractors.

From a portrait by Thomas Sully. Prints and Photographs Division, Library of Congress. LC-USZ62-2429

cate a more comprehensive library than the one in his charge. Writing in the *National Intelligencer* in March 1817, Watterston pointed out that in other countries a library of deposit was "an object of national pride" and suggested that the United States use as a model for a new structure the "elegant and splendid . . . national library at Paris."

The contrast between the ideal and the reality on the third floor of Blodget's Hotel could not have been greater.

James Monroe had handled foreign affairs during the War of 1812. He was a Republican and a confirmed member of "the Virginia dynasty," and he became president in 1816. He did not replace Watterston, whose passion for a national library seemed to have found sympathizers in the Senate. On January 6, 1817, a bill was passed there authorizing the Joint Committee to make "from time to time, a selection of such books as they may deem proper . . . out of the books which by the existing laws are to be deposited by the authors or publishers in the office of the Secretary of State."

This did not become law, but it did prefigure later copyright deposits. Meanwhile, the Library had again become a center of some socializing. According to a local commentator, it was "much resorted to as a place of relaxation." This did not improve the Librarian's relations with certain members of Congress, however. In his novel, *The L . . . Family at Washington*, Watterston would write of this, the so-called garret period of the Library, and of the unhappy Librarian officiating in cramped quarters, looking "devilishly sour."

In 1818, Watterston's opponents in Congress called for his resignation and for the appointment of someone less staunchly Republican. Senator Jonathan Roberts had to defend Watterston to Monroe, pointing out that the Librarian had several children to support, had recently bought a new house on credit, and—most important—had long defended in print "Republican principles." Monroe declined to replace him.

The president also signed into law a bill, on December 3, 1818, authorizing the joint committee "to cause suitable apartments, in the north wing of the Capitol, to be fitted up and furnished for the temporary reception of the Library of Congress." The books were returned to the Capitol, with an appropriation of $2,000 for additional ones.

The new attic quarters were preferred by Watterston to the old ones. He described them hyperbolically in another fictional work as "a region of learning, where like the Alps, books on books arose."

Too many books, in fact, for the available shelf space, another source of irritation to visiting congressmen described by Watterston as "honourable members and their ladies, more intent, I thought, on gazing at pictures, than on feasting their reason. . . . I thought it was best to stalk about . . . and take no notice of any body."

Clearly Watterston lacked necessary diplomacy, which probably had more to do with his political problems than any failures of management. The new books were gradually assimilated, but Congress continued to complain about the bibliographic disorder and the paucity of reference books.

A gradual awakening was in process, fueled by the global library movement and the examples set by other nations. The *National Intelligencer* crusaded for a national library of significance, pointing out that, in 1823, two thousand people visited the library in the British Museum in a single day. The national library in Paris contained half a million volumes, the *Intelligencer* added. "Among the things that please us most in our Capitol, is the noble room destined to contain the Library of Congress."

Designed by the Capitol architect, Charles Bulfinch, it sat in the center of the West Front of the Capitol; the books were transferred there on August 17, 1824, Monroe's last year in office. He had already signed a bill raising the annual appropriation to $5,000, and the new Library quickly became a showcase of learning and congressional intentions. The *National Journal* described the room reverentially as "decidedly the most beautiful, and in the best taste of any in this country."

Frances Trollope, mother of the English novelist Anthony Trollope, while traveling in America visited Congress. She found the new library quarters "very handsome . . . elegantly furnished; rich Brussels carpet; library tables, with portfolios of engravings; abundance of sofas. . . . The view from it is glorious."

And possibly short-lived. History was poised to repeat itself, sadly and ironically. The slow resurrection of this Library, fraught with politics, the vision and finances of the third president, and the administrative problems of an obscure Librarian with a vision of national significance, was threatened by the old enemy of book collections everywhere—fire.

In 1824 the reconstituted Library of Congress took up new quarters in
the West Front of the refurbished U.S. Capitol. Designed by Boston-
born Charles Bulfinch, appointed Architect of the Capitol in 1818, the
work and its executor exemplified the transition from amateur to professional architect that occurred at the time in this and other fields.
Bulfinch completed the Capitol's Senate and House wings, begun by
Latrobe, redesigned and constructed the rotunda and dome, and added
the Library of Congress and the western front on the Mall side of the
rotunda. The beauty and majesty of the room were much acclaimed,
but in less than two years the building—and the Library—would be
threatened yet again by fire.

Andrew Jackson Davis, "View Congress Library. Capitol. Washington," pen-and-ink
wash on paper, 1832. New York Public Library, New York, New York.

On the night of December 22, 1825, someone left a candle burning in a gallery of the Congress, in the midst of the Christmas season. The resulting conflagration threatened the entire Capitol; it and the Library were narrowly saved from a second destruction. No blame was ever assigned, although Watterston was subjected to vague accusations of neglect by Federalists in and out of government, including members of the Joint Committee on the Library, accusations that echoed the problems of the former Librarian, Patrick Magruder.

These prompted Watterston to respond, in character. He wrote to W. C. Bradley, with typical stylistic excess, of "so many greedy & hungry expectants of office who flock to the seat of govt. . . . who, at a distance, pester & harass for positions, that, upon the occurrence of the slightest accident, & indeed where no cause exists, they rush forward open mouthed & in full cry to fill the vacant space."

That vacant space might well be his own position; clearly, Watterston feared for his job.

A positive outcome of the 1825 fire was the raising of the question of fire prevention. But fire-proofing was deemed by Congress impractical and too expensive, and so the stage was set for a subsequent disaster.

John Quincy Adams had been narrowly elected president in 1824; he kept Watterston on. Edward Everett, representative from Massachusetts, was made a

By the late 1820s the Capitol building, shown here in a view of the West Front, had begun to take on its now-familiar form, with a dome higher than Latrobe had originally envisioned, as it was redesigned and constructed by Bulfinch. The cows shown grazing on the Mall belie the Industrial Revolution rapidly transforming U.S. cities in the north. Watercolor by John Rubens Smith, ca. 1829.

Marian S. Carson Collection of Americana, Prints and Photographs Division, Library of Congress. LC-USZC4-3579

Andrew Jackson, whose defeat of Henry Clay in the bitter presidential race of 1828 spelled the end of George Watterston's tenure as Librarian of Congress.

Painted by Thomas Sully, engraved by James B. Longacre. Published by William H. Morgan, ca. 1820. Prints and Photographs Division, Library of Congress. LC-USZ62-435

(right) President John Quincy Adams, who in 1828 authorized the position of Assistant Librarian of Congress. Earlier in his public career, Adams had been one of the first authorized book-buyers for Congress.

From National Portrait Gallery, *The Life Portraits of John Quincy Adams* (Washington, 1970), original in the collections of Harvard University.

member of the joint committee. Keenly interested in the collection, Everett busied the Librarian with queries. When the House of Representatives had the opportunity to expand the Library by acquiring manuscripts and books relating to America owned by Obadiah Rich, Everett championed the purchase. The collection included the letters of Amerigo Vespucci, Fracanzano da Montalboddo's *Itinerarium Portugalensium*, and another two hundred-odd items. The offer was declined by Congress, one of several missed opportunities, but Everett was successful in acquiring a lesser collection. This struggle between books perceived as practical and those seen as "antiquated" would persist.

Andrew Jackson and Henry Clay were pitted against one another in the upcoming 1828 election. Watterston, writing regularly for the *National Journal* to supplement his income and to strike blows for the emergent Whigs, championed Clay, Virginia statesman, "Great Pacificator," and currently secretary of state. In his new novel, *Wanderer in Washington*, the Librarian described Clay favorably and castigated supporters of General Jackson, hero of the Battle of New Orleans.

This was daring—and reckless—behavior for a man dependent upon the goodwill of a sitting president for his job, with Clay's prospects for election far from certain. But Watterston had never been circumspect in his dealings with those in power, and his tenure in the service of Congress had increased his invective.

General Jackson won the bitter contest and decided to replace Watterston, a predictable consequence of Watterston's partisan extracurricular activities. But the Librarian was outraged. He launched a journalistic campaign against his perceived enemies, among them anyone who considered himself worthy of succeeding him, referring to "the ignorance or stupidity of those who have been put into a situation for which they may be wholly unfit."

His friend Henry Clay melodramatically compared the replacing of Watterston to the burning of the Alexandrian library, and attributed the former to "the despotism" of the new Jacksonian regime.

Watterston was forced from the Library anyway. He took with him some of the records, including the manuscript of the catalog of Jefferson's library, which he turned over to his children to use as copybooks. It was an ignoble final act for a Librarian, however self-dramatizing and intemperate, who had envisioned a national library considerably beyond the needs of the men it currently served. Watterston would beseech succeeding presidents for reinstatement, without success, for two decades.

The object of his specific scorn was John Silva Meehan, a thirty-nine-year-old former publisher of more even temperament than his detractor. A native of New York, Meehan had published two Baptist periodicals since arriving in Washington a few years before, but had felt the allure of politics and had gone on to edit the newspaper *United States' Telegraph*. This had as its motto the thoroughly Jacksonian sentiment, "Power is always stealing from the many to the few." It had advanced the cause of the new Democrats, and this contributed to Meehan's appointment.

The job of Librarian had grown in both influence and in responsibility. The Library's holdings now included about sixteen thousand volumes and innumerable maps and periodicals. The fourth Librarian's time was occupied with cleaning and rearranging books while Congress discussed the advisability of making the law library available to the Supreme Court and of acquiring rare volumes, always a contentious issue. Meehan also visited the libraries of Baltimore, Philadelphia, New York, West Point, and Boston to learn about library management and the preservation of his valuable charge.

A separate law library was established in 1832, with purchases to be stipulated by the chief justice of the United States. Two years later, a joint resolution of Congress signed by the president called for twenty-five copies of every work printed by "order or at the expense of the United States" to be made available to the joint committee, which could use them to procure donations to the Library.

The fourth Librarian, John Silva Meehan, was a populist former publisher and editor whose vocal support for Jackson's new Democratic Party helped secure his appointment. Taking up the post in May 1829, Meehan would serve for more than thirty years under nine presidents.

Prints and Photographs Division, Library of Congress. LC-USZ62-43063

Once again the Library, located between the two houses of Congress, had become a functioning social center for lawmakers and their wives and friends, a fact that apparently did not displease Meehan as it had his predecessor.

A contributor to a local literary magazine, the *Champagne Club*, wrote in 1835: "A group of laughing, chatting ladies were *nonchalantly* turning over the elephant sheets of Audubon's ornithology; a sort of *obligato* amusement, like a flute accompaniment in a concerto, for all the fashionable idlers, who put to the test the urbanity of the Librarian."

Expansion of the Library was being advocated beyond the confines of Congress. Secretary of War Lewis Cass, addressing the American Historical Society in 1836, called for expanding the Library "in all the departments of human learning, as will render it worthy of the age and country, and elevate it to an equality with those great repositories of knowledge." But the bias against books perceived as nonessential persisted.

In 1836, the Joint Committee on the Library recommended purchasing twenty-five thousand volumes in the library of a Count Bourtoulin, of Florence, for "fifty or sixty thousand dollars." It would have more than doubled the books in the Library of Congress; included in the Bourtoulin collection were, in addi-

tion to early, rare works in Greek, Latin, and Italian, "419 copies of Aldine editions, 368 from the Bodoni press, and many hundred volumes printed in the fifteenth century."

The joint committee chairman, Senator William C. Preston of South Carolina, pointed out that this, one of the world's extraordinary private collections, was strong in areas where the Library was weak, including belle lettres and the history of art and literature; he echoed Jefferson's sentiments that no area of inquiry was beyond the possible requirements of Congress. But Henry Clay, among others, opposed the purchase, and the Senate narrowly declined to acquire Bourtoulin's library to augment its own.

View of the Capitol in 1840. The Library of Congress, roughly in the center of the building, had by this time become not only a locus of scholarly and legislative research but also a social gathering place for Washington's elite.

From William Dawson Johnston, *History of the Library of Congress*, vol. 1 (Washington, 1904).

The Library Committee called for the first official exchange of publications with another nation in 1837, an important precedent. The country was France, and it was a Frenchman, the colorful Alexandre Vattemare, ventriloquist as well as bibliophile, who would be recognized by Congress a few years later as the Library's representative in effecting the exchange of documents with various foreign countries.

At the time, France's national library contained more than twice the number estimated to exist in the entire United States. The Vatican library contained some 400,000 books and manuscripts, and the Imperial libraries of Vienna and St. Petersburg about 300,000 each. The Library of Congress could only aspire to such intellectual bounty.

Alexandre Vattemare, a French bibliophile and an early advocate for international exchanges among libraries. His ideas found favor in the Joint Committee on the Library, which in 1837 authorized the first such exchange between the United States and France and later made Vattemare the Library's first foreign acquisitions agent. These foreign acquisitions became the foundation for a solid program in area studies and collections that supported research in many cultures.

From William Dawson Johnston, *History of the Library of Congress*, vol. 1 (Washington, 1904).

Jackson did sign a bill authorizing a $5,000 appropriation for law books, apparently the sort most in favor during the egalitarian reign of the outgoing chief executive. The hero of the Battle of New Orleans did not have a high regard for scholarship.

Meehan apparently took no philosophical position on questions relating to the proper contents of the Library. He kept careful records and performed other duties calculated to please Congress, and specifically members of the Joint Library Committee. His devotion to detail and ability to avoid politics, after politics had put him there, enabled him to retain the office of Librarian long after the departure of the man who first appointed him.

Charles Dickens, the British novelist, otherwise a harsh critic of the United States during his visit here in 1842, found Meehan's Library of Congress "pleasant and commodious," with a balcony and "a beautiful prospect of the adjacent country."

Caleb Cushing, representative from Massachusetts, was one of the few allies in Congress of President John Tyler, a Whig. Cushing championed the president's right to conduct his own foreign affairs and to fund foreign missions. Rejected in the Senate as Tyler's nominee for secretary of the treasury in 1843, Cushing was made "Commissioner, Envoy Extraordinary and Minister Plenipotentiary" and sent to China.

An attorney, a linguist, and an accomplished politician, Cushing successfully negotiated a treaty opening the commercial avenues of China to Americans. During most of his diplomatic service in the Far East, he acted as an unofficial agent of the Library of Congress, acquiring rare books and manu-

scripts that launched the Chinese, Japanese, Korean, and Indic collections.

In 1845, Texas was becoming one of the United States, and the war with Mexico was about to begin. The shifting political center in Washington had left the Library largely unaffected; it was a bit larger, and better appointed. The book collector and writer William Q. Force remarked at the time in his book about Washington: "Within the Capitol is a Library of about forty thousand volumes, in a large and elegant room, and disposed in order by an excellent librarian . . . a gentleman of amiable manners."

Meehan had survived as Librarian of Congress under four presidents by now—Jackson, Martin Van Buren, Tyler, and James Polk (five if the tenure of William Henry Harrison, dead after a month in office, is considered). Meehan was recognized as an able administrator, but the Library still lacked stature at a time of rising sentiment for a national institution devoted to books.

Senator Rufus Choate of Massachusetts, outgoing head of the joint committee, publicly criticized the Library, as did Congressman George Perkins Marsh, of Vermont. Choate publicly stated that the small appropriations would

(above left) Massachusetts Senator Rufus Choate chaired the Library Committee in the period leading up to the establishment of the Smithsonian Institution in 1846. The idea of a national library had gained momentum in Congress and among opinion makers, but many—Choate included—favored the Smithsonian as its seat.

Smithsonian Institution Archives.

Congressman George Perkins Marsh, who like Choate supported a national library and considered the Library of Congress ill-suited, and woefully ill-equipped, to assume the role.

Smithsonian Institution Archives.

Senator James A. Pearce of Maryland, the scholarly and patrician successor to Choate as chair of the Library Committee. Pearce would become a major figure in the Library's administration during the tenure of John Meehan.

Daguerreotype. Prints and Photographs Division, Library of Congress. LC-USZ62-109962

forever keep the Library from greatness, and Marsh added that "there is no one branch of liberal study . . . in which it is not miserably deficient."

Even the new chairman of the joint committee, Senator James Alfred Pearce of Maryland, had a dim view of the Library's indices ("crude, meager, and deficient"). But Pearce brought to bear considerable intellectual power, and discipline, and he soon dominated the Library. The relationship between the senator and the Librarian was a good one, but it did not allow flexibility on the larger question of a national library—which Pearce envisioned not in the Capitol, but just down the Mall.

The nascent Smithsonian Institution threatened the Library of Congress's sovereignty and national aspirations at a time when those ideas were still speculative and controversial. Established with a bequest from the late James Smithson, a wealthy English scientist, the Smithsonian was struggling with its vague mandate, "The increase and diffusion of knowledge among men."

On one side was Joseph Henry, secretary of the Smithsonian, a respected physicist devoted to scientific research who opposed the notion of a national library located there, and on the other the brilliant young Charles Coffin Jewett, Henry's librarian. Jewett was determined to make the Smithsonian *the* great American repository of books. Among his allies in Congress were Choate, Marsh, and Pearce.

The act establishing the Smithsonian stipulated that both it and the Library of Congress were to receive, on deposit, one copy of every copyrighted "book, map, chart, musical composition, print, cut, or engraving." The copyright deposits were considered a burden by almost everyone at the Library, which now possessed more than fifty thousand volumes and was expanding its international exchange program and the acquisition of books abroad. Meehan would probably have welcomed relinquishing his copyright deposit duties to the messianic Jewett, who was comparing the establishment of a national library to the writing of the Declaration of Independence.

Meehan had earned a reputation for prudence in money matters; he had acquired duties additional to those performed for the Library. He kept the records and attended to correspondence for the Wilkes Fund, set up to publish the results of Charles Wilkes's global explorations, a fund for the purchase the works of John Adams, the Botanic Garden Fund—Meehan occasionally had to ensure that congressmen wanting botanical specimens for their gardens got them—and a $20,000 fund for acquiring art for the Capitol.

(above left) Joseph Henry, scientist and pioneer of electromagnetism, became the first secretary of the Smithsonian Institution in 1846. Henry's opposition to locating a national library within the new institution was at odds with the ambitious vision of his own librarian, Charles C. Jewett.

Prints and Photographs Division, Library of Congress. LC-USZ62-14760

Charles Coffin Jewett, the brilliant Smithsonian librarian whose impassioned dream of building the nation's preeminent library under Smithsonian auspices was not to be. The librarian's break with Joseph Henry and subsequent departure over the issue would signal a new, and essentially permanent, shift of momentum in favor of the Library of Congress.

Prints and Photographs Division, Library of Congress. LC-USZ62-13081

He also managed the fund to print the Library's catalog—according to the plan put forward by the Smithsonian—and separate funds for the publication of Thomas Jefferson's, James Madison's, and Alexander Hamilton's papers, and yet another for acquiring portraits by G. P. A. Healy of the presidents of the United States. But it was Jewett on the Mall who made the daring, and popular, proposals regarding books and libraries.

One was that the Smithsonian Institution become "a center of bibliographical reference" with "one class of books most immediately important to American scholars . . . to place American students on a footing with those of the most favored country of Europe." Jewett's vision included a centralized cataloging system for all American libraries produced by the Smithsonian on stereotype plates that would be generally distributed.

A committee appointed by the new president, Millard Fillmore, generally approved of Jewett's ideas, including the proposal for the Smithsonian to catalog all the books of the Library of Congress. The chairman of the Library's Joint Committee approved as well, also being a member of the inner group helping to shape the Smithsonian. A new, alphabetical arrangement of the Library of Congress's books would appeal to congressmen who had complained for decades about the old system, if not about the comforts the Library afforded them.

The main Library hall was now hung with portraits of the first three presidents by Gilbert Stuart, plus portraits of other noted Americans and foreigners, including one of Christopher Columbus over the south mantle. A bust of Jefferson stood next to the door leading to the balcony, on a pedestal held up by fluted black marble, opposite a bust of Lafayette. The books were arranged in twelve arched alcoves, and a fine carpet set off these symbols of learning and decorum.

Then in the early hours of Christmas eve, 1851, a blaze broke out, another holiday alarm and the third fire for the Library of Congress. A coalition of firemen and citizens battled it until noon, cutting the burning roof and dome away with axes and so saving the rest of the Capitol. Frozen hoses made their work more difficult.

Meehan wrote to Senator Pearce that same day: "It is my melancholy duty to inform you that a fire originated in the principal room of the Library . . . and that nearly everything in the room was destroyed before the flames were subdued." He added that "the late beautiful room, with its invaluable contents" was nothing but "a smoldering mass of ruins."

Gone were some thirty-five thousand volumes, including two-thirds of Jefferson's irreplaceable library. Almost completely destroyed were the collections of parliamentary debates, congressional reports, maps, the documents of the Committee for International Exchanges and those attained by Vattemare, medals, portraits, and busts, among them a bronze of George Washington, and the marble likeness of Jefferson.

Among the salvaged material were Jefferson's books categorized as ancient, American, and ecclesiastical history, "Mineralogy and Conchology," moral philosophy, "Law of Nature and Nations," religion, politics, music, "Dialogue and Epistolary," logic, rhetoric, and "the Theory of Criticism." The law library had also survived. The fire had been a real—and in the minds of some, a symbolic—disaster.

A faulty chimney flue, not human error, had been the culprit. Faced with the absence of what it had come to take for granted, Congress quickly appropriated money to pay for the fire-fighting, and for a temporary room for the books that remained. Another $10,000 was provided for replacements, a start at the daunting task of reacquisition.

In March 1852, the Architect of the Capitol, Thomas U. Walter, proposed repairs and a significant enlargement of the Library quarters to include all of the western projection of the Capitol, at a cost of $72,500. At last a fireproof material was to be used—iron. This, too, was quickly approved by the president, as were a subsequent cost overrun in August and an additional $75,000 for the purchase of books and furniture.

Private gifts of books and art work arrived throughout the year from concerned Americans and foreigners, among them members of the Royal Geographic Society. Books and documents were brought up from the cellar where they had

Architect of the Capitol Thomas U. Walter, who planned and oversaw a major new expansion of Library of Congress quarters in the Capitol following the disastrous fire of 1851, the third to befall the Library. After a two-year reconstruction —this time using fireproof materials— the Library's quarters were pronounced more impressive than ever, yet the institution itself remained without even a stated mission or acquisitions policy.

Smithsonian Institution Archives.

been stored after the fire. Meehan had a staff of five, and kept the temporary Library open every day when Congress was in session, and three times a week during recess, waiting for what promised to be an ideal new architectural creation.

Construction proceeded. On each side of the main room—ninety-one feet long, thirty-four feet wide—three stories of iron bookcases slowly rose. Semicircular stairways were erected, works of art arrived to replace those lost, and overall the structural vision took shape. But there was no vision for the collection itself, neither from Meehan nor from Senator Pearce.

"The new Library, in a safer room, was to be merely a replica of the old," wrote David Mearns in *The Story Up to Now*. "No one took advantage of the opportunity to devise a definition. No acquisitions policy, for which the Library had waited for half a century, was contrived. No imagination was any-

where discernible, save for the ingenuity of the architect."

Meehan survived the transition to yet another administration, and in the spring of 1853, President Franklin Pierce approved $3,000 for a general catalog that Charles Coffin Jewett had proposed, the stereotype plate system. Sentiment still tilted in Congress toward the establishment of a national library at the Smithsonian when the secretary, Joseph Henry, faced with the prospect of spending most of the institution's resources on books, pronounced that "the idea ought never to be entertained" that the Smithsonian would provide enough books to "ever be sufficient to meet the needs of the American scholar."

This prefigured the formal break between Henry and Jewett and clearly signaled that a preeminent national library, if there was to be one, would not be housed at the Smithsonian. Jewett was dismissed by Henry in July 1854; the Library of Congress would a dozen years later receive many of the books and documents Jewett had so eagerly assembled, as part of what became known as the Smithsonian deposit.

The more likely residence for a national library had always been the Library of Congress. The previous August, 1853, had seen the completion of the orna-

President Franklin Pierce was among the first visitors to admire the new Library quarters in 1853, the last year of his presidency.

mented ceiling in the new Library, with its elaborate ironwork and paneled walls adorned with frescoes that pleased the Librarian (" . . . most elegant," Meehan wrote to Senator Pearce). The upper gallery, including pilasters and pillars, was painted and repainted a deep cream color, and the ornamentation gilded. Carpets were laid, and most of the Library's approximately twenty-five thousand volumes shelved.

On July 6, 1853, a month before the official opening, the president of the United States paid a visit, the first in years to show any active interest in this extension of his executive privilege. President Pierce was accompanied by the British scientist Sir Charles Lyell, who pronounced the new Library "the most beautiful room in the world."

The Library had come to serve not just Congress but also the Supreme Court, the State Department, the president, judges, and various government agencies. Visitors were so plentiful that an admission charge was contemplated; anyone present was allowed to read and peruse books and to engage in private colloquies that on occasion combined reference, statesmanship, and socializing.

An illustrated article that appeared in an 1856 edition of *United States Magazine* portrayed both the Library's exquisite architectural detail and groups of top-

Abraham Lincoln, who took office in 1861, chose not to follow the wishes of the Joint Committee on the Library but instead exercised his prerogative as president and brought the decades-long tenure of John Meehan as Librarian of Congress to a close.

Quarter-plate daguerreotype by Nicholas Shepherd, ca. 1846. Prints and Photographs Division, Library of Congress. LC-USZC4-2439 (color); LC-USZ62-12457 (black and white) hatted, frock-coated men with canes conversing while women gazed on admiringly. The Library had become a de facto public institution, if not a formally recognized one; it served Congress well enough but was still far short of the universal demands of American scholarship.

In 1857, James Buchanan was elected president and, like so many before him, allowed the Librarian, the aging Meehan, to stay on at the Library. President Buchanan's only significant act relating to the collection was to repeal the copyright deposit provision. The quality and scope of the materials received by the Library, and by the Smithsonian, had been uneven. Meehan, like Joseph Henry, was glad to be free of the obligation—for the time being.

Meehan was sixty-seven years old and had served as Librarian for twenty-eight of them. His sophistication, business acumen, and diplomacy had kept him somewhat above the Capitol fray, but at the outset of the new decade, politics caught up with him at last.

John G. Stephenson, appointed the fifth Librarian of Congress by Lincoln in May of 1861. The appointment of Stephenson, a physician and Republican activist, was largely a matter of political patronage, though by all accounts he served ably and delegated well — especially in bringing on the young Ainsworth Spofford to be his principal assistant.

Prints and Photographs Division, Library of Congress. LC-USZ62-614319

President Abraham Lincoln took office in 1861, when members of Congress, like so many Americans, were at odds over the questions of slavery and secession. Senator Pearce, still chairman of the Library Committee, quickly wrote to Lincoln to remind him that for years the president had acceded to the wishes of Congress in the choice of its Librarian, and that the committee wanted to retain Meehan and his staff.

These "men of books," Pearce assured the president, would be unaffected "by political changes & safe from the influence of political partisanship."

One month later, the bombardment of Fort Sumter in South Carolina by the Confederates launched open warfare between the North and South. Meehan, like many others in Washington, had relatives sympathetic to the South and was automatically associated with a cause that had little real claim on him. But Lincoln was distracted, and intensely political, and a month later he relieved Meehan of his duties and replaced him with a Lincoln supporter from Terre Haute, Indiana, a physician named John G. Stephenson.

One of Meehan's final acts as Librarian was to write a letter to a London bookseller. Meehan advised him that the bookseller would in the future be dealing with someone else and predicted that the man's relationship with the Library of Congress would continue to be "satisfactory and happy." That statement is free of the vituperation characteristic of former dismissed Librarians; if nothing else, Meehan stands as a paragon of civility at the outset of the least civil time in American history.

Catawba and Good Fellowship

Visiting Washington in 1861 was a young man with the unlikely name of Ainsworth Rand Spofford, the son of a New England clergyman who had gone west—to Cincinnati—to overcome physical handicaps, including weak lungs. There Spofford had become a partner in a book-selling and publishing firm; "energy, great memory, and knowledge of books," according to a friend, "soon made him indispensable for the business."

Known for voracious reading in politics, history, and biography, Spofford also founded Cincinnati's Literary Club. He and other young members, considered radicals by the city's gentility, debated current issues and ideas while imbibing local catawba wine. Spofford was enthusiastic about the New England Transcendentalists; he convinced Ralph Waldo Emerson to come to Cincinnati to speak. Spofford and Emerson became friends, and Spofford—tenacious, serious—was able to bring other noted writers westward, among them Theodore Parker and Bronson Alcott.

Spofford, too, proved to be a writer of uncommon literary sensibility and good sense. An ardent "Free-Soiler," opposed to slavery, Spofford wrote an essay justifying defiance of the Fugitive Slave Law that was published as a book in New York in 1851. It so inspired Emerson that he wrote to Spofford admitting that he, Emerson, would "not hide the most unblushing plagiarisms" when he, too, wrote on the subject.

Spofford gained something of a national reputation. Senator Salmon P. Chase, the Free-Soiler defeated by Lincoln in the 1860 presidential election, knew of him and wrote to a friend urging that Spofford be made the editor of a liberal newspaper in Cincinnati. Chase spoke of Spofford's "talent, principle, and business qualities." Instead he became the editorial writer for the *Cincinnati Daily Commercial*, closely aligned in the 1850s with the budding Republican party. His first editorial castigated Cincinnati's librarian for his choice of books, and subsequent ones dealt with the antislavery movement, politics, existing lecture practices, "national history," literary taste, and the U.S. copyright.

These were all potent subjects in Washington,

D.C., where Spofford had been sent by the newspaper in January to write about the opening of the Thirty-seventh Congress. Spofford described Washington in a letter to his wife, Sarah, as "the city of mud & politicians." He praised the abolitionists, criticized the Democrats, and generally reflected upon the capital scene. At the Library of Congress, he wrote in March, "a herd of sightseers press continually around, gazing into the quiet, well-stored alcoves, and reading aloud the titles of books they never saw or heard of."

Fate played some role in Spofford's burgeoning career. In the Cincinnati Literary Club he had included among his friends two crucial individuals, Rutherford B. Hayes and Reuben H. Stephenson. The former was destined for the ultimate political distinction in America; the latter happened to be the brother of the man who had just become President Lincoln's new Librarian of Congress.

Ainsworth Rand Spofford, publisher, book dealer, and editorialist.

Prints and Photographs Division, Library of Congress. LC-BH826-452-A

James A. Garfield, born in Ohio, joined Spofford in the Literary Club of Cincinnati before the Civil War. After the war, he spent seventeen years in Congress, but his presidential career was cut short by his assassination.

Prints and Photographs Division, Library of Congress. LC-USZ62-209

Essayist Ralph Waldo Emerson, another friend of Spofford's youth, spoke in Cincinnati at Spofford's invitation and so liked Spofford's writing against the Fugitive Slave Law that he accorded it the prospective flattery of his own imitation of it.

Prints and Photographs Division, Library of Congress. LC-USZ62-084673

Rutherford B. Hayes and his wife, Lucy Ware Webb Hayes. Spofford's friendship with future president Hayes would have deeply fortuitous consequences for the Library of Congress.

Photograph by Fabian Bachrach. Prints and Photographs Division, Library of Congress. LC-USZ62-32420

3

The Crystal Fountain ⸻

(1861–1896)

An institution is the lengthened shadow of one man.

Ralph Waldo Emerson

The mystic chords of memory, stretching from every battlefield and patriot grave to every living heart and hearthstone all over this broad land, will yet swell the chorus of the Union, when again touched, as surely they will be, by the better angels of our nature."

The conciliatory words spoken by President Lincoln in his inaugural address in March 1861 had not prevented the subsequent secession by more Southern states; hostilities, real and unappeasable, pulled at official Washington in unprecedented ways after the fall of Fort Sumter.

Those better angels charged with the conduct of government and the passage of laws—i.e., members of Congress—were also torn by national and factional loyalties, while those serving them often showed more enthusiasm for war than for their official duties. One of these was the new Librarian of Congress, John G. Stephenson. An ardent speaker in Republican causes, one of Lincoln's early supporters, and apparently a mediocre doctor, Stephenson had come to Washington seeking the appointment for the financial benefits that came with it; once ensconced, he set about replacing the Library staff. It was a disordered and neglected facility, in his view: dust-ridden and ill-managed, the books disintegrating and no suitable accounting system, and the collections woefully lacking in modern encyclopedias and newspapers.

The autocratic, courtly head of the Library Committee since 1845, Senator Pearce, a Southern sympathizer whose resistance to change was one of the Library's problems, was accustomed to pliant underlings and was taken aback by Stephenson's action. Pearce complained of the new Librarian's presumption with regard to the dismissals, but Stephenson was not dissuaded. He wanted subordinates capable of running an improved facility on their own while he

A later portrait of Ainsworth Rand
Spofford, whose forty-seven-year career at
the Library of Congress transformed the
Library from a legislative resource into a
genuinely national institution.

Photograph of a portrait by Bayard H. Tyler.
Library of Congress Archive.

attended to a matter of greater concern to him—achieving distinction in the
fighting south of the Potomac as a commissioned colonel in the Indiana militia.

Stephenson's contribution to the Library of Congress may well have been
inadvertent but it would prove to be of lasting significance, for he offered the
position of chief assistant to the Librarian to the slight, bearded literary man
from New Hampshire, the pseudonymous editorializer in the pages of the
Cincinnati Daily Commercial against slavery and secession, A. R. Spofford.

A staunch Republican, Spofford had witnessed and reported upon the battle of Bull Run and could claim valuable prior experiences as a bookseller and
leading light in the literary fellowship of Cincinnati. But it was connections, as
always, that had counted most: a fellow member of Cincinnati's Literary Club,
Reuben H. Stephenson, brother of the new Librarian, had recommended
Spofford as an assistant.

Spofford weighed his response in his meticulous way. On August 5, 1861,
he wrote to his wife, Sarah, to list nine reasons for declining the job and seventeen for accepting, among them "Largely increased opportunities of
acquaintance, especially with public men, editors, & scholars" and "Escape from

disagreeables of a coal-smoked city." He went to work at the Library in September; on his first day at the Library, Spofford had to sign documents for Stephenson who, having attended Union wounded in a makeshift hospital set up in the Patent Office, was soon off to the battlefield.

Spofford's editorials in the *Commercial*, written under the names "Sigma" and "Spero," according to historian John Y. Cole, "illustrated their author's ardent sense of purpose, his concern with 'educating' his audience," "his self-righteousness," and "an inordinate degree of intellectual zeal and self-confidence." All these traits became apparent as Spofford plunged into what he had predicted would require "no exhaustion of brain" but which in fact absorbed him.

Within a month Spofford was writing to the still unhappy Senator Pearce announcing a new binder for the catalog that Spofford had ordered without consulting the chairman and asking that the joint committee authorize payment. This was followed on December 16, 1861, by a hand-written, thirty-five-hundred-word "Annual Report of the Librarian," unsigned but certainly written by the Assistant Librarian, criticizing the condition of the Library and appealing in strong terms to the committee to "repair its deficiencies and to promote its usefulness to those who are entitled to its benefits."

The Library contained about seventy-two thousand volumes and pamphlets, about fifteen thousand of those duplicates, and Spofford wanted permission to auction off what he indelicately referred to as "rubbish" and to use the funds for other purchases. In addition, almost a thousand books had been lost or assigned to people no longer in Congress. In general, Spofford's discussion of circulation practices, bookkeeping, and physical conditions at the Library was both dismal and damning.

Spofford also introduced in the report what would be the central theme of his tenure: the need for a well-stocked national library, "the only one commonly visited by travelers and by the American people." This rich, dependable, handsome source of books and other reference materials would serve as an inspiration to the nation, he felt, but not as the core of a nationwide library system. Instead, the Library of Congress would symbolize America's intellectual achievement and potential. Spofford thought a marble floor to replace the present carpeting would be good place to start, pointing out that the British Museum's floor was made of slate.

No fewer than eight appendixes were attached to the exhaustive report which had been compiled in three months with the help of only two clerks, a momentous achievement that covered everything from expenditures to government publications required. Its clear intimation was that the committee, the committee chairman, and the former Librarian were remiss; it isn't difficult to imagine the effect of such criticism on old Senator Pearce, whom Spofford considered the dead hand of the past.

In January 1862, Ralph Waldo Emerson came to Washington. Spofford showed his renowned literary friend around the Library, pointing out its deficiencies and blaming them on "Southern domination." The slowness of congressional response to his report may have spurred Spofford to publicly criticize congressmen in the *Commercial*, again under the moniker Sigma, asking why $3,000 per annum was paid "for a third of a year's attendance in Washington for a body of men two-thirds of whom could not earn as much in a whole year at home." And: "There is no use disguising the fact—the halls of Congress are full of little men . . . gifted with no power of broad or comprehensive vision."

This was risky behavior for a man in Spofford's position, who could have lost his job at the hands of the "little men." But as he explained in a letter to a friend, he intended to avoid being identified with "partisan journals," and then gave vent to more strong feelings: "For myself, despising, perhaps unduly, the whole tribe and generation of politicians, I have . . . engrossed myself in intellectual pursuits connected more or less intimately with acquiring a thorough knowledge of a great Library."

He managed to keep from being identified with Sigma's public sentiments and meanwhile began to build political bridges on Capitol Hill that he thought necessary for the eventual success of a national library. He was no longer openly identified with the Republican party or any special interest group. The Assistant Librarian, for all his criticism and scholarly remove, would prove himself to be a calculating, and effective, member of the tribe.

The English novelist Anthony Trollope, visiting Washington, wrote that the streets "were always full of soldiers. Mounted sentries stood at the corners . . . with drawn sabres,—shivering with cold and besmeared with mud." In this climate, the Librarian who was also a physician, Stephenson, was assigned to the relief of soldiers of the Army of the Potomac.

Spofford, with strong views on the need to preserve the Union, concentrated nevertheless on Library business. As Stephenson's official representative he traveled to Philadelphia, New York, and Boston, visiting publishers and bookstores to obtain books for the Library and making arrangements for binding books already in the Library's possession. The average cost of new books was almost halved by him and the cost of bindings also reduced, while the quality improved.

Stephenson did find time to dabble in Library affairs. He summarily dismissed a member of the Library staff taken on by Spofford, without consulting anyone and without offering an explanation, prompting Spofford to write of Stephenson's "weakness of character" in a letter to a friend. "I knew that he had many strong impulses—somewhat quick and prone to act upon half views—but I have never before (fortunately) been compelled to see & suffer from an exhibition of his prejudices. He has left me so free to act in all things after my own judgement."

Spofford told Stephenson unequivocally that he would not stay on unless Stephenson agreed to support him, and consult with him about all hiring and firing. Faced with the prospect of finding a replacement, or running the Library himself, Stephenson readily agreed. Spofford considered this "a clear business understanding as to the future conduct of the Library," as well as a de facto recognition of his own autonomy.

The death of Senator Pearce just before Christmas, 1862, alleviated some of Spofford's problems and contributed indirectly to his control. The late senator was succeeded as head of the committee by Vermont's Jacob A. Collamer, more sympathetic to Spofford's desires. A second hand-written report was submitted to the joint committee by Spofford in January 1863, again compiled but not signed by Spofford, frankly assessing the Library's shortcomings. There were three other collections in the United States larger and more comprehensive than the Library's, he said, and conditions for storage of the Library's valuable books was poor.

But into Spofford's prose crept a more solicitous note, indicating that he was learning diplomacy: ". . . if it should appear to the Committee that I am overearnest they are asked to remember that the Library has become of such size and value, will require such care and expense . . . and is intended to fulfill such important purposes in connection with National Legislation, as to make earnestness necessary."

He would need that diplomatic skill in the years ahead, pressing as he was for extension of Library hours and of lending privileges to people outside of Congress, among them judges and solicitors in the Court of Claims, and for expanded and improved facilities. It was the beginning of a long campaign for a national library with universal relevance and integrity, housed in a grand, independent structure already built in the Assistant Librarian's active mind. Surely he would receive help from his Ohio friends moving into positions of prominence in Washington.

During 1863, Librarian Stephenson, a volunteer aide-de-camp now with the rank of colonel, participated in the battles of Fitzhue Crossing, Chancellorsville, and Gettysburg, the last a bloody encounter beyond the imaginings of most Americans. "Colonel Stephenson, Librarian of Congress . . . exposed himself freely on all occasions," wrote Maj. Gen. Abner Doubleday, "and rendered many valuable services." The First Division of the First Army Corps

An artist's eyewitness depiction of a scene from the devastating battle at Gettysburg, in which Librarian of Congress John Stephenson served with the First Army Corps.

Drawing by Alfred R. Waud, July 2, 1863. Prints and Photographs Division, Library of Congress. LC-USZ62-15837

in which Stephenson served suffered 1,153 casualties in the battle, and he was recommended for promotion and subsequently decorated.

Washington was full of Union wounded, attended by volunteers, among them the poet Walt Whitman. During this preoccupation with the hostilities and their effects upon the nation and the capital city, Spofford put aside his strong feelings about the war and continued to press Congress for more money and space for books. He made up a list of documents the Library should but did not possess and later wrote to the secretary of war, Edwin McMasters Stanton, informing him of which of the U.S. Army *Registers* could not be found in the Library, asking for duplicates "in case of fire."

When for the first time Spofford would directly appeal to a friend from Ohio, Secretary of the Treasury Salmon P. Chase, for $1,000 for the contingency fund, so that the Library might acquire new furniture, catalog drawers, and other necessities, Chase would comply. Political capital was being collected by Spofford, who acted as book-buyer, at the Library's discount, for Chase and other friends—Congressman James A. Garfield and Senator John Sherman, also from Ohio, and Rutherford B. Hayes. Garfield extended to Spofford his franking privilege, eliminating some of the Library's postal costs.

Meanwhile Spofford was compiling a new four-volume Library catalog in

A month after the end of the Civil War, army troops marched in review in Washington, D.C. Among those that marched was the Twentieth Army Corps of Georgia, parading here from the Capitol toward the White House along Pennsylvania Avenue.

Prints and Photographs Division, Library of Congress. LC-B811-3398

which all books were listed alphabetically, an innovation, Spofford explained, in the best interests of "facility of reference." The new catalog was released in the fall of 1864 and, unlike previous classification systems contemplated by the Library, caused no dissension in Congress.

The war officially ended with the surrender of Robert E. Lee at Appomattox on April 9, 1865. It had cost 620,000 lives and, as Mark Twain wrote a few years later in *The Gilded Age*, had "uprooted institutions . . . changed the politics of a people, transformed the social life of half the country, and wrought . . . profoundly upon the entire national character."

At the end of December 1864, Stephenson had announced his retirement from the position of Librarian. He had other, vague aspirations, and questions had arisen about his possible involvement in inappropriate wartime speculations. Though these were not proved, they cast a shadow over the affairs of a man who had never pretended that the Library was anything more to him than a political and financial opportunity. He apparently hoped for another patronage job and might have gotten it but for the tragic aftermath of the war's conclusion that initiated, for Stephenson, a drift into obscurity.

Spofford's command of Library affairs was undisputed, and he had the support of the head of the Library's Joint Committee, Senator Collamer. But these things did not assure him the mantle of Librarian, always the prerogative of the president of the United States. The second-ranking member of the committee favored the librarian of the House of Representatives to be Librarian of Congress, and so Spofford's relations with members of the political tribe were to be crucial. Passionately desiring a sphere he had once viewed coolly, Spofford sought the support of everyone sitting in the House and Senate, eliciting sixteen letters of recommendation that he sent to Lincoln, soon followed by eight more. He also sent a petition signed by eighty-seven representatives, and on New Year's Eve, 1864, President Lincoln made Spofford the sixth Librarian of Congress.

Mathew Brady, Photographer

Throughout the Civil War an unlikely bearded figure appeared on battlefields in a dirty white linen duster and straw boater, armed with a strange contraption mounted on a tripod. He traveled at the end of the Union columns in what he called a "what's-it wagon," covered with canvas and pulled by two horses because of the weight of its contents: work benches, cabinets full of equipment and chemicals—silver nitrate, acetic acid, thiosulfate of soda—and a tub of water used in a miraculous process that reproduced images of real events. His name was Mathew B. Brady, and the nascent craft he pursued so diligently and so well was photography.

Brady was already well known as a practitioner of a new art form. His portraits of the famous, in daguerreotypes and collodion prints, included Abraham and Mary Todd Lincoln, Stephen Douglas, Edward, Prince of Wales, Edgar Allan Poe, Clara Barton, Horace Greeley, Zachary Taylor, and many others, but it would be his and his assistants' pictorial record of determined generals and vulnerable soldiers and the overall desperation and waste of war that would earn him a place in history.

The son of Irish immigrants, Brady grew up in the commercial and artistic ferment of New York City. He intended to be a portrait painter but studied under the artist and inventor Samuel F. B. Morse, who had also mastered the early photographic process invented by Louis Daguerre in France. Brady showed great aptitude with it; he opened his own gallery in 1844 at the age of twenty-one and was soon the city's leading society daguerreotypist.

Mathew B. Brady, whose early aspirations toward portrait painting gave way to pursuit of the new technologies of photography.

He switched to wet-plate collodion photography in 1855, and three years later opened the National Photographic Art Gallery in Washington, on Pennsylvania Avenue near Brown's Hotel. Washington was still a provincial backwater with broad, tree-lined avenues of mud overshadowed by huge classical edifices, many of them unfinished (Brady photographed the Capitol while it was under construction, a dank canal extending westward across what is now the Mall toward the bog of the Potomac), and dominated by officials, favor-seekers, and providers of goods and services.

Brady was soon part of the city's social fabric: President-elect Lincoln visited his studio for his first official photographs, and members of his Cabinet and other notables followed. A dandy in expensive tailored clothes and a silk cravat, Brady responded to the allure of war despite its logistical difficulties and its dangers. "Destiny over-ruled me," he later recalled. "Like Euphorion, I felt I had to go."

He obtained permission from his friend, General Winfield Scott, commander in chief of the Union Army and the subject of one of his most notable portraits, to take two what's-it wagons onto the battlefield.

Brady as well as the Union Army were routed at the first battle of Bull Run in July 1861. He took few photographs, and as if in recompense established thirty-five bases of operation from which to photograph the rest of the war. As many as twenty other photographers followed the Army of the Potomac for Brady and captured in searing detail Antietam, Fredericksburg, and other engagements, including those of General Ulysses S. Grant in the last eighteen months of the conflict. They took thousands of photographs. Included in the Brady collection was the famous portrait of Robert E. Lee after his surrender.

Brady's popularity waned toward the end of the war; he waited in vain for the government to publish the negatives of his Official Records of the Rebellion, and was finally declared a bankrupt in

1873. Two years later Congress appropriated
$25,000 to pay the storage fees on what was left of
Brady's archives of negatives and prints, which
represented the majority of approximately seven
thousand prints and negatives from the Civil War
now at the Library of Congress.

Brady lived the rest of his life in Washington
but the career of this bright photographic meteor
had been permanently eclipsed.

Brady's traveling photographic lab—
with which he pioneered the art of
documentary photography during the
Civil War—shown here in Petersburg,
Virginia, around 1864.

Prints and Photographs Division, Library
of Congress. B8184-B-5077

Camp of the Thirty-First Pennsylvania Infantry, just outside of
Washington, D.C., ca. 1861–62.

Photograph by Mathew Brady. Prints and Photographs Division,
Library of Congress. LC-B811-2405

General U. S. Grant, who entered service in the Civil War as a colonel leading a volunteer regiment from Illinois, eventually commanded all the Union armies, drove the Confederates to surrender at Appomattox, and was made general. During his presidency, in 1870, he signed the bill centralizing copyright registration and deposit in the Library of Congress. Following his two terms, Grant made a trip around the world, future Librarian John Russell Young both accompanying him and writing a book about the journey.

Prints and Photographs Division, Library of Congress. LC-USZ62-21986

During the first sixty-four days of 1865, the Library of Congress moved closer toward assuming the role of national library than at any prior time. Spofford was largely responsible. "The Librarian's reputation for honesty and fairness," as John Cole has observed, "combined with his impressive knowledge of books and undeniable energy, naturally led the Committee members to defer to him in virtually all library matters." This influence extended to the body of Congress, where momentous decisions were being made.

On March 3, a bill was passed giving the Library, in addition to the annual appropriation, the unprecedented sum of $160,000 for enlargement, "so as to include in two wings, built fire-proof, the space at either end of the library, measuring about eighty feet in length by thirty feet in width, in accordance with a plan to be approved by the committee." Spofford, who had called attention to the cramped quarters in his 1862 annual report, would now get triple the shelf space and, more importantly, official recognition of the need for expansion, now and in the future.

The same act addressed the old, unresolved question of copyright. The concurrence of Stephenson's predecessor, Meehan, in the 1859 repeal of the copyright law had been negligent, in the view of Spofford, who had championed copyright protection in editorials for the Cincinnati *Commercial* and as Assistant Librarian. When the bill to extend copyright to photographs was raised in 1865, Spofford used the opportunity to propose copyright deposit at the Library once more, and not at the Patent Office, which had been designated as the recipient of copies of all new works. With the support of the Library's Joint Committee, he took his proposal directly to the Committee on Patents.

The bill that emerged amended the copyright law and then stipulated that "a printed copy of every book, pamphlet, map, chart, musical composition, print, engraving, or photograph, for which copyright shall be secured . . . shall be transmitted free of postage . . . to the library of congress at Washington." This would be the basis of the Library's extraordinary accumulation over the years and of its unique status as a national collection for the use not just of Congress but also of the people of the United States.

Two weeks after the bill's passage, Spofford was notifying American publishers of their legal obligation to comply. He also launched an effort to obtain copies of all government publications.

Characteristically, he paid close attention to the details of the Library's physical expansion, differing with the engineer in charge over changes in the original plans and calling for the use of steam heat because it was cleaner and more even than that from proposed "old-fashioned hot-air furnaces."

The assassination of President Lincoln in Ford's Theater on April 14, 1865, threw the country into turmoil once again and set it on a political course that might have been more conciliatory toward the South had Lincoln lived. His successor, Andrew Johnson, beleaguered and unequal to the postwar challenges, made no move to replace the Librarian of Congress.

Spofford's views had found ready acceptance with the head of the joint committee, Senator Collamer, who died in the autumn of 1865 and was replaced by another Spofford supporter, Senator Timothy Howe, of Wisconsin. Shortly thereafter there arrived in Washington an old friend from the Cincinnati Literary Club, Rutherford B. Hayes, who had been elected to Congress and joined the Joint Committee on the Library.

Spofford could now complain with confidence to the Architect of the Capitol of deviations from the expansion plan and insist upon modifications, like adding two overhead passages so more light would be let into the galleries. He wanted proper furnishings for the new wings and put a request directly to the Appropriations Committee for $10,000 for "sliding cases for illustrated books" and other specifics, and he got it.

In his first annual report as Librarian, in 1866, Spofford pointed out that one wing was complete and the other almost so. Space existed for 210,000 books, and the iron construction "is now impregnably fire-proof" and "future accessions to its stores, as well as the present accumulation of valuable works, are secure from a casualty which has twice consumed our national library."

The Library's space was permanent at last, a significant accomplishment for Library advocates. There was room for two important libraries that Spofford hoped to bring into this handsome new realm, if only he could convince members of Congress to accept a beneficence from a sister institution in one case, and in the other to spend an unprecedented amount of money on that enduring subject of congressional debate—books.

The large library of the Smithsonian, long disputed as the adjunct of a basically scientific institution, again came under discussion. The secretary of the Smithsonian, Joseph Henry, had dismissed his librarian, Charles Coffin Jewett, and limited the institution's collection to "original contributions to human knowledge." That left forty thousand other works that needed a home elsewhere. Henry, impressed with Spofford's dedication and the creation of new, permanent space at the Library of Congress, suggested that the Smithsonian's collection be moved there.

Spofford considered any consolidation of government documents and books at the Library a positive step. The Smithsonian international exchange program for the dissemination of scientific information, which would be con-

The Mall in Washington, D.C., as it looked in 1865, with the Smithsonian Institution in the foreground and the Capitol—by then looking almost as it does today—in the far distance.

Photograph by Mathew Brady. Smithsonian Institution Archives.

tinued at the Library, would provide it with a new category of publications and ensure that their flow continued—the basis of what would become a library resource unique in the world.

The transfer of the Smithsonian's books would increase the number at the Library to 139,000. Among the books were the copyright deposits collected by the Smithsonian between 1846 and 1859, another boon to the Library. Spofford convinced the committee of the wisdom of accepting Henry's offer; there was no objection from Congress, and the Smithsonian's collection was officially accepted in April 1866, bringing to a close the long discussion over the relative merits of the Smithsonian and the Library as the locus of national inquiry and documentary resources.

In the process, Spofford secured a valuable ally in the renowned scientist Joseph Henry, who also believed in the need for a national library. Henry would assist in Spofford's long quest for the systematic collection of public documents to vastly enhance the Library's range and in Spofford's bid for what was probably the most illustrious private library in America—a unique collection of Americana housed within blocks of the newly expanded Library of Congress, but not part of it, belonging to the aged Peter Force.

For years, historians and book-lovers had been aware of a unique library belonging to a former mayor of Washington, also formerly a journalist and printer, named Peter Force. He owned two houses not far from the Capitol, one for himself and a number of cats, the other for a collection of books, manuscripts, maps, and pamphlets related to American history. Force had published

Archivist and historian Peter Force, whose preeminent collection of Americana became, in 1867, the Library's most important single acquisition since it took possession of the library of Thomas Jefferson.

Smithsonian Institution Archives.

part of his documentary of the Revolution, *American Archives*, with the support of the federal government, but the project had been dropped by Congress in 1853. Force had mortgaged his property to keep the collection intact; now aged seventy-seven, he was badly in need of a bibliophilic angel to save him and his precious library.

It contained 22,529 books, some 40,000 pamphlets, and almost 1,000 volumes of bound newspapers, many of the pamphlets and newspapers having been published before 1800. In addition, there were 429 volumes of manuscripts of historical importance, many from the Revolutionary period, 250 works published before 1600, and 161 examples of incunabula (books printed before 1501, in the infancy of printing). As early as 1848, Joseph Henry's nemesis in the Smithsonian library, Jewett, had written of the need to keep Force's "invaluable collection" in Washington, and Henry had concurred.

Before the outbreak of the Civil War, however, the New-York Historical Society began discussions with Force about the possibility of purchasing his library and moving it to New York City. The price was $100,000, an enormous sum. Spofford had meanwhile become acquainted with Force. Books ordered by Force from dealers outside Washington were often included in Library shipments, and Spofford and Force also exchanged duplicate volumes. It is easy to imagine Spofford's interest in the old man's collection and how he would have longed to see it at the Library of Congress. The effect of such an acquisition would have been second only to that of the library of Thomas Jefferson.

Spofford raised this remote possibility with the latest chairman of the Joint Committee on the Library, Senator John A. J. Creswell. When the New-York Historical Society's fund-raising efforts failed and acquisition by the Library at least seemed possible, Spofford wrote to a society member, the historian George Bancroft who was serving as American minister to Germany, asking his opinion of the value of the Force collection. "Congress will never again have such another [sic] opportunity," Bancroft replied.

The prospect of Congress appropriating $100,000—"a liberal price but not extravagant," in Bancroft's estimation—was not bright. Lawmakers had turned down the Bourtoulin library in 1836, and no large appropriation had been approved since the acquisition of the library at Monticello, with the exception of the $85,000 provided for replacement of books destroyed in the Library fire of 1851. The last annual appropriation for books, newspapers, and periodicals had been only $9,000, and that a significant increase. If the Library acquired the Force collection, Congress would be committing itself in the future to expending large sums for other collections and for suitable accommodations for a national library, not just for a servant of legislative needs and curiosities.

Spofford was asked by the committee in the summer of 1866 to conduct an inventory of Force's collection and to prepare a report. Force, anxiously following the debate in Congress, was disappointed that it was not purchased outright; he wrote sadly to his son of the library that "I have been near fifty years gathering up in the expectation that some public body would gladly purchase and preserve it. I may have been mistaken."

Spofford undertook this task with enthusiasm and thoroughness, spending a part of each day at Force's house at the corner of Twelfth and D Streets, Northwest, rummaging amid the shelves. By the fall his examination was complete. He recommended unequivocally that the collection be purchased and lobbied for it, successfully soliciting letters of support from various historical societies, from members of the political tribe, and from noted men of letters.

Bancroft wrote as requested to Senator Creswell, recommending purchase; so did the well-known bibliographer Henry Stevens. He informed the head of the joint committee that the collection was "like the embodied spirit of American History," that there was nothing to equal it in Europe, "and it is too late in the progress of the world to form anything like it again in America."

Spofford secured the active support of his friend Congressman Hayes of Ohio, who supported the purchase as a member of the joint committee. Spofford addressed the committee and spoke passionately of the Force collection and of its ability to "illustrate our history and progress as a nation." Also, the Library of Congress, "as the great national library of the United States . . . should contain all publications relating to our own country. . . . That these sources of so much hitherto unpublished history should go into private hands to be scattered, or consumed by fire, could not but be regarded as a national misfortune."

Spofford knew his audience. He raised the question of intellectual inferiority to Britain, a sore subject with some. Each year that country spent the equivalent of $100,000 on its "national repository of knowledge" at the British Museum and at that moment had a larger collection of books relating to American history than did America. The Force collection would "repair this deficiency." The implication was that the United States surely could spend as much, once, for "the largest and best collection of the sources of American history yet brought together in this country."

The joint committee unanimously recommended the purchase to Congress. Hayes then saw to it that the $100,000 was attached to a larger appropriations bill, and on March 2, 1867, the Thirty-ninth Congress voted in accordance with the committee's wishes. Within the month the Force collection had been moved into the safekeeping of the Library, to join the newly acquired Smithsonian deposit and the accumulation of recent publications received as a result of the new copyright legislation.

The Librarian's combined successes already pointed toward a new dilemma —a congressional library too ample for the building that contained it.

The Force library not only contributed to the assembly of Americana already there but also served as the foundation of what became the rare book collection. Ironically, old Peter Force, who could not bear to be separated from his beloved library, daily walked to the Capitol to be among his books, and died before the following year was out.

Spofford's views on books, copyright, and other matters were not lost upon those who employed him. Many congressmen depended on his knowledge and expertise in library matters, just one of these being his friend, James A. Garfield, who quoted a colleague in his diary as saying, "I don't read books, I read Spofford."

This Librarian was the first to have final say on what books were obtained—including the "Lover's Dictionary" that was a collection of quotes and a medical treatise "Abuses of the Sexual Function," both objected to by a straitlaced congressman whose criticism Spofford successfully deflected. A prominent librarian attending the first American Library Association convention in the nation's centennial year would remark, "What every library needs is a printed Spofford."

The perennial subject of copyright arose again just two years after the

Drawing of the Library of Congress "old Congressional Reading Room" in the Capitol by W. Bengough, as published in *Harper's Weekly* on February 27, 1897. The bearded Ainsworth Rand Spofford *(right)* was almost overwhelmed by the piles of books and other materials that had come into the Library, their quantity greatly increasing after the copyright law of 1870.

Prints and Photographs Division, Library of Congress.

Library had again begun to receive copies for deposit. The Patent Office wished to reform the patent laws, and Spofford used the occasion to propose that the Library of Congress directly receive all applications for copyright, in addition to the deposits, relieving the Patent Office of that responsibility. It so happened that his friend and another member of the Cincinnati Literary Club, Samuel S. Fisher, was commissioner of patents; apparently he was delighted that Spofford might take the burden off his shoulders.

Spofford wrote to another friend, Representative Thomas A. Jenckes, of Rhode Island, head of the Committee on Patents, arguing for locating all copyright activity in the Library. "We should have one comprehensive Library in the country, and that belonging to the nation." By now his theme was familiar. Jenckes agreed with the Librarian, and he and Garfield maneuvered the proposal through Congress. President Ulysses S. Grant signed the bill into law during the summer of 1870.

Spofford considered this "by far the most important step forward in the annals of the Library"—the exclusive duty to register copyright and hold on deposit America's published works, the assured flow of books that would include two copies of every new one, and official recognition of Spofford's achievement.

The steady flow into the Library soon became a torrent: 11,512 new books, periodicals, musical and dramatic works, maps, photographs, and prints that year. In 1871, new items approached 20,000. By 1872 the Library had 246,000 volumes. One possible solution to caring for them was to extend the west front of the Capitol to accommodate the burgeoning collection, but Spofford favored something altogether different, and audacious: a new building.

It should, he said, be capable of holding three million books. This seemed a preposterous number to some observers, but not to Spofford. After calculating the number of new arrivals in the years ahead, he predicted that in a century the Library would contain about 2.5 million volumes. He had very specific ideas about what sort of building should house them, one circular in design, capable of growing in all directions.

The Library, he wrote in his 1872 annual report, "can be arranged in alcoves rising tier above tier around the whole circumference . . . , while the desks and catalogues for the use of readers occupy the centre. This circular apartment should be surmounted by a dome of iron and glass, thus yielding adequate light at all seasons." The reading room would be 100 feet in diameter, the exterior walls about 65 feet in elevation. The building would front on two or three streets, with "suitable approaches and decorative shrubbery" and "will look out upon a park the dimensions of which are about 500 by 800 feet"—the specific vision of a man who lived for, and thoroughly understood, the place of books in the national imagination.

Spofford used the proposal to again advance the argument for a national library, one that echoed an egalitarianism ahead of its time: "In every country where civilization has attained a high rank, there should be at least one great library, not only universal in range, but whose plan it should be to reverse the rule of the smaller and more select libraries, which is exclusiveness, for one of inclusiveness. Unless this is done, unless the minor literature and the failures of our authors are preserved, as well as the successes, American writers will be without the means of surveying the whole field trodden by their predecessors."

The Joint Committee on the Library approved his suggestions and convinced Congress to promptly create a commission charged with selecting a plan and a site. It appropriated $5,000 to cover expenses. But there was still disagreement among senators, some favoring extension of the Capitol, others wanting a new building altogether.

Twenty-seven architects submitted plans for the latter; the commission eventually chose an Italian Renaissance design by the Washington firm Smithmeyer & Pelz.

John L. Smithmeyer, born in Austria, had served an apprenticeship in Chicago and had practiced in Cincinnati; Paul J. Pelz, a German, had served an apprenticeship in New York and worked as an architect and construction engineer for the U.S. Lighthouse Board. The project, launched in so timely a fashion, eagerly responded to, would surely come to fruition before the Library ran out of shelf space.

But Spofford had not counted on further congressional disagreement about the style and location of the new building. Another design competition was launched and arguments sounded over the various merits and disadvantages of Judiciary Square, East Capitol Park, and the area west of the Capitol where the Botanic Garden stood. Smithmeyer & Pelz submitted new designs for each site, including a Romanesque one, but a final decision proved elusive.

In 1875, Spofford's friend, Congressman Garfield, wrote to a fellow Ohio Republican, "I send you this letter to show you the operation of a machine known as the Typewriter." Mechanization was gaining a foothold in literary affairs, though not at the Library of Congress. Inundated by new books, Spofford warned Congress in his annual report that, because of the influx of new publications, he was presiding over the "greatest chaos in America."

His former associates were now men of great influence. Garfield would eventually occupy the White House, but Rutherford B. Hayes had temporarily gone back to Ohio to be governor, depriving Spofford of that support in Congress. Meanwhile the Library did indeed run out of shelf space, its polyglot collection of books, pamphlets, periodicals, sheet music, maps, and assorted publications mounting in various stacks around the Library floor, empirical evidence of the need for new quarters.

Congress finally passed the legislative authorization for the new building. President Hayes, returning to Washington in 1877 after a close, rancorous national election that had focused on the corruption of the Grant administration, referred to the Library of Congress in his State of the Union message as "national in its character . . . it cannot be doubted that the people will sanction any wise expenditure to . . . enlarge its usefulness." The words had almost certainly been suggested by Spofford.

But plans for the proud, capacious new building languished. "Congress will hardly be held to have discharged the trust reposed in it as the custodian of what President Jefferson called with prophetic wisdom the Library of the United States," Spofford warned in his annual report. He and his staff had difficulty responding effectively to demands under the new burden of the copyright provisions. There was criticism among historians and other librarians and among those in a Congress served by the Library. Then the index of debates and documents of Congress undertaken by Spofford had to be abandoned, and in 1880 Spofford stopped publishing the alphabetical catalog.

Spofford's old friend President Garfield died in 1881 after being shot and was replaced by Chester Arthur, who retained the Librarian. Spofford's most dependable supporters in Congress were still his friends: Daniel W. Voorhees of Indiana, characterized as "the Tall Sycamore of the Wabash," chairman of the joint committee, and Justin S. Morrill, of Vermont. In a speech about the Library in 1880, Voorhees stressed the morality of books and intellectual exertion: "The mind fed at the crystal fountains of accumulated knowledge will continue its growth, and its expansion until it makes its final transition to a sphere of endless and unlimited development." It was a colorful view of eternity, with libraries as cathedrals. "I cannot believe that the plain and imperative duty of Congress on the subject of its Library will be longer neglected."

Smithmeyer and Pelz's winning Italian Renaissance Revival design for the new Library building provoked a series of fresh congressional debates, ranging from proposed alternative sites to the nature of the Library itself and its proper architectural expression. Following much delay, inaction, and further consideration of other designs, a modified version of Smithmeyer & Pelz's design was finally settled upon. By the time excavation for the new building had begun, however, the notion of making the Library a national cultural showpiece— with appropriately grand and beautiful interiors—had begun to take hold.

Drawing by Smithmeyer and Pelz, September 1888. Prints and Photographs Division, Library of Congress. LC-USZ62-51463

A Joint Select Committee on Additional Accommodations was formed to promptly resolve the disputed issues, which it did not do. Meanwhile Spofford's memory remained the Library's most active "fountain," as he was often called upon to use it in locating something within the chaos. Spofford found so little time for letter writing that the London bookdealer Henry Stevens referred to him as the world's worst correspondent, implying not negligence but ceaseless toil in the shadow of tottering—and growing—stacks of books.

Senator Daniel W. Voorhees of Indiana, one of the most prominent and eloquent articulators of the Library as a national symbol of knowledge and, as such, a basic and indispensable bulwark against tyranny and barbarism. In his speech to Congress in May 1880, Voorhees voiced his opinion that "Knowledge is power, the power to maintain free government and preserve constitutional liberty."

Prints and Photographs Division, Library of Congress. LC-USZ62-117814

In early 1882, Spofford received a letter making a proposal unlike any other he had seen. The writer, a Washington physician named Joseph M. Toner, owned a library of medical and scientific books and source materials, plus extensive writings by and about George Washington; he wished not to sell his collection but to give it to the Library of Congress. The Librarian's duties did not prevent him from responding enthusiastically to the prospect of yet more books, and he wrote back to Toner expressing his "earnest hope that your life-long labors in the cause of letters and science will be fitly crowned with this great public service to the American people, and that this first example of the gift of a library to the nation will be the precursor of many in the future."

The joint committee and consequently Congress agreed to accept the gift, and a bust of Toner was commissioned to rest on a pedestal in the new building outside a room containing Toner's forty thousand volumes.

Meanwhile the collection was unceremoniously stored in a boarded-up quarter of the crypt under the Capitol rotunda, not a fate calculated to impress other prospective donors. The bust, when completed, waited patiently in a niche over the door in the office of the superintendent of the old reading room.

The plan for the new public building ran afoul of some members of the

American Library Association who favored a more sequestered atmosphere for research than Spofford's grand public spaces. Spofford had not been an active member of the association, believing as he did that though the Library of Congress should be a national institution, it should not be the nucleus of a national library system. He was also too busy. So some of those who should have been his allies in the profession became instead countervailing voices in the long struggle for supremacy.

The architect, John L. Smithmeyer, was sent to Europe to tour the libraries of London, Paris, Berlin, Munich, Vienna, and Rome, to collect impressions and what amounted to preponderant evidence in favor of his and Spofford's classical choice. Smithmeyer returned to defend the Italian Renaissance design in a thirty-one-page pamphlet, and then the *Library Journal* published an editorial supporting Spofford. At last the stage seemed set for an affirmative vote in Congress, but a last minute proposal to raise the Capitol dome to contain the new Library caused further delay. This preposterous notion was dismissed after due consultation with a noted engineer.

On April 15, 1886, Congress considered the bill to erect a new Italian Renaissance Library building on the East Capitol Street site. It passed both houses; Morrill and Voorhees, overcome with victory, blew kisses to one another on the floor. A page was sent to fetch the Librarian, who came "ambling in," according to a contemporary account, and returned the senators' embraces. This august figure, closely identified with the institution of the Library, had visibly aged in service to it; Spofford was on the verge of what would be his last resounding victory.

The new building would symbolize Spofford's idea of a national library, a greater accomplishment than the securing of copyright authority or the Smithsonian, Force, and Toner collections. He would remain as Librarian for another decade, dealing as he knew best with a vast repository of knowledge in cramped quarters. The amount of material he was responsible for and his casual record keeping would cause criticism. But for the moment, as Spofford wrote to a friend the day president Grover Cleveland signed the bill into law, "I am . . . the happiest man in Washington."

The new library building was not assured in 1886 by the mere passage of legislation. Disputes over the nature of such a national institution, present at the idea's inception, carried over into its painfully slow realization. They pitted statesmen, architects, builders, book-lovers, and artists against each other in a continuing political saga.

The three-man commission appointed to supervise construction—Spofford, the Librarian of Congress, Edward Clark, Architect of the Capitol, and Secretary of the Interior Lucius Q. C. Lamar—was split immediately by an argument between Clark and the architect for the project, John L. Smithmeyer, over placement of the building. The site chosen lay east of the Capitol near First Street and Independence Avenue. Smithmeyer wanted the building in the central west portion of the lot, but Clark feared it would block the view of the Capitol and argued for an alternate site. His view was supported by the renowned landscape architect Frederick Law Olmsted. Both were overruled.

Ground-breaking occurred in 1887. Then Smithmeyer became involved in a dispute with a supplier of concrete who had friends in Congress; the architect was accused of padding his payroll and at the same time pressured by congressmen to provide patronage jobs for their friends. An investigation proved little more than that discord existed within the building commission, where Spofford was too busy to pay sufficient attention to details and Clark wished to resign.

Then the noted portrait painter A. G. Heaton announced that his heroic canvas was near completion and depicted the eighteen men who had contributed most to the creation of the new building. Spofford was to be represented, as was Smithmeyer but not his partner, Paul Pelz. Also featured were Senators Justin S. Morrill and Daniel W. Voorhees. A member of the Joint Library Committee was left out because he demanded a more central position and was later found to have improperly sought contracts for marble from a company owned by his father.

Smithmeyer was fired and the commission dissolved; some began to doubt that the daring new building would ever become a reality.

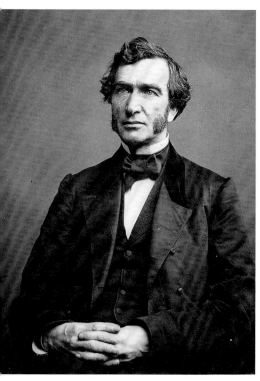

Senator Justin Morrill of Vermont, another prominent congressional ally of Librarian Spofford. In 1857 Morrill had sponsored the land grant college act, which passed and was signed by Abraham Lincoln in 1862. The agricultural colleges —enabling more widespread public education—helped move the country from an agrarian focus toward an emphasis on science, commerce, and technology. Like his colleague Daniel Voorhees, Morrill wanted to broaden access to science and education, and for seventeen years he led the congressional committee in charge of constructing the new Library building, now called the Thomas Jefferson Building.

Brigadier General Thomas Lincoln Casey, chief of the U.S. Army Corps of Engineers, had overseen the completion of the Washington Monument and the State, War, and Navy Building next-door to the White House, and Congress chose him to build the Library of Congress. Casey, with a reputation for both efficiency and monumental structures, was asked to submit a plan for $4 million worth of construction. He produced two plans—the one requested, and another for $6 million.

Both were prepared by architect John L. Smithmeyer's former partner, Paul Pelz, under Casey's direction. The general then put in charge of the work itself Bernard R. Green, a civil engineer who had been Casey's superintendent of construction on the earlier projects and who was prominent in Washington's scientific and cultural circles. Green's businesslike manner and penchant for recording daily advances in construction appealed to his boss's military disposition and to Congress's desire for material progress.

He and Casey expanded the existing plans with the help of Ainsworth Spofford, who urged that the building be as large as possible and "capable of extensions in the future." Spofford also recommended room dimensions, shelving in both alcoves and stacks, a central reading room lit by a glass dome, and an art gallery for "the many thousands of objects of graphic arts and arts of design now buried in immense piles in the basement of the Capitol and elsewhere in the Library."

During preparations for the inaugural of President Benjamin Harrison, Congress approved the more expensive Library plan. When construction began in earnest, it incorporated the latest technology in heating and lighting equipment, a tunnel for transporting books to and from the Capitol, and nine tiers of steel bookstacks serviced by the first pneumatic tube system in the country. Casey and Green were so efficient that money was left over for interior murals, sculpture, and architecture on an unprecedented scale, part of what was to be an American monument. The two engineers shared Spofford's ideal of an inspiring national library and increased the reading room dome from the 70 feet in height requested by Spofford to 195 feet.

Pelz was let go, and the general's son, Edward Pearce Casey, trained as an architect at the Ecole des Beaux Arts, arrived from New York to design the building's interior. Green and the two Caseys agreed to commission twenty American sculptors and nineteen American painters to represent subjects suggested by the artists but subject to Casey's and Green's approval. Busts of nine writers suggested by Spofford would be placed in the portico of the front entrance pavilion: Demosthenes, Dante, Goethe, Macaulay, Scott, Franklin, Hawthorne, Irving, and Spofford's friend Emerson. (Spofford later complained of the sculptor's failure to reproduce Emerson's "finely chiseled" nose.) On the balustrade of the Main Reading Room were to stand sixteen bronze statues of illustrious men, from Moses to Joseph Henry, secretary of the Smithsonian Institution, chosen by Spofford. He also chose the writers to be represented across the front entrance, and the quotations in the Great Hall on the second floor.

The Casey-Green triumvirate subjected their commissioned artists to military-style scheduling and freely criticized any aspects of the art that did not appeal to them. One artist, Paul W. Bartlett, commissioned to produce bronzes of Columbus and Michelangelo, would stalk out of a meeting with Green, but most submitted.

The building began to take shape in the final years of the century, in defiance of the doubts and acrimony it had spawned, rumored to become a monument beyond the imaginings of the populace who might one day be allowed to view it. Meanwhile Pelz pursued his personal grievances against the builders in the courts, while his former partner, Smithmeyer, his reputation destroyed by his dismissal, lived in poverty. When he died, Pelz borrowed $172 from "fellow architects and others" to have him buried.

Bernard Green, a civil engineer who had worked with General Thomas Lincoln Casey on such edifices as the Washington Monument, supervised the work of constructing the new Library building.

Prints and Photographs Division, Library of Congress. LC-USP6-6496-A

(opposite top) Workmen laying the foundation of the new building, November 1889.

Prints and Photographs Division, Library of Congress. LC-USZ62-73540

(opposite bottom) By July of 1890, exterior stonework was well under way.

Prints and Photographs Division, Library of Congress. LC-USP6-6545A

Nov 1889

JULY 30, 1890.

S.W. CLERESTORY ARCH, ROTUNDA
JUNE 28 1892

(above) In June 1892, the keystone was placed in the southwest clerestory arch of the Jefferson Building's rotunda.

Prints and Photographs Division, Library of Congress. LC–USZ62–51462

Edward Pearce Casey, the general's son, joined his father and Green in overseeing the architectural details of the Library, including interior murals and sculptures and exterior stonework.

Photograph courtesy of Columbia University of the City of New York. Photograph by Blank & Stoller, Inc.

Following completion of the exterior and interior structures, many prominent artists were engaged to decorate the vast interior spaces and surfaces. This photograph shows the painter Edwin Howland Blashfield on a scaffold in the rotunda.

From the collections of the National Museum of American Art, Smithsonian Institution.

(below) An early view of the completed building, whose construction had used 400,000 cubic feet of granite, 3,000 tons of iron and steel, and 70,000 barrels of cement.

Prints and Photographs Division, Library of Congress. LC-USP6-6534-A

Of the nine busts set into the portico above the entrance pavilion, centered in the front were *(from left to right)*: Emerson, Goethe, Benjamin Franklin, Thomas Macaulay, and Nathaniel Hawthorne. Spofford, who chose the mix of European and American notables, thought the bust of Emerson was not a good likeness.

Photograph copyright © Anne Day.

4

The Round Table

(1897–1939)

A powerful agent is the right word.

Samuel Langhorne Clemens

Towering bronze doors at the entrance of the new Library of Congress, representing Tradition, Writing, and Printing, were opened to the American public in early 1897. Even Washingtonians accustomed to the city's heroic architecture were impressed. The Capitol dome nearby had a rival here near the corner of Independence Avenue and First Street, Southeast, not as large, perhaps, but resplendent in twenty-three-karat gold leaf which had cost $3,800. Somewhere beneath its symbolic radiance were eventually to be gathered some 800,000 volumes; already present was the work of fifty American painters and sculptors that demonstrated the depth of native talent and complemented the building's broad-shouldered classicism.

Before entering, visitors passed an ornamental fountain without equal in the country: a scene from the court of Neptune, fifty feet wide, a triumph of ornamentation by the sculptor Roland Hinton Perry that had cost taxpayers $22,000. In the marble corridors, visitors were greeted by a host of historical luminaries and mythical figures, among them four tympanums by George W. Maynard in the Pavilion of the Discoverers representing Adventure, Discovery, Conquest, and Civilization. A series of murals in the corridors adjoining the Great Hall depicted Labor, Rest, Study, Recreation, and Religion.

A fifteen-foot marble mosaic of Minerva by Elihu Vedder faced those who approached the entrance to the Visitors' Gallery. Murals, sculpture, bronze doors, and sumptuous decorative painting had deprived the Treasury of another $364,000, but overall the building had been finished for $200,000 less than the $6.5 million Congress had agreed to earlier, a triumph of discipline attributed to the autocratic building supervisor, Brigadier General Casey.

All the costs, like the memories of political, contractual, and artistic squab-

The new Library building in 1898,
its copper dome covered in gold leaf.
Bernard Green and Brigadier General
Thomas Lincoln Casey worked to make
it a cultural monument embellished on a
grand scale. A circular drive separated the
Library and the Capitol.

Library of Congress slide, no. LOC-8, no. 5,
LJ, 1898.

The central bronze door greeting
visitors at the top of the granite steps at
the entrance to the new building represented in sculpted relief *The Art of Printing*.
Its sculptor, Frederick Macmonnies, was
one of the founding members of the
American Academy of Arts and Letters,
along with William Dean Howells, John
Singer Sargent, Henry Adams, Theodore
Roosevelt, and others. His portrayals of
Minerva in the tympanum and young
women representing the Humanities, in
the left panel, and Intellect, on the right,
suggested through allegory and idealization
the optimistic view of American civilization
that suffused the institution.

Photograph courtesy of the Architect of the
Capitol.

bling, were set aside in the enthusiasm for what was unde-
niably a national institution. If only six of the twenty-four
statues and figures destined for the Main Reading Room
had arrived before the deadline of January 1, all would be
in place within a year, with the exception of the straggler,
Michelangelo.

A local guidebook proclaimed, "America is justly proud
of this gorgeous and palatial monument to its National
sympathy and appreciation of Literature, Science and Art."
The writer speculated that the Library was "a fitting temple for the great thoughts of generations past, present, and
to be." One rapturous future visitor would write to the
Librarian, "[N]ot until I stand before the judgement seat of
God do I ever expect to see this building transcended."

In 1897, the grand new building
opened on November 1, and special tours
attracted forty-seven hundred visitors on
Thanksgiving Day. Visitors admired the
Neptune Fountain in front of the main
entrance. Roland Hinton Perry, born in
New York in 1870, sculpted the Roman
god of the sea in bronze, with a sea nymph
astride a sea horse on either side of him.
The sea god Triton, turtles, frogs, and a
serpent inhabit the fountain as well.

Photograph by Frances Benjamin Johnston. Prints
and Photographs Division, Library of Congress.
LC-USZ62-4546

One of those happiest with the new building's reception was the Librarian
of Congress who had first envisioned it, Ainsworth Rand Spofford, now seventy-one. The 326,000 square feet would well accommodate the rich national
collections. Spofford had prepared the way for national services that would cor-
respond with the Library's national stature: shared cataloging and a new classification system that was badly needed with the influx of so many new books.

In testimony before special sessions of the joint committee on Library
affairs, Spofford had defended his classification system as adequate in relation

A series of murals in the north corridor of the first floor of the new Library building represented Labor, Study, Recreation, Rest, and Religion. Charles Sprague Pearce (1851–1914) painted them in oil on canvas, which was then affixed to the wall. In his painting *Religion*, a young man and a young woman kneel before an altar made of two stones topped with a blazing fire.

to the Library's other, vast responsibilities: preserving 200,000 musical scores, 250,000 pieces of graphic art, 40,000 maps and charts, some of them quite rare, and a host of manuscripts—among them the letters of John Paul Jones and Robert Fulton and George Washington's Revolutionary War journal—18,000 volumes of newspapers, and an annual accumulation of more than 15,000 copyright deposits.

Noted librarians of the time, Melvil Dewey, originator of the decimal classification system, and Herbert Putnam, librarian of the Boston Public Library, had also testified. Duly impressed, Congress soon increased the number of Library workers from 42 to 108, but even that number would struggle under ceaseless duties and acquisitions.

In July 1897, the Library of Congress was illuminated at night, an experiment that drew thirteen thousand people to Capitol Hill. The same month Spofford was replaced as Librarian by a former journalist and diplomat, John Russell Young. A friend of President William McKinley, Young had written in his diary two months earlier, "Saw the President . . . he said that he would have an important nomination very soon. Would rather be paralyzed than in any way disturb Spofford."

Spofford was kept on as Chief Assistant, an indication that the new Librarian

At the approach to the Visitors' Gallery overlooking the Main Reading Room in the new building, Elihu Vedder fashioned a fifteen-foot-high marble mosaic of Minerva, Roman goddess of wisdom, whose counterpart in Greek mythology was Athena. He shows olive trees, associated with Athena, to represent peace, and Minerva holds a scroll listing arts and sciences that flourished in a civilized society. Vedder was born in New York in 1836 and painted mostly classical, ideal, or mythological scenes that resembled those of contemporary British Victorian artists.

Photograph copyright © Anne Day.

One of sixteen bronze statues on the balustrades of the galleries surrounding the Main Reading Room, *Michelangelo* was the last to be put in place. Paul Wayland Bartlett's much praised sculpture of the great Italian painter and sculptor portrayed an artist-laborer restless with creative energy and suggested commitment to honest work and human aspiration, values that were espoused by the flourishing Arts and Crafts movement.

LC-P6-5010A

knew enough to retain the Library's chief asset and knew that Spofford was better acquainted with the place than anyone else. After twenty-six years of advocating a new Library building, Spofford constituted an institution in his own right.

McKinley's appointment of Young came at the end of the Library's first century. Mrs. John A. Logan, wife of an Illinois congressman, described the Library at that time, in her book *Thirty Years in Washington*, as "a monument of a nation which has emerged from the darkness of doubts and dangers into the full glory of conscious power." A new era loomed in which the United States was to play a pivotal role, the Library part of it: a repository of knowledge and resources for an era of risks and responsibilities that were only dimly envisioned by its founders.

The new Librarian, born in Ireland, was as diffuse in worldly experience as Spofford was focused on the affairs of the book. Formerly managing editor of Horace Greeley's *New York Tribune*, and an official agent abroad for the departments of Treasury and State after the Civil War, Young had accompanied General Grant on his globe-girdling journey and written a two-volume account of it. He was named as minister to China by President Chester Arthur, and he moved easily between the realms of journalism and diplomacy. John Young knew everybody, as David C. Mearns wrote in *The Story Up to Now*: "statesmen, cardinals, poets, actors, duchesses, people great and people . . . 'little.'" He was also an intensely loyal Republican, and he was given to bouts of physical and mental exhaustion.

Once again, political connections had proved more important than knowledge or skill as a bookman in the appointment of the Librarian, a fact that did not please members of the increasingly influential American Library Association. But Young's intentions were serious. As if to prove this, he set about reorganizing the Library, as was called for by Congress, to include a reading room, an art gallery, a hall for the maps and charts, separate departments for manuscripts and music, and a law library. All would have their own superintendents, and candidates for these and other Library jobs were evaluated by a board chosen by Young and headed by the redoubtable Ainsworth Spofford.

John Russell Young was appointed Librarian of Congress in 1897 by William McKinley and presided over the opening of the new Library building, appointing new staff and improving financial record-keeping. Young's diplomatic travels motivated him to augment the Library's international holdings. He died in office in January 1899 at the age of fifty-eight.

Photograph, 1897. Prints and Photographs Division, Library of Congress. LC-USZ62-6011A

They included Thorvald Solberg, involved in copyright procedures since 1876, as Register of Copyrights, and David Hutchison, a Library veteran for twenty-three years, to supervise the Reading Room. Other thoroughly respectable appointments moved the *Library Journal*, heretofore critical of Young, to express the opinion: "[T]he new librarian of Congress continues to give the best of evidence of his intention to make the library worthy of its opportunities."

The dog days of summer, 1897, saw the beginning of the transfer of books and other materials—some eight hundred tons—from the Capitol to the new Library in wheelbarrows and horse carts, a long and arduous process. Finally, on November 1, the Library opened officially, with the collections intact, and on Thanksgiving day some five thousand visitors trooped through rooms filled with one of the finest, most extensive assemblies of books and published materials on earth.

The Fifty-fifth Congress even considered a bill stipulating that "the Library of Congress shall be known as and styled the 'national Library.'" No action was taken, but clearly the sentiment was there.

This did not mean a central lending library for the United States. Young wanted the Library of Congress to be a great institution of research and he worried about the nature, extent, and condition of the collection. In December 1897, he announced that the catalog would be brought up to date. He characterized it as "the home of America's literary and artistic genius, supplemented and strengthened by that of all lands and all time. And now, when the work of organization is in a plastic condition, before what is done hardens and consolidates and becomes difficult of undoing, no step should be taken without considering . . . what will be most useful a hundred years from today."

In the summer of 1897, wheelbarrows and horse carts carrying books, pamphlets, maps, manuscripts, prints, and music moved back and forth between the Capitol and the new Library building, taking an enormous number of items to their new home, as Bernard Green kept track. Copyright deposits piled up in the halls waiting to be sorted, counted, classified, recorded, and shelved.

Young considered the collection of foreign publications deficient for a great Library. "Its original classification by Thomas Jefferson," he wrote in a letter to foreign service officers, seeking additional material, "contemplated a national Library, universal and representative in character, with all knowledge for its province."

The Librarian advised them that any addition to the collections that "would add to the sum of human knowledge, would be gratefully received and have due and permanent acknowledgement." Spofford favored more selectivity, but he and Young respected one another and both men possessed sufficient decorum to resolve most differences of opinion. Both wished to obtain publications from government agencies, but the Assistant Librarian did not believe that book-buying agents here and abroad should procure "every edition of Milton, Chaucer, Spencer, Dryden, Pope, etc."

Young continued to cast an exceedingly wide net. Foreign emissaries were pressed by him for exchanges of books and publications of all sorts. So successful was he that the agent in charge of receiving orders at the Library wrote, "My narrow quarters are becoming quite buried up by books." Young wrote to the secretary of war and the quartermaster general of the army seeking further additions for the Library and petitioning for—and attaining—passage for a Library official to travel to Puerto Rico and Cuba in search of more books.

There was in Young's efforts a feverish, almost desperate quality. In poor health much his life—a recurrent theme in Librarians of Congress until more recent times—Young was now faced with the infinite diversity of a library with a national charter, large, distinguished, and rapidly expanding collections, and myriad responsibilities to Congress and to the public. This would have

taxed a seasoned administrator, and Young had no previous experience as such. He was habitually racked by aches, chills, and unsteadiness on his feet, all exacerbated by insomnia, depression, and, according to his diaries, occasional hallucinations.

At times, as Librarian, Young lacked the strength to sign official documents; he sought cures in milk diets, various medicines, even shock treatment, but nothing had more than temporary effect. His friends feared he was working himself to death.

The Great Hall of the Library building in 1904. Much of the ornamental sculpture, including the figure of the woman in bronze holding a torch at the bottom of the grand staircase, was done by Philip Martiny. Overseeing the stucco and color decoration of the extravagant interior was Elmer E. Garnsey, who had directed similar work at the Boston Public Library and the Columbian Exposition in Chicago in 1893.

Prints and Photographs Division, Library of Congress. LC-USZ62-60743

Young's accomplishments included a room specially appointed for the blind, where books with raised print were available, and readings were held. During the first year it had received some ten thousand visitors, far in excess of what Young had anticipated. And he had begun to reassemble Thomas Jefferson's library, the remnants of which had been widely scattered among the

Library's shelves. In late 1898, he survived a particularly intense period of physical and mental duress, but by Christmas Eve felt reasonably well again.

He left his office early to help his wife put up the Christmas tree, but before reaching home he slipped and fell. Young was confined to his bed, where he remained through Christmas. Two days afterward he noted in his diary, "Very ill."

Gardiner Greene Hubbard

"I hereby offer to the Congressional Library, for the benefit of the people of the United States, the collection of engravings made by my husband . . . and in addition thereto the art books, to be treated as part of the collection."

The letter, addressed to the Librarian of Congress by the widow of Boston businessman Gardiner Greene Hubbard, had arrived in early 1898. Gertrude M. Hubbard wished to give the Library, in addition to the collection, $20,000 for purchasing more engravings. But there was a stipulation: a gallery must be named for her late husband, an unprecedented request that, if met, would have important implications.

Gardiner Greene Hubbard had been a founder of the National Geographic Society, in association with such distinguished men as John Wesley Powell, the first man to run the Colorado River, and Alexander Graham Bell, inventor of the telephone. The founding had taken place in the Cosmos Club, where figures in science, literature, and politics gathered for intellectual discussion when in Washington. Hubbard had also been the Geographic's first president, and was a promoter of special education for the deaf. His deaf daughter, Mabel, was married to Bell.

Hubbard was an important figure in the developing telephone industry, and his business success had enabled him to pursue his interest in art and to assemble the most extensive collection of Rembrandts, for instance, in the United States.

This was just part of a much larger collection — some twenty thousand items — that also included works by Dürer, Callot, and other ranking printmakers, as well as portraits and historical prints relating to Frederick the Great and Napoleon Bonaparte. A total of three hundred items pertaining to Napoleon were offered to the Library by Hubbard's widow.

Librarian Young quickly responded to "this act of munificence" and passed the offer on to the Joint Committee on the Library. He pointed out that the collection was considered "by expert judges of art . . . as in many respects the most instructive and valuable in the country." He favored creating such a special gallery within the new building, and offered to assign "a competent person" to catalog the collection and make it available to the public, as requested.

Congress, however, balked at naming part of a public building after an individual citizen, and offered instead to officially name the collection after Hubbard and to administer it as such. Mrs. Hubbard eventually agreed to this, and made the bequest she had promised Young, for the acquisition of more art. This was an important precedent of another sort and illustrated the need for a special trust to deal with donations and bequests made to the Library.

In 1898, Mrs. Gardiner Greene Hubbard donated to the Library its first major collection of fine prints, assembled by her husband. Gardiner Greene Hubbard (1822–1897) was a pioneer in the telephone industry. Among the twenty-seven hundred prints was *The Expulsion from Paradise* or *The Fall of Man* by Albrecht Dürer, with his ideal images of a man and woman drawn in classical proportions.

Woodcut, 1510. Prints and Photographs Division, Library of Congress. LC-USZ62-99461

The Three Trees, a landscape by Rembrandt van Rijn, is one of an extensive collection of works by Rembrandt purchased by Gardiner Greene Hubbard that became part of the collections of the Prints and Photographs Division.

Etching, drypoint, and engraving, 1643. Prints and Photographs Division, Library of Congress. LC-USZC4-3883 (color); LC-USZ62-17353 (b&w)

In January 1899, Chief Assistant Librarian Spofford cabled the Library's agent in the Caribbean: "Please return."

The Librarian of Congress had died without recovering from his latest fall. This left vacant the position of leadership within two years of John Russell Young's having assumed it.

The "chaos" Spofford had once used to characterize complex and urgent Library affairs had not ended with the erection of the new building or the recognition of a national role but, if anything, it had been exacerbated by new duties and expectations. Young's untimely death brought renewed demands for professional and managerial skills never before applied at the Library.

Recommendations for his replacement flowed directly to President William McKinley, from various quarters. Professional librarians thought one of their own should lead the Library, a sentiment echoed by the *New York Tribune*, which called attention to the caliber of those who had testified on Library matters in 1896. "At this juncture it seems entirely feasible to secure the services of one of these eminent men ... in keeping with the requirements of a truly National institution."

The president was also opportuned by persons seeking a ripe political plum. They included members of Congress and others working on the Hill; a member of the Library staff, the chief clerk, Thomas Alvord, Jr., was so convinced of the power of his candidacy that he told Thorvald Solberg, register of copyrights, "Shake hands with the next Librarian of Congress."

But Solberg and other professional librarians arranged a meeting in New York to propose what they considered a suitable replacement for Young. McKinley first offered the post to a retiring Massachusetts congressman and only after a member of the Library Committee objected did he recognize the wisdom of appointing a professional. The president settled the job upon the slight, resolutely squared shoulders of the head of the Boston Public Library, Herbert Putnam, an austere young man of thirty-seven known for his buttoned-up frock coat, silk cravat, starched collar, thinning red hair, and intense gaze.

Putnam had graduated from Harvard with honors in classical studies and studied law at Columbia University before undertaking the role of librarian, first at the Minneapolis Athenaeum, then in Boston. He had established a reputation as an effective, even inspiring, leader interested in library expansion and services provided to other libraries around the country.

His view on the collections had been expressed three years earlier in a letter written to supplement his congressional testimony. Putnam thought that legislation of the United States and other countries should be of foremost concern at the Library of Congress, followed by copyright material, law, Americana ("so far as practicable"), and, finally, "general literature," including history.

Putnam took over in April 1899. His first day of duty included a tour of the building conducted by Spofford, recognized as an invaluable resource by this new Librarian, too, and retained to ensure a smooth transition. So the aging, casually attired, ever dedicated Chief Assistant Librarian Spofford showed the slight, almost dapper and punctilious Putnam all that had been accomplished and all that needed to be done.

Putnam requested an inventory of the Library's awesome mass of undigested material which, he discovered, included almost a million volumes and pamphlets to be reclassified, more than 50,000 prints to be cataloged, and as many volumes of documents, plus some 20,000 manuscripts, 50,000 maps, 237,000 pieces of music, and 50,000 copyright items. Putnam estimated that to reclassify, shelf list, and catalog all this in the space of year would require 448 workers and would cost $383,000.

There were also 100,000 volumes and pamphlets that needed to be repaired or rebound, and deterioration that had to be stopped among most of the collections. The new Librarian designated new divisions to replace the old departments, and four new entities were created—order, bibliography, documents, and binding departments. The physical demands of Library maintenance were also considerable. A single horse-drawn wagon was available for assistance in moving items, a wistful symbol of an age coming to an end, both for the country and the Library. The innovative new Librarian wanted to replace the horse and wagon with an electric car.

Herbert Putnam, librarian of the Boston Public Library, was William McKinley's choice to follow John Russell Young as Librarian of Congress, a role he filled from 1899 to 1939. One of his early requests was for an electric car to replace the Library's one horse-drawn wagon. The woman who photographed him here, Frances Benjamin Johnston, took up photography in 1889 and became one of the first successful women practitioners of the art. Besides doing portraits, she documented architecture, industry, and education.

Prints and Photographs Division, Library of Congress. LC-USZ62-6012A

In his budget estimates for the year 1900, Putnam asked Congress for a hiring increase, from 134 employees to 230; he also needed $50,000 to increase the collections. Congress, in an accommodating mood, accepted his estimates and provided the funds for cataloging and classification, the new Librarian's primary focus.

Putnam knew that Melvil Dewey, who had also testified before Congress in the Library hearings, was reworking the decimal classification system, and he wrote to Dewey inquiring about it. But Putnam subsequently determined that a collection as large as that at the Library of Congress required its own system. Library holdings exceeded those of any other library in the western hemisphere at this time, and he had plans for greatly adding to them, augmenting particularly the international character of the collections.

The Library should be an unparalleled source of information for Congress and for scholarship, Putnam thought. He obtained from Congress permission to lend books outside of Washington, initiating interlibrary loans and other extended Library influence that would grow over the years. In 1901 Putnam announced that the Library would undertake printing catalog cards in a standard format, making available the bibliographic information resulting from the classifying and cataloging of books in the Library's collections. Printed catalog cards were sold to libraries throughout the country; the Library was now serving as both an example and a resource.

The Librarian wanted this role officially recognized by the White House and requested, with typical self-assurance, that the new president, Theodore Roosevelt, include remarks about the Library in his first message to Congress in December 1901. Roosevelt, a noted bibliophile, complied. The Library of Congress, he told the assembled congressmen, "had a unique opportunity to render to the libraries of this country—to American scholarship—service of the highest importance . . . not merely a center of research, but the chief factor in great cooperative efforts for the diffusion of knowledge and the advancement of learning."

No Librarian had been so well responded to in public by a president of the United States.

Putnam retained the best of the Library's staff and fought for compensation for these professionals equal to what he saw as the importance of their duties. When the position of chief of the manuscripts division became vacant, Putnam informed the secretary of the treasury that he was waiting "until the salary shall be placed at a sum which will enable me to secure for it a thoroughly adequate person." Likewise, he sought the best collections for the Library in all fields.

The State Department was ordered by the president to transfer to the Library what was referred to as the Revolutionary Archives: the records of the Continental Congress and the papers of Washington, Jefferson, Madison, Hamilton, and other founders of the nation. This was another step in the accumulation of historical documents to augment the Library's rich resources for scholarship and historical reference. The Library also gathered, with assistance from the Carnegie Corporation and the American Historical Association, copies of documents pertaining to American history from the British Museum and the Bodleian Library, Oxford, a collection that within ten years comprised 175,000 folio pages.

Library acquisitions included Albrecht Weber's four-thousand-volume library of Indica. Putnam made the wise but somewhat risky comment in the annual report for 1904 that he "could not ignore the opportunity to acquire a unique collection which scholarship thought worthy of prolonged, scientific, and enthusiastic research, even though the immediate use of such a collection may prove meager." The Carnegie Corporation would provide a grant for expanding the collection.

Putnam attempted to obtain the well-known John Carter Brown library near the beginning of his tenure but failed. In 1907 the Gennadii Vasil'evich Yudin collection of Slavica became available, a treasure in the eyes of collectors and librarians everywhere. Yudin, a wealthy Siberian and amateur bibliographer, had amassed the largest personal library on the Russian empire: more than eighty thousand volumes that included early editions of eighteenth- and nineteenth-century literary works (among them a first edition of Dostoyevsky's first published novel), literary magazines and provincial gazettes, a Slavonic ABC book published in Rome in 1753, the first Russian geometry book, and 333 drawings of Chinese subjects executed about 1860.

Putnam successfully negotiated the purchase, and a Library staff member was dispatched by him to Russia to supervise packing and shipping the collection, an extraordinarily bold move for a Librarian at that time. The Yudin collection formed the basis at the Library for what would be the largest collection of Orientalia in the Western world.

Then the acquisition of the Albert Schatz collection added more than twelve thousand printed librettos in German and Italian, mostly from the seventeenth and eighteenth centuries, to the resources of the Music Division, plus assorted, valuable materials relating to early opera. Other, significant collections of Hebraica and Chinese and Japanese books followed.

Ainsworth Rand Spofford died in 1908. He had been the primary force behind the Library's phenomenal growth, and Putnam's decision to extend the Library's reach beyond the confines of Washington had been the logical extension of his Chief Assistant Librarian's national library vision. Putnam eulogized Spofford as a man who never wavered "in fidelity to the institution nor enthusiasm for its interests." His tribute concluded with a poem of his own composition that said as much about the current Librarian's values as it did about Spofford's:

He toiled long, well, and with Good Cheer . . .
He had no Strength that was not Useful
No Weakness that was not Lovable
No Aim that was not Worthy . . . .

There had accrued to Putnam the status of ranking American bookman, a public role for which he was obviously suited. He belonged to the Cosmos Club, the respected center of social and intellectual life in Washington, and every day lunched in a private dining room next to the public one on the top-most floor of the Library. There he was joined by various assistants, scholars, and distinguished people from the realms of literature, commerce, and politics; this floating group came to be known as the Round Table, although the Librarian was indisputably first among equals.

The Round Table soon acquired a wide reputation for conviviality and polished discourse. The British novelist H. G. Wells visited Washington in 1906 and wrote of the city, in *The Future in America: A Search after Realities*, as an intellectual wasteland alleviated only by the literary assemblage at the Library of Congress—"a small raft upon a limitless empty sea. I lunched with them at their Round Table, and afterwards Mr. Putnam showed me the Rotunda, quite the most gracious reading dome the world possesses, and explained the wonderful mechanical organization that brings almost every volume in that immense collection within a minute of one's hand."

The Librarian dealt authoritatively with the inevitable complaints from Congress about its services, which some members saw as too limited. He pointed out that the Library performed functions commonly the responsibility of a legislative office and enumerated the Library's other considerable, wide-ranging duties. Increasing them, he said, would require additional staff and expenditure.

He added that "whatever the appointing or administrative authority, the selection of the experts and the direction of the work should by law and in fact be assuredly nonpartisan." Within a few years Congress would appropriate sufficient funds to create the type of office Putnam spoke of: the Legislative Reference Service.

Meanwhile President Roosevelt's successors, William H. Taft and then Woodrow Wilson, retained Putnam as Librarian, in what was becoming a tradition. The new chief executive's fondness for detective novels did not escape the Librarian, who sent a number of such books to the White House in the spring of 1913 and received an appreciative note from Wilson. America was entering an era of foreign involvement that would have unimagined, lasting consequences, and the president—like the Librarian—was representative of it.

President Wilson proclaimed neutrality in the hostilities developing in

Europe, a reflection of popular sentiment, but this began to change with the mounting sympathy for the Allies. The participation of young Americans in the foreign brigades of Canada and France, the naval blockade of France and England by the Germans, and the subsequent loss of American lives foreshadowed direct American involvement.

The Library now had more than forty miles of book shelves. It possessed two million books and about one million other items—manuscripts, maps, prints, and musical compositions. Classification and cataloging had prevailed, so that the speed of retrieval was equal to or better than that in other American libraries. The various collections grew apace. In 1915 an emissary from the Department of Agriculture traveled to the Far East with a commission from the Library and returned with 5,000 Chinese volumes containing thousands of individual works, 770 Japanese volumes, 7 from Korea, and thousands of bound periodicals. Other materials flowed steadily into Library stacks.

Putnam insisted upon, and rigorously conducted, weekly meetings of the Library staff. His manner could be imperious. Absolute protocol prevailed, and strict operating procedures extended even to the answering of Library telephones. But the Librarian also inspired hard work and loyalty.

The entry of the United States into the First World War in early 1917 brought new duties; the American Library Association formed a Library War Service, and Putnam found himself in charge of it. He helped supply reading material to camps for the diversion and enlightenment of American servicemen in this country and abroad. He paid close attention to the lists of books requested by the soldiers and wrote feelingly of the diversity of subjects in a typical day's requests—business law, mining, physics, electricity, chemistry, physiology, aviation, military signaling, agriculture, motors, and war.

"Among other miscellaneous titles," he later wrote, "are Kipling's Departmental Ditties, Service's Rhymes of a Red Cross Man, Taylor's Practical Stage Directing, a life of Grant, a history of Missionaries and—The Iliad of Homer!"

The war put financial and emotional stress on his staff. In the summer of 1918 Putnam wrote an open letter to them to bolster morale: "You have much to discourage you in the present situation. Your expenses are increasing; your salaries aren't. . . . But don't for a moment believe that—outside of the fighting ranks themselves—there is any 'war work' more necessary than you are doing here. It is our country as a whole which is at war."

The Library had an indispensable part to play, he went on. "Its efficiency *must* be maintained. You can feel also that in 'standing by your job,' patiently, steadily, at a serious personal sacrifice, you are proving a loyalty as unselfish— as fundamentally patriotic—as any shown in this crisis."

During the period of direct American involvement in the World War I and immediate postwar activities, the Library of Congress joined the American Library Association in creating the Library War Service Program, whose general director was Librarian of Congress Herbert Putnam. Born from a belief in the vital importance of books and reading in sustaining American soldiers, the program quickly evolved into a complex effort involving overseas book services and the establishment of libraries in dozens of U.S. training centers—one of which is shown here.

Prints and Photographs Division, Library of Congress. LC-USZ62-04077

The fighting ended that fall with the American success in the Meuse-Argonne offensive, but much of the country, and the Library, remained on a war footing. The military's bibliographic needs still had to be met, and the Library assembled a comprehensive collection of books to accompany the American delegation to the conference at Versailles the following year. One of those in greatest demand by the delegates, and by Library patrons at home, was *The Economic Consequences of the Peace* by John Maynard Keynes.

For years the two most precious documents to the people of the United States—the Declaration of Independence and the Constitution—had rested in an ornate vault at the State Department. On September 30, 1921, State's curator of manuscripts, Gaillard Hunt, former chief of the Manuscript Division at the Library of Congress and a friend of Putnam's, suggested that Putnam come to the stone building on Seventeenth Street, south of Pennsylvania Avenue. There, with the assistance of Library personnel and a panel truck, he transferred the splendidly engrossed parchments to the Library of Congress.

President Warren G. Harding had issued an executive order to accomplish this, and Congress subsequently appropriated $12,000 for "providing a safe,

permanent repository of appropriate design, with the Library of Congress Building." This would be a second-floor shrine designed by Francis H. Bacon to keep the documents safe from light and from handling by viewers while otherwise making them readily accessible. The transfer served a symbolic function as well, proclaiming the Library as a repository of American icons and an essential part of the enduring democracy.

The duties of Library staff had become highly specialized. In many cases, staff responses had been perfected only through years of experience; in 1923, a review of jobs and personnel was conducted and the results used to compare Library workers to those in other government agencies. It

Woodrow Wilson, who in 1913 had received the favor of some detective novels sent him at the White House by Putnam, in 1917 found himself leading the nation into active participation in World War I. In January 1919 he traveled to Paris, where he spent nearly six months with the Allies determining the terms of peace. The Library sent a variety of books to the conference at Versailles for the use of the American delegation there, including *The Economic Consequences of the Peace* by John Maynard Keynes.

Prints and Photographs Division, Library of Congress. LC-USZC4-4936

The Declaration of Independence and the Constitution were transferred from the State Department, where Gaillard Hunt and Secretary of State Charles Evans Hughes supported this move, to the Library of Congress, where Herbert Putnam received them on September 30, 1921. In 1952 these fundamental official documents would go to the National Archives. The papers of Founding Fathers, including George Washington and other presidents, that Putnam had received from State in 1903 remained at the Library of Congress.

Prints and Photographs Division, Library of Congress. LC-USZ62-399

revealed a woeful discrepancy in compensation at the Library, and Putnam wrote a forceful memorandum to the Personnel Classification Board pointing out that the Library of Congress was "unique," with a collection twice the size of any other in the country and one of the three largest in the world.

In addition, he wrote, the Library was "a central cataloguing bureau for 3,000 American libraries, to which it furnishes results in its printed catalogue cards." The specialized knowledge possessed by the chief of each division was equivalent to that of a college professor, and their expertise and relevant experience "cannot be replaced." Salary and professional recognition should be commensurate, a claim that would take two decades to implement.

The precedent of receiving gifts had been established by Putnam's predecessors, but the opportunities increased under him, owing in part to the Librarian's influential Round Table. One guest, Mrs. Elizabeth Sprague Coolidge, the daughter of a wealthy Chicago businessman and a musically gifted mother, lunched at the Library in 1924. Carl Engel, chief of the Music Division, had corresponded with her about the possibility of her supporting music at the Library of Congress. She subsequently offered to sponsor a series of concerts, and, with Engel, convinced Putnam of the advisedness of it. Putnam in turn convinced Congress to accept her gift of private funds to support the concerts.

In the fall of 1924 the first concert was staged in the Freer Gallery of Art, a bureau of the Smithsonian Institution. Putnam gave his full support to the series and to the formation of the Elizabeth Sprague Coolidge Foundation to promote

Elizabeth Sprague Coolidge (1864–1953), a patron of music who established the foundation at the Library of Congress for the encouragement of chamber music. Her contribution led to legislation setting up the Library of Congress Trust Fund, which allowed the Library to promote the arts in general. The Coolidge Foundation commissioned the composition of new works by such musicians as Aaron Copland, whose work *Appalachian Spring* was first performed in the Library's Coolidge Auditorium.

Portrait by John Singer Sargent, 1923. Prints and Photographs Division, Library of Congress. LC-USP6-1532A

"study and appreciation of music in America." At the same time, the Library announced that Mrs. Coolidge's initial gift of $60,000 would be used to build the Coolidge Auditorium in the Library (considerably more money would be required), for a festival of chamber music beginning the following year. Concerts held in the Library and, less and less frequently, elsewhere would be underwritten by an endowment, as would original compositions from noted composers, competitions, lectures, publications, and other activities in the interest of music.

Putnam wrote in his annual report that the Coolidge gifts were "absolutely consistent with the scheme and policy of the Library as a National Library and an agency of the Federal Government, which is . . . to do for American scholarship and cultivation what is not likely to be done by other agencies."

With the Hubbard and Coolidge bequests, the Library of Congress had become a noted institution of "cultivation," as well as one for scholarship and research; it was an obviously worthy object of independent largesse and attracted the attention of an increasing number of philanthropists. The Library's Trust Fund Board was created to deal with what had become a broad range of gifts and a loan account set up into which donors might deposit money for the Library's projects. The funds were to be administered by the board, authorized by Congress on March 3, 1925.

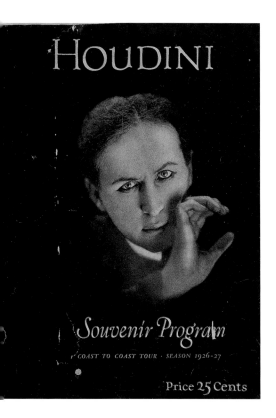

HOUDINI

Souvenir Program

COAST TO COAST TOUR · SEASON 1926-27

Price 25 Cents

Harry Houdini, born Ehrich Weiss in 1874 in Budapest, Hungary, moved that same year with his family to the United States to settle in Appleton, Wisconsin. As a boy, he earned money performing as a contortionist and joined a circus. Later to become a master magician and a renowned escape artist, Houdini read widely about magic. He left to the Library of Congress at his death in 1926 a bequest that included works on spiritualism, magic, and psychic phenomena and scrapbooks of such things as theater notices, playbills, and news clippings. His gift attracted other collections about magic to the Library, such as the McManus-Young Collection that includes this dramatic photograph of the magician.

Rare Book and Special Collections Division, Library of Congress.

The Library acquired less conventional gifts as well. Harry Houdini bequeathed to it what he described as "one of the largest libraries in the world on psychic phenomena, Spiritualism, magic, witchcraft, demonology, evil spirits." Then in 1927 John D. Rockefeller, Jr., informed the Librarian that he was making yet a different sort of gift— $50,000 a year for five years for preparation of a bibliographic "apparatus."

This was to be more than a catalog, a comprehensive list for scholars and researchers of what books and other materials existed and where in the country they might be found. When completed, it would be the most exhaustive catalog of books in American libraries in existence and would serve as another example of the Library of Congress's growing national influence. At the end of the five years, this "union" catalog would contain eight million entries, and five years after that, fourteen million entries.

Several wealthy Americans, among them Andrew Mellon, contributed money for acquiring and recording American folk songs, an activity that became the mission of a separate entity within the Music Division. (The cylindrical recording of the voice of Kaiser Wilhelm II was the first recording acquired by the Library; expansion of that capability led to recordings made specially for the blind.) James B. Wilbur made a donation for photocopying manuscripts pertaining to American history in European archives, and Richard R. Bowker contributed to the bibliographic service. Chairs were established by William Evarts Benjamin in American history and by Archer M. Huntington in Spanish and Portuguese literature, and the Carnegie Corporation established a chair in the fine arts.

The collections and their "interpretation" had gained an ascendancy in the Librarian's mind, sometimes at the expense—or so it seemed to professionals elsewhere—of cooperative book lending and the technical aspects of librarianship that had marked the initial years of his tenure. Putnam seems to have never doubted the wisdom of any course he chose, and so it was with the emphasis now on the cultural role played by the Library and the securing of outside funds for specialists steeped in their respective disciplines.

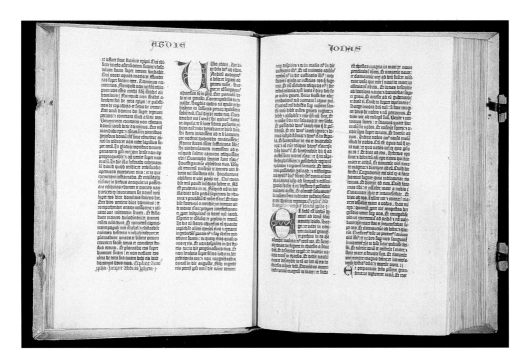

In 1929, the inauspicious year of the stock market collapse, an appropriation was made for buying the land for the construction of an Annex for the burgeoning collection of books and other objects that were again outstripping the Library's capacity. More space was needed; a site had been chosen just to the east of Library, and the cost of construction projected at $6.5 million. Authorization came in 1930, but the project languished with the deepening of the Depression.

Putnam worked for what promised to be a great Library acquisition: the three-thousand-volume Vollbehr collection of fifteenth-century books that included one of three perfect copies of the Gutenberg Bible in existence. A retired scientist, Otto H. F. Vollbehr had located the Bible at a Benedictine monastery in Austria and contracted to buy it. His collection of incunabula, worth approximately $3 million, included books produced at 635 early printing establishments, some in vernacular languages, and a hand-written inventory by the collector, Wilhelm Schreiber.

Vollbehr wished for the Bible and incunabula to reside in the United States but had failed to find a private sponsor to reimburse him for half the collection's value, which was all the compensation he required. A bill was introduced in Congress to provide the funds. Putnam was at first hesitant to champion

One of three known perfect copies of the Gutenberg Bible printed on vellum in 1455 came to the Library as part of the Vollbehr collection. The Bible had only three owners before the American people: Johann Fust, business associate of Johannes Gutenberg, took the Bible to Paris. There it was purchased by the monks of Saint Blasius, who owned it until after World War I, when they sold it to Otto H. F. Vollbehr to raise funds to restore their monastery. Despite the stock market crash the previous fall, the U.S. Congress, with the support of the public and the press, in 1930 approved a special appropriation for this purchase.

what he considered an important acquisition because funding of the construction of the Library's own Annex was pending, but after scholars and other experts testified to the collection's value—and after the Annex appropriation was approved—Putnam publicly advocated buying the collection. The cost was a bargain $1.5 million.

In August 1930, the three-volume Bible was brought from the monastery to the American legation in Vienna and transferred to Paris by special courier; then it went to Cherbourg and into the hold of the *Leviathan*, bound for the United States.

The Library had by now amassed some four million books and pamphlets on an almost infinite variety of subjects. The other collections were similarly diverse. A random sampling included the Library's published report on the original musical manuscripts for "The Star-Spangled Banner," "Hail Columbia," and "Yankee Doodle," "A Preliminary List of Books by Negro Authors for the Paris Exposition and Library of Congress," and "A List of Maps of America." It possessed two drafts of the Gettysburg Address and Theodore Roosevelt's papers.

Almost all the Library's holdings were available to citizens in one form or another. "As one looks down on the general reading room . . . ," wrote the historian James Truslow Adams in his work *The Epic of America*, published in 1931, "one sees the seats filled with silent readers, old and young, rich and poor, black and white, the executive and the laborer, the general and the private, the noted scholar and the schoolboy." Even allowing for hyperbole, the description reflected a thoroughly democratized institution.

Putnam's aloofness, however, had created a distance between himself and other librarians and between himself and his staff. "That he was subjected to an impenetrable dignity cannot be denied," David C. Mearns later wrote in a tribute to Putnam. "He possessed no gifts for glib or sudden intimacy. He rarely gave or asked a confidence. . . . No associate ever called him by his given name."

He insisted upon ruling on the activities of all thirty-five divisions and eleven hundred employees, an impossible task even for a seasoned administrator. Morale declined, and cataloging arrearages, the old Library complaint, were again in the ascendancy. Success in attracting donors was crowned in 1935 by the stunning gift of Stradivari instruments by Mrs. Gertrude Clarke Whittall; almost simultaneously, Putnam rejected an idea backed by the American Library Association for locating a federal library bureau within the Library of Congress. It would have been a distraction, in his view, and a clear threat to his autonomy.

By the end of the decade the Library required a change of leadership. Putnam himself recognized this and indicated to President Franklin D. Roosevelt that he was prepared to relinquish a post he had held for almost forty years, the longest tenure of any Librarian. His contributions had been incalculable. The Library of Congress was, in the estimation of American Council of Learned Societies, "the peer in all respects of its great prototypes, the British Museum and the Bibliothèque Nationale." Putnam, in the council's view, had "made it an indispensable instrument on the American continent for the promotion of learning and the increase of knowledge."

Library influence in scholarship and culture reached into every sector of the country. An Aeronautics Division and the crucial Annex had taken shape out of the ashes of the Depression. The day the Annex reading rooms opened — April 5, 1939 — a bust of Putnam was given to him by his luncheon guests in the main Library, as a tribute. The Librarian was also presented with a letter from the White House.

"My dear Doctor Putnam," Franklin Roosevelt wrote, "I wish it were possible for me to be with my friend of the 'Round Table.' Under your direction our national library has become one of the great libraries of the world. I have an unshaken conviction that democracy can never be undermined if we maintain our library resources." The Library of Congress, he added, "has become universal in scope and national in service."

Gertrude Clarke Whittall

A precious gift was offered to the Library of Congress in 1935 by Gertrude Clarke Whittall, a wealthy widow who, like her philanthropic rival Elizabeth Sprague Coolidge, wished to make a unique, lasting contribution to music in America. Her offer — three violins, a viola, and a violoncello made by Antonio Stradivari (1644–1737), the famous luthier of Cremona, Italy, with bows by François Tourte — came after Mrs. Whittall had sought out the noted instrument dealer H. Blakiston Wilkins and asked him to purchase for her a collection of Stradivari instruments suitable for use by a resident string quartet.

The most famous was the Betts violin, made in 1704 and named for an English violinmaker who had owned it previously. The Castelbarco violin and violoncello had been named for a Milanese count who owned them until 1862. The others were the Ward violin and the Cassavetti viola, one of ten made by Stradivari. These instruments were among the finest musical instruments in existence. Librarian Putnam gladly accepted the offer. Mrs. Whittall stipulated that all the instruments had to be played regularly and donated money to the Trust Fund Board to start a foundation to pay for a chamber music ensemble; in the tradition established by Mrs. Coolidge in 1925, it would perform before the public without charge. Mrs. Whittall later provided funds for construction next to the Coolidge Auditorium of the Whittall Pavilion, where the instruments were to be displayed. In addition to the Strads, as they were called, and the Whittall Pavilion, Gertrude Clarke Whittall donated rare musical works to the Library, including holographs of great European composers such as Bach, Haydn, Mozart, Beethoven, Schubert, and Brahms. From there, the extraordinary musical trail branched repeatedly, leading from the arcane to the popular, from Modest Mussorgski's *Night on Bare Mountain* rearranged by Leopold Stokowski for a Disney animated film to ephemera associated with Jelly Roll Morton.

Gertrude Clarke Whittall (1867–1965) presented the Library with five Stradivari instruments and a Tourte bow for each in 1935–36, later providing funds for construction of the Whittall Pavilion to house them. The Gertrude Clarke Whittall Foundation supports concerts by string quartets using the instruments. Another gift in 1950 would establish the Whittall Poetry Fund to support lectures and poetry readings.

Photograph. Poetry Office, Library of Congress.

Mrs. Whittall gave the Library music manuscripts reflecting her interest in the classic tradition, including autograph scores and original manuscripts by Brahms, Beethoven, Haydn, Mozart, and Schoenberg. Music manuscripts and other materials related to Johannes Brahms formed the largest Brahms collection in any repository outside of Vienna, including this manuscript score for his *Symphony no. 1 in C minor, opus 68.*

Music Division, Library of Congress.

Three Stradivari violins—the Ward (1700), the Castelbarco (1699), and the Betts (1704)—from among the five Stradivari instruments donated by Mrs. Whittall that have been played regularly in the Coolidge Auditorium by the resident string quartet supported by the Gertrude Clarke Whittall Foundation. The Budapest String Quartet was the resident ensemble from 1940 to 1962, followed by the Juilliard String Quartet.

Photograph copyright © Dane Penland.

5

The Comet and the Ploughman

(1939–1954)

What are the dead to us in our better fortune?
They have left us the roads made and the walls standing.
Archibald MacLeish

The anxious spring of '39 saw President Franklin Delano Roosevelt reminding Adolf Hitler and Benito Mussolini, in Roosevelt's typically cordial manner, that "throughout the world hundreds of millions of human beings are living today in constant fear" of war. The United States was hampered by unemployment and other effects of a decade of economic stress, and now from abroad came the threat of "the new philosophies of force" the president had warned of in his address to Congress.

In Washington, leaders were required who would be capable of dealing with challenges to America from abroad and at home. One job infused with new potential—and attracting an unprecedented amount of presidential interest—was that of Librarian of Congress. Roosevelt took the appointment seriously; he wanted a new Librarian with broad experience to replace Herbert Putnam.

But the professional librarians wanted one of their own. The American Library Association, grown increasingly influential over the years, sought an audience with the president to discuss the matter, and when Roosevelt declined, the ALA—without being asked—put forward its own executive secretary as a candidate.

Roosevelt was not one to be pressured. He himself had a candidate in mind, and he wrote to Felix Frankfurter, recently appointed to the Supreme Court, asking, "What do you think of Archie MacLeish? . . . he has lots of qualifications that . . . specialists have not."

Frankfurter responded that what was required was "imaginative energy and vision. [The Librarian] should be a man who knows books, loves books and makes books . . . only a scholarly man of letters can make a great national library

Archibald MacLeish (1892–1982), Pulitzer Prize-winning poet, lawyer, playwright, professor, and champion of democratic principles, became ninth Librarian of Congress despite some initial resistance from professional librarians. He proved to be an able and charismatic Librarian who reorganized the institution administratively and inspired Library staff during the very trying wartime years.

Prints and Photographs Division, Library of Congress. LC-USZ62-614321

a general place of habitation for scholars, because he alone really understands the wants of scholars."

The president had met Archibald MacLeish—"a charming 'mixer,'" as Frankfurter described him—early in his first administration. Although some former Librarians of Congress had pursued literary interests, MacLeish would attain real recognition as a writer. Also, he had studied and taught law and successfully pursued a separate career in journalism. MacLeish would bring an unprecedented degree of celebrity to the Library, should he be chosen.

The choice, however, was seen as a radical departure from the sober professionalism of Herbert Putnam's regime. MacLeish's lack of experience in library affairs and his liberal politics seemed certain to bring on a bruising confirmation fight in the U. S. Senate. Nevertheless, the president remained determined to follow his inclination.

Born in 1892 in Glencoe, Illinois, Archibald MacLeish was the product of parents who believed in education and public service. His father, a successful Chicago merchant, was a founder and trustee of the University of Chicago and his mother president of Rockford College and a force in the Women's Foreign Mission Society. The well-to-do MacLeish was raised on the family estate on Lake Michigan, attending Hotchkiss preparatory school and later Yale University. There he displayed a remarkable aptitude for mastering dissimilar activities—writing for the literary magazine, playing sports, earning a Phi Beta Kappa key.

Franklin Delano Roosevelt (1882–1945), thirty-second president of the United States, led the country through two of the worst crises of the twentieth century: the Great Depression and the Second World War. In 1939, in search of a new Librarian of Congress with broad experience, he nominated Archibald MacLeish to the post. MacLeish would later serve the Roosevelt administration as director of a wartime agency, the Office of Facts and Figures, and as assistant secretary of state.

National Archives and Records Administration.

MacLeish went on to Harvard Law School but left to serve in the field artillery in France during World War I. He returned to Harvard, where he studied under Frankfurter and edited the *Harvard Law Review*. He taught government at Harvard while also working for a Boston law firm. What promised to be a distinguished career built around teaching and the law ended abruptly in 1923 when MacLeish and his wife, Ada, and their two small children sailed for Europe.

MacLeish had decided to pursue his primary interest, poetry. In Paris, he wrote and published several collections of verse and shared the celebrated expatriate life with members of what came to be called the Lost Generation, among them Ernest Hemingway and John Dos Passos. He also traveled to Persia with the League of Nations, an early association that he continued for most of his life.

After returning to the United States in 1929, MacLeish went on to Mexico, where he traced the path of Cortés's invasion and wrote the poem on the subject that eventually earned him a Pulitzer Prize.

MacLeish later wrote on political and cultural subjects for Henry Luce's *Fortune* magazine. He worked long enough each year to earn enough to support his more literary endeavors, which he single-mindedly pursued on a farm in western Massachusetts. In 1933 he published a complimentary piece about the New Deal in *Fortune*, and that and his avid championing of the Loyalists against the fascists in Spain best reflected his liberal politics. Soon he resigned from his position at *Fortune*.

In 1939, MacLeish edited the writings of Frankfurter, who urged him to come to Washington to discuss with the president the position of Librarian of Congress. MacLeish did so, and was offered the job in May but declined on grounds that it would not allow him time to write. "I should therefore feel, in taking it," MacLeish wrote to Roosevelt, "that I have given up my own work pretty much for the rest of my life." A subsequent White House visit followed, and MacLeish changed his mind.

Roosevelt was pleased, and he wrote to MacLeish in a way that illustrated rapport between the two men. It also revealed Roosevelt's lightness of touch and sense of humor. On his new job, MacLeish would "be able to take 'time off' for writing, especially if you like travel to distant parts where you could also improve your knowledge of ancient literature ... you should become thoroughly familiar with the inscriptions on the stone monuments of Easter Island ... [and] sign writing alleged to exist on ancient sheepskins in some of the remoter lamaseries of Tibet. If you go on such a trip I would like to go along as cabin boy. ...."

Not amused by MacLeish's appointment, however, were certain members of Congress and most of the American Library Association. One congressman accused MacLeish of being sympathetic to Communism because of his attendance at the leftward-leaning Second American Writers Congress. And the president of the ALA deplored MacLeish's lack of experience: "I should no more think of him as librarian of Congress than as chief engineer of a new Brooklyn Bridge."

The ALA sent a letter to the president deploring the "calamity" of MacLeish's appointment despite the fact that many professional librarians and scholars did in fact endorse MacLeish. The appointment was similarly attacked in the *New York Herald Tribune* as "shocking" and in the *New York Sun* as "the eccentric favoring of a personal friend" of Roosevelt's.

The *Boston Herald* did remind readers that Putnam and John Russell Young had made contributions to the Library when neither of them had had professional training as a librarian and that MacLeish had displayed considerable organizational abilities by setting up the Nieman fellowship program at Harvard for distinguished journalists.

After holding hearings, the Senate Committee on the Library approved unanimously of MacLeish. Opposition in the Senate itself proved limited and ineffective, if highly vituperative, and Roosevelt's appointment was confirmed. MacLeish chose to be sworn in as Librarian in an unconventional and inconspicuous manner—by the postmaster of Conway, Massachusetts, in the post office where MacLeish picked up his mail.

The Nazis invaded Poland in the fall of 1939. The country and the world were focused on other impending conflicts when MacLeish reported to the Library in early October, a controversial forty-seven-year-old poet, journalist, lawyer, and presidential confidant who wore tweeds as well as pinstripes and who gazes out of a photograph taken that year with a wry, challenging expression.

The Library had grown sevenfold in the last half century. Demanding the new Librarian's attention were almost six million books and pamphlets, one and a half million maps and related material, more than one million pieces of music and books about music, and half a million prints. No one had counted the manuscripts.

MacLeish threw himself into the task of dealing with this intellectual trove. "His drive was tremendous," David C. Mearns wrote of MacLeish in *The Story Up to Now*, "and the fresh air he brought with him was invigorating." Working with the new Librarian, he added, "was almost never easy, but it was almost always fun."

MacLeish was impulsive and unpredictable; many of the demands made upon him were decidedly not "fun." The Library employed eleven hundred people in thirty-five administrative units, all reporting directly to the Librarian, a system that had suited Putnam but dismayed MacLeish. He later wrote, "I have a constitutional disinclination to signing documents I do not know to be right."

MacLeish called for a broad review of Library operations and learned that one and a half million books and pamphlets were not found listed in the main catalog and that the backlog was increasing by thirty thousand items annually. Furthermore, there were serious deficiencies in the collections. Fifteen of the forty major subject fields had no specialists, and only twelve of those that did received adequate attention.

In addition, separate accounting records were kept by various administrative units. Salaries throughout the Library were well below those for comparable positions in other government and research units.

The new Librarian asked Congress for $4.2 million for fiscal 1941, an increase of $1 million over the previous year; he received about a third of that. He had proposed the creation of 287 new positions and was granted only 50, all for book processing. The requests for new area specialists, additional staff for reference, and salary increases were denied. A thorough review of salaries was launched, however, and that would lead to job reclassification and more equitable compensation for the Library's large, uniquely talented staff.

One crucial appointment made by the new Librarian was that of Luther H. Evans, formerly head of the Historical Records Survey, a nationwide archival survey sponsored by the Works Progress Administration. Evans had been recognized by a member of Roosevelt's "brain trust" and shared the political views of the New Dealers, among them MacLeish. Somewhat daringly, MacLeish put Evans in charge of the Library's important Legislative Reference Service.

Congress called for a Librarian's Committee of distinguished outsiders to evaluate the processing operations less than a year after MacLeish took office, and he began to reorganize the Library according to the committee's recommendations. In the process, fresh air began to work its way into the fabric of the Library. The poet cum "charming mixer" proved adept at bureaucratic maneuvers and at employing such a modern business concept as the Statement of Objectives.

Librarian MacLeish appointed longtime staff member Verner W. Clapp to be budget officer in charge of administration and, later, head of the newly created Acquisitions Department. Clapp also supervised the wartime evacuation of irreplaceable items from the collections to facilities outside of Washington—including the U.S. Constitution and the Declaration of Independence—but here he performed the more mundane task of delivering a book to a reader in the Library's Main Reading Room.

Library of Congress Archives.

First MacLeish consolidated day-to-day activities in three departments and elevated two trusted associates: Verner W. Clapp, a seventeen-year Library veteran, who became budget officer in charge of administration, and the newcomer, Evans, who was to head Reference. The highly varied activities of receiving, cataloging, preparing, and shelving books and other items were concentrated in a processing department, and to head it, MacLeish brought in another professional destined for a stellar Library career, L. Quincy Mumford, on temporary loan from the New York Public Library.

This was just the beginning. Within three years MacLeish had created the Acquisitions Department and moved Clapp over to run it. Evans had become chief assistant librarian in charge of all administration, and the authorial David Mearns had been made head of Reference. The Library's "nearly incredible metamorphosis" was cited in an article in the *Saturday Review*, and subsequent observers commented on the surprising fact that this amateur Librarian had brought off a reorganization that would have proved impossible a few years later. It vindicated Roosevelt's appointment.

Among MacLeish's objectives was obtaining for the Library "all books and other materials … which express and record the life and achievements of the people of the United States." The Library should also possess "in original or in copy" materials pertaining to other societies "past and present," and full, representative collections "of most immediate concern to the people of the United States."

The unequivocal nature of these assertions put MacLeish firmly in the camp of Thomas Jefferson and others who had equated knowledge and the general well-being of the nation throughout the Library's history.

Prevented by the press of his official duties from writing poetry, MacLeish did initiate a poetry reading series at the Library, bringing such established figures as Robert Frost before appreciative audiences. Frost's association with the Library would continue over the years: he served as the Library's Consultant in Poetry (1958–59) and as Honorary Consultant in the Humanities (1958–63). He also recorded his poetry for the Library's Archive of Recorded Poetry and Literature.

Library of Congress Archive.

To achieve these admittedly idealistic objectives, MacLeish recruited young scholars with fellowships paid for by the Carnegie Corporation to fan out through the Library, assessing its holdings in individual fields and making recommendations for additional purchases. In the process, they strengthened crucial ties between Library staff and American universities.

Even the august annual report was touched by the transforming hand. Formerly a compendium of colorless accounts of Library activities, the report received a literary gloss from the new Librarian. In it, in 1941, MacLeish made an attempt to formally elucidate his vision: "We propose . . . to exhibit the Library in action—not what it possesses only, but what it *does* with what it possesses."

The cultural component of the Library, firmly established during Herbert Putnam's long reign, was further strengthened by MacLeish. The Library welcomed refugee writers from Europe, among them Thomas Mann, who became a special consultant in Germanic literature. Naturally concerned with poetry —and unable to write it while Librarian—MacLeish initiated a poetry reading series underwritten by the publisher of the *Washington Post* that placed established literary figures before an appreciative public. They included Robert Frost, Carl Sandburg, and Stephen Vincent Benét.

Meanwhile, conflict had enveloped Europe. The bombing of London by the

Nazis riveted the attention of Americans, and at the Library, preliminary steps were taken to guard the collections against possible air raids. A survey to determine what should be removed began in early 1940, and first priority went to irreplaceable manuscripts, maps, prints, musical scores, and, of course, rare books. Next came those volumes and pamphlets relating to American history that might be used as a foundation upon which to start a new Library, should harm come to the existing one, a reminder of the fate of the Library during the invasion of British troops more than a century earlier.

Staff volunteers working overtime tagged all items. Thousands of wooden packing cases were purchased for transportation and various college campuses chosen as possible storage sites.

The bombing of Pearl Harbor by the Japanese the following year drew America into the war, and the Library joined an overall readiness campaign in Washington. It was an exciting—and distracting—time. A reference service with a twenty-four-hour telephone bank was set up to serve various war agencies and provide books and bibliographies. Government researchers were provided space in the Annex, including an entire floor for what became the Research and Analysis Branch of the Office of Strategic Services.

The Library's various divisions found themselves preoccupied with war-related needs: Legislative Reference with translations and abstracts, the Map Division with updated military campaign maps, the Music Division with foreign-language training and music courses for the U.S. Army, and the Division for the Study of Wartime Communications with reports on public opinion and propaganda. As a kind of symbolic action, a "Democracy Alcove" was established in the Main Reading Room.

All this activity taxed the Library's already overworked staff and led to massive defections as employees took jobs at other government agencies. Some of these staff members were uniquely qualified and were lost, as MacLeish reported, "because the Library . . . is at a permanent disadvantage in competing with other employers. It is unable to offer equal salaries for equal work." The reclassification study undertaken by the Civil Service Commission was far from complete.

The Library's evacuation plan was put into effect under the supervision of Verner Clapp. First the Declaration of Independence, the Constitution, the Bill of Rights, the Gutenberg Bible, and the Stradivari instruments were sealed in waterproof containers and provided a military escort to the U.S. Bullion Depository at Fort Knox, Kentucky. Also included in the precious shipment was the Magna Carta, which had been placed in the care of the Library by the British government.

Within five months some five thousand cases of additional items had been stored in fireproof buildings at Thomas Jefferson's University of Virginia, at

In the late 1930s, as World War II began to engulf the globe, a number of the cultural and intellectual treasures of foreign nations were sent to the Library of Congress for safekeeping. One of the most precious of these was the Lincoln Cathedral copy of the Magna Carta, which had been on display at the 1939 World's Fair in New York City. After the Japanese attacked Pearl Harbor, the Magna Carta was sent with the Library's treasures to Fort Knox, Kentucky. Accompanied by future Librarian of Congress Luther Evans (*left*), it was removed from the Library on December 26, 1941, under Secret Service protection.

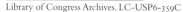

Library of Congress Archives. LC-USP6-359C

Washington and Lee University, at the Virginia Military Institute, and at Denison University in Ohio. The Union Catalog—and its staff—were also sequestered in Virginia and eight million cards from the Library's main catalog and shelflists were recorded on microfilm and shipped out of the capital.

MacLeish often assisted the president when that assistance had nothing to do with the Library. He contributed to Roosevelt's 1941 inaugural address and would do so again in 1945; he was also responsible for Roosevelt's 1944 State of the Union address. "Sometimes we would send a call for help to Archibald MacLeish," presidential adviser Robert Sherwood later wrote, ". . . who would come in late at night to help bring a diffuse speech into focus." Clearly the Librarian had his hands full.

It was logical that the president would turn to MacLeish to help in the general readiness effort. This indirectly affected the Library, for Roosevelt appointed MacLeish to direct a new war agency, the Office of Facts and Figures, to be housed in the Annex. MacLeish's dual role would divide his responsibilities; worse, it provided an opening for his critics.

Luther Evans was designated Acting Librarian while MacLeish turned his attention to the new agency. It was to be a clearinghouse for information put out by the government, envisioned as an important part of the burgeoning defense effort, but in fact it possessed insufficient authority to control or even coordinate government releases.

Hostile members of Congress, mindful of MacLeish's close relationship with the president, questioned his qualifications for the job and his objectivity.

When a pamphlet describing Nazi propaganda tactics was published in 1942 by the agency, before the excesses of Naziism became widely known, members of Congress and editorial writers criticized it as the product of liberal bias.

MacLeish was subsequently grilled by a subcommittee of the House Committee on Appropriations on the close relationship between the Office of Facts and Figures and the Library of Congress and the difficulty of meeting obligations toward both. "Like a lot of other people in town," MacLeish responded, "I have stopped sleeping and given up Sundays."

Some congressmen were not impressed. The Library's book budget was slashed from $173,000 to $55,000. Although the funds were later restored, MacLeish was stung by the act, which he saw as representative of a larger failing among elected representatives. He publicly charged them with anti-intellectualism and the news media with indifference to a basic American need—access to knowledge of all kinds.

In an address to the American Library Association, which had rallied to MacLeish's support, he elaborated: "Fifty years ago an attack upon a great library, an attempt to deprive the people of this country of their books, would have brought down upon the politician who attempted it a storm of criticism in the public press. Today it passes almost without comment." That criticism would resonate in the years following World War II, when the House Un-American Activities Committee called into question some basic American freedoms.

The Office of Facts and Figures was moved out of the Annex and merged with the Office of War Information. MacLeish acted as assistant director for policy for the larger organization but resigned from that position in 1943. Much of his subsequent tenure as Librarian was devoted to increasing the ratings and salaries of employees and encouraging them to take part in discussions of Library policy. A Staff Advisory Committee drafted a policy for airing employee grievances that attracted the attention and praise of other government agencies.

Despite the distractions of war and politics, MacLeish had kept the Library's cultural programs alive. He made the poet Allen Tate a special consultant and charged him with further developing the literary collections, editing a new quarterly, and organizing a group of distinguished American writers to advise the Library that included Carl Sandburg and Katherine Anne Porter. The poet Robert Penn Warren would follow Tate as the special consultant.

Acquisitions made by the Library had been inadequately described and reported for years. In the summer of 1943 MacLeish announced the publication of the *Library of Congress Quarterly Journal of Current Acquisitions* to correct this problem. Under Tate's guidance it would contain "cooperative scholar-

Folklorist Alan Lomax in a 1940 publicity photograph for CBS. Lomax directed the Library's Archive of American Folk Song from 1937 to 1942, working with his father, John A. Lomax, who was in charge of the archive from 1932 to 1942. Both at the Library of Congress and working as private citizens, the Lomax family created a significant collection of documentary field recordings, mostly in the South, that would become an important part of America's cultural heritage.

Archive of Folk Culture, American Folklife Center, Library of Congress.

ship" of staff, consultants, and scholars and make the Library's many acquisitions more accessible to all.

MacLeish, weary of the feverish activity during the war years, wished to resume his career as a writer. Given to bouts of depression, according to his biographer, Scott Donaldson, and a tendency to create subjects about which to worry, MacLeish never gave up "contemplating 'the shine of the world.'" He wrote to Roosevelt asking to be relieved of his duties as Librarian, foreseeing a retreat from official Washington to the relative calm of New England.

The president responded, "It is going to be difficult and I honestly believe impossible to find anybody to occupy your chair." MacLeish suggested as a replacement the librarian at Princeton University, Julian P. Boyd, who was intent upon publishing an edition of Thomas Jefferson's papers and declined Roosevelt's offer. But MacLeish planned to depart early in 1944 even if a replacement had not been found.

His other interests diverted him from the Library that spring—to write a series of radio broadcasts for NBC's Inter-American University of the Air and to travel to London as a delegate to what became the United Nations, a cause he supported consistently. MacLeish felt that his reorganization had "provided a sensible, orderly, and manageable structure, strong enough to support the great future of which the Library of Congress is so manifestly capable" and that he was free to follow his inspiration.

The president was not through with him, however. At the end of the year MacLeish was appointed assistant secretary of state in charge of public and cultural relations, and Luther Evans became Acting Librarian.

MacLeish's new post required congressional confirmation and provided another opportunity for an acrimonious discussion of the role of literary men in American affairs. During hearings before the Senate Foreign Relations Committee, MacLeish was closely questioned about his verse. "The word *poet*," he later wrote, "was pronounced with a particular intonation. . . . The implication . . . being that this man [MacLeish] regards himself as a poet and this obviously disqualifies him not only for public life, but for those sensible conversations . . . by which ordinary men communicate."

He was confirmed in his new State Department post. The president wrote to compliment him, adding, "The only trouble is that you jump from one mausoleum into the other. This is not meant to be derogatory on my part, for both the Library of Congress and the Department of State have long and honorable histories. This ought to hold you."

It would not, MacLeish's energies being protean and his interests peripatetic. His eye was always on some new opportunity. He headed the delegation to the United Nations conference where the infant United Nations Educational, Scientific, and Cultural Organization (UNESCO) was founded, and later returned to Harvard. By then Roosevelt was dead of a cerebral hemorrhage and the Armistice and the surrender of Japan had brought World War II to a conclusion.

The world was about to be remade, and the Library of Congress reverberated with MacLeish's brief tenure there, fondly characterized by Luther Evans as a "brush of the comet."

Collecting in Unexpected Ways

The collections had expanded in varied and unexpected ways under MacLeish. Using funds from the Carnegie Corporation, the Library installed in the Music Division a laboratory for duplicating phonograph recordings, for making its own recordings, and for radio broadcasting. A sound truck and six portable receivers were acquired to facilitate recordings in the field, to make and preserve phonographic records of American music and other cultural achievements.

Fifteen hundred flutes and related instruments from all over the world—the most extensive such collection in existence—were obtained from Dayton C. Miller, a professor of physics and an authority on acoustics. Included in his unusual bequest were flutes by the masters Theobald Bohm and H. F. Meyer, and three thousand volumes relating to flute playing published between 1488 and 1940, plus a wealth of ancillary material.

A bequest from Lincoln's granddaughter, Mary Lincoln Isham, in 1937, included the contents of the president's pockets on the night he was shot at Ford's Theater in Washington, D.C., which had stayed in the family more than seventy years.

The history of aviation was documented in the Library's holdings by letters from aeronautical pioneer and engineer Octave Chanute and over thirty thousand diaries, notebooks, scrapbooks, and glass plate negatives recording the careers of Wilbur and Orville Wright. The history of film was captured in the personal film library and papers of George Kleine, which the Library purchased in 1947. An American distributor of European films, Kleine collected footage from the period 1898 to 1926, including motion pictures produced by Thomas A. Edison, Inc., between 1914 and 1917, which provides today's researchers with examples from the early film industry.

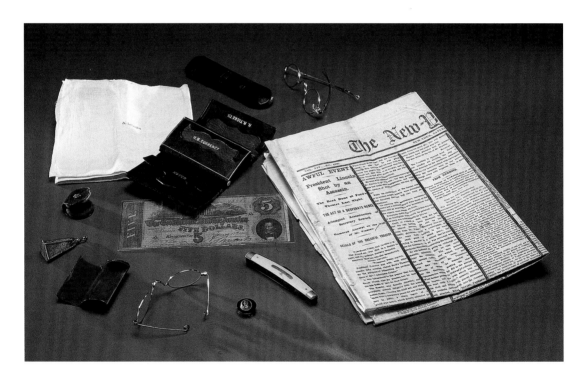

Among the items visitors to the Library often asked to see were the contents of Abraham Lincoln's pockets on the night he was shot at Ford's Theater, April 14, 1865. These included two pairs of spectacles, a pocketknife, a linen handkerchief, and a Confederate note and newspaper clippings in a leather wallet. They were bequeathed to the Library in 1937 by Lincoln's granddaughter, Mary Lincoln Isham. An issue of the *New York Times* reporting Lincoln's assassination was part of Alfred Whital Stern's collection of Lincolniana.

Rare Book and Special Collections Division. Photograph by Roger Foley.

Sounds—not only of music but of folk ceremonies, radio broadcasts, and other audible events interwoven into daily life and important to a rounded understanding of history—were recorded, duplicated, and preserved by Library of Congress laboratories, sound trucks, and portable receivers.

Library of Congress Archives. LC-USP6-431C

(below) Taken at the exact moment of liftoff, this historic photograph labeled "First Flight, December 17, 1903. Distance 120 feet. Time, 12 seconds. Orville Wright at controls" came to the Library when the papers of Wilbur and Orville Wright were given to the Library in 1949 by the executors of Orville Wright's estate.

Photograph by John T. Daniels. Prints and Photographs Division, Library of Congress. LC-USZ62-6166

128

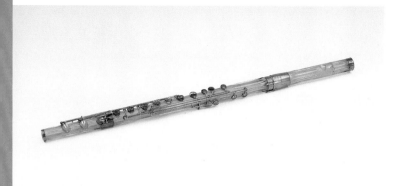

A crystal flute by Claude Laurent was among the more than sixteen hundred flutes and other wind instruments from all cultures of the world and dating from pre-Columbian times that Dayton C. Miller donated to the Library in 1941, along with music, prints, and three thousand books that represented practically everything written about the flute and flute playing before 1940.

Music Division, Library of Congress.

Bandmaster and composer John Philip Sousa (*center, with beard*) posed with his band at Willow Grove Park in Philadelphia in 1905. Known as America's "March King," Sousa directed the U.S. Marine Band from 1880 to 1892, after which he organized his own band and toured the country with great success. The Library's John Philip Sousa Collection eventually contained autograph music manuscripts of most of his works—not only the marches like "The Stars and Stripes Forever" but also his popular tunes and comic operas.

Music Division, Library of Congress.

The appointment of Luther Harris Evans as Librarian of Congress by President Harry S. Truman in 1945 seems in retrospect an inevitable decision. The president, himself a bookman, invited Evans to the White House to explain, as Evans described the meeting to a friend, that Truman wanted the Library "to give service to Congress, but he wants it also to be 'the Library of the United States' and give increased service to the little libraries all over the country."

This was not the same thing as serving as a central administrative library, a notion rejected periodically throughout the Library's long history. Neither was it a departure from the role envisioned by Ainsworth Rand Spofford years before. Truman was reaffirming in his own words the rightful place of this national institution.

Evans—despite Archibald MacLeish's failure to recommend him as his replacement—was an obvious choice for heading the Library, conversant with it and successful in realizing some of MacLeish's innovations. It was Evans who had moved the Library toward greater efficiency, helping devise new cataloging procedures that formed the basis of the National Union Catalog of Manuscript Collections. He had initiated regular meetings of department directors and encouraged others to communicate freely with staff.

The Library now possessed about twenty-five million items. They had become the direct responsibility of the son of a railroad section foreman. Librarian Evans was the social antithesis of the privileged MacLeish, having attended a one-room schoolhouse in rural Texas and worked his way through the University of Texas and Stanford University. After teaching political science at several universities, including Princeton, Evans brought a dedication to Roosevelt's Washington rooted in his own experience with hard times.

Having established a reputation as a wise and careful administrator with an eye for detail, Evans was sworn in two months after the fall of Nazi Germany and three months before the surrender of Japan. In the months and years that followed the war, the United States assumed a new, sober, dominant role in world affairs; it found itself—like the Library of Congress—manifestly concerned with *all* intellectual and cultural matters.

As the new Librarian himself wrote late in 1945, "[D]estruction has been avoided only through an unprecedented mobilization of man's knowledge of himself and his environment. No spot on the earth's surface is any longer alien to the interest of the American people." The words echoed Thomas Jefferson's belief that no subject lay outside the potential interest of the people's elected representatives.

Efforts to improve services and salaries at the Library and to increase the collections received fresh impetus. Evans estimated the needs for fiscal 1947 at almost $10 million; he called for an extensive study justifying that unprece-

Appointed head of the Legislative
Reference Service by Librarian MacLeish,
Luther H. Evans later became chief assistant librarian in charge of all administration.
Some six months after MacLeish's resignation, President Harry Truman nominated
Evans to be Librarian of Congress. He
took the oath of office on June 30, 1945,
and served until July 5, 1953.

Prints and Photographs Division, Library of
Congress. LC-USZ62-58936

dented request from Congress and called it the most important paper to emerge
since the 1802 report of the committee considering the Library's organization.

Congress didn't share his enthusiasm. It provided more than $6 million to
the Library but the increases in the appropriation were earmarked for the
Copyright Office and the Legislative Reference Service.

Congress wanted to know what the Librarian had in mind for the future.
Evans appointed a planning committee composed of distinguished Americans
outside the Library—professional librarians, scholars, and government officials,
chaired by Harvard University librarian Keyes D. Metcalf. It broadly considered
the functions of the Library in the years ahead. When issued, the report reflected
Evans's expansive view of the Library's role in American life, with enhanced collections to meet the needs of government, academia, and commerce.

Again, Congress was not persuaded. Any budget increases were absorbed by
higher costs for books and materials and by long overdue salary adjustments. The
controversies surrounding Evans's predecessor, and anti-intellectual sentiments in
many quarters of the country, may also have affected the mood of Congress.

The Lincoln Cathedral copy of the Magna Carta, kept safe by the Library during
World War II, was returned to England. For two years thereafter the Lacock Abbey

copy of the 1225 Great Charter, the only perfect copy, with its original wax seal, was exhibited at the Library as a token of deep British appreciation.

The war had taken a toll on the Library's own collections and had revealed their inadequacies. Evans, writing in the Washington *Sunday Star*, pointed out that the Library's data on meteorological conditions in the Himalayas had assisted the Air Force in crossing those mountains, but that a deficiency in the collection of periodicals from Germany had prevented American policymakers from anticipating the rise of Naziism.

Similarly, a better collection of plans of European cities might have prevented the destruction of important monuments. "[T]he lesson which the war has taught us is the lesson that, however large our collections may now be, they are pitifully and tragically small in comparison with the demands of the Nation."

Despite postwar frugality, Evans envisioned a Library twice the size of the current one. He was determined to increase the collections, particularly of research material from foreign countries. Cooperative arrangements brought in a torrent of new material, and microfilming projects further expanded the Library's resources from abroad.

Evans—a steady, undramatic, dedicated westerner—anticipated two significant future trends in America: the emphasis upon cultural variety and its continuing relevance and the moral obligation to return works improperly removed from other countries.

In 1949 Evans announced that the Library would not buy or accept any foreign document that appeared to have been removed illegally. He also made arrangements for the return of such documents, among them a letter written by Christopher Columbus in 1504 and removed from the Real Academia de la Historia in Madrid during the Spanish Civil War.

Meanwhile, the Library acquired from abroad the manuscript of Somerset Maugham's *Of Human Bondage*, the manuscripts, letters, and first editions of Hans Christian Andersen, Leonard Kebler's Cervantes collection, and the autograph manuscripts of the Russian composer Sergei Rachmaninoff.

Acquisition of domestic material also accelerated, including that of valuable American manuscripts, correspondence, and books. The Library obtained the papers of Orville and Wilbur Wright, landscape architect Frederick Law Olmsted, General John J. Pershing, and the novelist Owen Wister.

Two life masks of Lincoln—one from before his presidential campaign and the other made by Clark Mills in February 1865, about two months before Lincoln's assassination—came to the Library in 1953 with the the most extensive collection of Lincolniana ever assembled by a private individual. The Alfred Whital Stern collection included publications, contemporary newspapers, sheet music, broadsides, prints, stamps, coins, and autograph letters and was supplemented by an endowment from Stern's family that allowed further purchases. The musical manuscripts of George Gershwin and John Philip Sousa were acquired, and Woodrow Wilson's nine-thousand-volume personal library was deposited in the Library of Congress, with special arrangements made for its display and use.

The massive backlog of unclassified material from the war years, added to the material then being acquired, put great stress on the staff. Evans was convinced that "firm and democratically-arrived-at answers to the cataloging problems can be found," but they persisted throughout his tenure—as indeed they had from the Library's inception.

Under Evans's guidance the Library issued *Rules for Descriptive Cataloging in the Library of Congress*, a groundbreaking codification of the standards of processing, and new rules were developed for dealing with the burgeoning collections of film, recordings, photographs, original manuscripts, prints, and books for the blind.

As President Truman desired, the nation's libraries had already come to depend upon the Library of Congress's schedules for classifying material. But these were revised and updated, particularly in the fields of medicine, military science, and the law, and the Library's card catalogs were published in book form. Local libraries were consulted with, and Evans traveled around the country explaining the Library's procedures and offering its support.

A Science Division was established in 1949 and became the most diverse in the country; it was followed by a Technical Information Division. European affairs were assigned to a new division, the Slavic countries to yet another, and a Korean specialist was added to the Orientalia Division. Evans created the Folklore Section in the Music Division and arranged to have authors recorded while reading from their works. Library concerts were broadcast to the public.

In general, a series of administrative and departmental reorganizations broadened and deepened the Library during the decade of Evans's stewardship. "There is no doubt that it was the personality of the Librarian that set the pace of this pressure for accomplishment," wrote Assistant Librarian Clapp. "His own long hours and merciless schedule were known to all."

Motivating Evans was a steadfast belief in free speech. He wrote of the recent past and "vicious, perverse and cunning men, [whose] false words corrupted and degraded and destroyed. It is . . . the principal duty of this generation to restore the dignity, the confidence, the influence, the benignity of words. Starved minds and starved spirits breed totalitarianism."

This belief involved Evans and the Library in a controversy as searing as any in its history. The Bollingen Prize in Poetry, established with a grant from the Bollingen Foundation in 1948, was to be awarded annually for the best book of verse by an American author. Making the selection the following year, the eve of the Library's sesquicentennial year, were the thirteen poets and authors of the Fellows in American Letters of the Library of Congress, which included Conrad Aiken, W. H. Auden, and Robert Penn Warren.

The first award went to Ezra Pound for *The Pisan Cantos*. Unfortunately, Pound was at the time under indictment for treason for his wartime activities in Europe, and residing in Saint Elizabeth's hospital for the insane in Washington, D.C. The fellows acknowledged that they were "aware that objection may be made to awarding a prize to a man situated as is Mr. Pound." But the objections surpassed anything they and Evans anticipated.

So acrimonious was the response in Congress and in segments of the American press that the Joint Committee on the Library demanded an end to the practice of making awards of any kind. Evans subsequently announced the demise not only of the short-lived Bollingen Prize but also the Elizabeth Sprague Coolidge awards in chamber music and three awards made for the national exhibition of prints. Thus ended the Library's role as cultural arbiter.

Evans had complied with the wishes of Congress at a time when questions of ideology and loyalty preoccupied Americans. But two years later, addressing librarians in California, he stated unequivocally that censorship was the "most serious threat to free libraries at home." Censors, he added, "are willing to deny the whole concept of freedom in order to strike a blow against ideas which they find unwholesome."

In early 1950, President Truman sent Evans an appreciative letter citing the Library for its services and vast collections that would not have been possible "without the power of the principle of free enquiry." Modest sesquicentennial celebrations that year included an address by Truman in the Coolidge Auditorium in recognition of the publication of the first volume of *The Papers of Thomas Jefferson*.

Evans announced another gift from Gertrude Clarke Whittall for establishing a fund to "promote the appreciation and understanding of poetry" through lecturing and readings, rather than prizes. Cleanth Brooks, himself a poet, and the actor Burgess Meredith would present an initial program about the poet Edward Arlington Robinson.

The American Library Association, which over the years had its differences with the Library, held a banquet in honor of its 150th year. Librarian Emeritus Herbert Putnam got up to speak about the Library's remarkable evolution. "[I]f you are summoning shades of the past," said Putnam, "you must not fail to summon one shade and keep *him* contemporary—the valiant, persistent . . . 'forecasting,' 'foretelling,' 'prophesying' shade . . . Ainsworth Spofford."

The current Librarian's personal interest in oral history led him to participate in the interpretation of the Library's past. Evans left a rich collection of commentary about the Library from the perspective of the late 1940s. Assisted by Clapp and Mearns—the three of them interviewed each other, as well as division chiefs and specialists—he put together a recorded, somewhat personal history. The interviews were broadcast during intermissions in the chamber music concerts in the Coolidge Auditorium.

But Evans might have heeded his predecessor Spofford's earlier example of dealing carefully and diplomatically with members of Congress, whatever his view of them. That Evans had neglected to do so soon became apparent.

Assistant Secretary of State Archibald MacLeish had asked Evans to join the U.S. delegation to London when UNESCO was first founded. Evans had continued his association with that organization, helping shape the Universal Copyright Convention and speaking often about UNESCO's mission before American audiences. Evans considered it and the Library's objectives similar—the promotion of peace through cultural exchange and international cooperation—and involved the Library in various UNESCO efforts.

In 1952, he attended a UNESCO executive board meeting in Paris instead of appearing at the House Appropriations Committee budget hearings on Capitol Hill. It proved to be a considerable tactical error. Hostility toward the Library's administration had persisted in Congress, exacerbated no doubt by the Bollingen Prize controversy and Evans's continuing association with MacLeish and the Department of State. This became evident in sharp criticism of Evans made to Chief Assistant Librarian Clapp, who represented the Library before the committee.

Clapp defended Evans as a dedicated leader who worked eighteen hours a day and maintained close communications with the Library when away, but some members were not assuaged. Congressman Walter Horan, of Washington State, asserted that Evans was "not running the Library." Christopher C. McGrath went so far as to suggest that Evans "get another job." The Librarian's effectiveness before Congress, despite his accomplishments, was clearly in question.

President Truman was succeeded in office by Dwight D. Eisenhower. On election night in 1952, CBS television experimented with the powers of the electronic computer UNIVAC I, which, with just 5 percent of the votes counted, predicted one of the biggest landslide victories in the country's history for Eisenhower. Disbelieving television executives withheld this information, only to find the next morning that the prediction had been accurate. Outdated thirteen years after its creation, UNIVAC I became part of the collections of the Smithsonian Institution in 1964.

A new era had clearly begun. In the summer of 1953, Luther Evans was elected director-general of UNESCO. To no one's surprise, he submitted his resignation to President Eisenhower. Verner Clapp was made Acting Librarian, and the search began for a permanent replacement for the poor boy from Texas.

Luther Evans had overseen the greatest expansion of the Library in recent times. The collections had grown by 28 percent, to almost thirty-two million items, but the quality of the acquisitions was as remarkable. Evans's tenure had seen a dramatic increase in the resources available to serve the nation's research needs.

Sight and Sound

In 1942, using a grant from the Rockefeller Foundation, the Library had begun to select certain American films for preservation that had been deposited for copyright. In 1946 Mary Pickford, the popular actress and cofounder of United Artists, donated her private collection to the Library for preservation and research. Included were one-reel films from the old Biograph Company made between 1909 and 1912, and feature-length films made between 1914 and 1931, among them *Rebecca of Sunnybrook Farm.*

In 1943 the Motion Picture Section was created. Although it was liquidated by budget cuts in 1947, it eventually became part of the Motion Picture, Broadcasting, and Recorded Sound Division. Included in the collection today are American feature and other films going back to 1894 and a collection of foreign films, including German, Italian, and Japanese films from the 1930s and 1940s.

In 1947 the collection of George Kleine, an early American distributor of foreign films, was purchased by the Library. Among the 456 motion pictures made between 1898 and 1926 were many produced by Thomas A. Edison, Inc. Fifty films had been made by foreign companies—Gaumont, Pathé, Cines, Ambrosio. These and the Kleine papers dealing with various aspects of early motion picture distribution totaled some twenty-six thousand items.

In the years and decades ahead, the film collection grew exponentially in number and in breadth of subject. There would be a trove of films about Theodore Roosevelt received from the National Park Service that showed Roosevelt as a Rough Rider and as a mature political figure, most of them made between 1909 and 1919.

The collection presented by United Artists contained some three thousand motion pictures from the film library of Warner Brothers made before 1949—*High Sierra, I Am a Fugitive from a Chain Gang,* and *Little Caesar.* There were fifty silent films and some four hundred cartoons such as Merrie Melodies, Looney Tunes, and Popeye.

Television programs also found their way into the division—copies of thousands of prime time telecasts made during the first decades of commercial broadcasting. Among these were videotapes of *Meet the Press,* first televised in 1949, as well as about sixty-four thousand items (most held in the Manuscript Division) in the collection of Lawrence E. Spivak, the producer of the program for the National Broadcasting Company, including transcripts, scrapbooks, autographs, and news clippings.

Charlie Chaplin —
m The Kid —

Jackie Coogan

Charlie Chaplin and Jackie Coogan in a scene from *The Kid* (Vitagraph Company of America, 1916). In 1942, the Library began to select for preservation certain American films that had been deposited for copyright. That same year Librarian MacLeish established the Motion Picture Division—which became the Motion Picture, Broadcasting, and Recorded Sound Division—in acknowledgment of the essential historical value of movies, radio broadcasts, and recordings in all their formats. At the end of the twentieth century the collections comprised well over 200,000 film prints, American films, and the most widely representative collection of foreign-language films in the world.

Motion Picture, Broadcasting, and Recorded Sound Division, Library of Congress. LC-USZ62-44820

Among the 456 motion pictures that came to the Library when it purchased the George Kleine film collection in 1947 were many produced by the Edison Manufacturing Company in Orange, New Jersey. One of these, from 1895, was *Annabelle Butterfly Dance*, a cinematic reproduction of the dance performances at the 1893 World Columbian Exposition in Chicago that had brought fame to Annabelle Whitford. The dramatic impact of Whitford's performances was heightened by the use of colored gels on the spotlights—an effect that was reproduced on film by hand coloring every black-and-white 35mm print, frame by frame, in the Edison studio.

Frame enlargements. Motion Picture, Broadcasting, and Recorded Sound Division, Library of Congress.

(above) Alfred Hitchcock used film to explore issues of identity, anxiety, and obsession in *Vertigo*, released by Universal Pictures in 1958. Kim Novak played the protagonist who was transformed physically to resemble a dead woman adored by a retired police detective played by Jimmy Stewart.

Frame enlargement. Motion Picture, Broadcasting, and Recorded Sound Division.

Theodore Roosevelt, here photographed in his late twenties, about 1885, collected books about big game hunting, natural history, exploration, ornithology, and sport, which revealed his strong personal interests. His grandson Kermit Roosevelt presented this hunting library to the Library of Congress in 1963 and 1964. The Theodore Roosevelt Association, founded in 1919, began collecting motion pictures related to Roosevelt in 1920 and eventually sent these early films to the Library of Congress where they became part of the National Film Collection.

Rare Book and Special Collections Division, Library of Congress. LC-USZ62-23232

6

A Delicate Balance

(1954–1974)

*As if I had measured the country
And got the United States.*
Robert Frost

Mid-century in America entailed prosperity and general contentment, but that mood had not affected the relationship between Congress and its Library. For fifteen years this had been uneasy and sometimes hostile, feelings that carried over into the assessment of the man appointed by President Eisenhower to replace Luther Evans. His name was Lawrence Quincy Mumford and he was the first professionally trained librarian to be nominated in the 154 years of the Library's existence.

A product of Columbia University's School of Library Service, Mumford had distinguished himself at the New York Public Library before being invited to the Library of Congress, back in 1940, to reorganize the thirty-four processing divisions. Mumford's efforts at that time resulted in some three hundred appointments and promotions and a dramatic increase in the rate of processing books, periodicals, and other material.

Mumford had gone on to the Cleveland Public Library, where he became director. In nine years there he doubled that library's budget and displayed administrative and diplomatic skills that would serve him in Washington, should Congress accept him.

But during the confirmation hearings he was pointedly asked by a member of the Senate Rules and Administration Committee, "[I]f you found that the Library of Congress was neglecting its primary duty . . . that of service to the Congress . . . would you be willing to correct that situation?"

Mumford, mindful of the tension that had existed between Congress and Archibald MacLeish and Luther Evans, and the disfavor that their outside activities had caused, was prepared to devote all his attention to his duties. For the Library had, in the words of Representative Frances Bolton of Ohio, a Mum-

In the mid-1950s, President Dwight D. Eisenhower appointed Lawrence Quincy Mumford, who had worked at the New York Public Library and directed the Cleveland Public Library, to lead the Library of Congress into a new era of technological advances. Distinguished among Librarians of Congress for his professional training, Mumford was a graduate of the Columbia University School of Library Service, the country's first such school, which was established in 1887 and trained librarians over the course of a century.

Courtesy of Harris & Ewing. Prints and Photographs Division, Library of Congress. LC-USZ62-96-470

ford supporter, "fallen into patterns of inefficient and unwise operations" and badly needed "housecleaning." Some wondered if Mumford had the resolve to wield the broom.

Like Evans, Mumford had been raised on a farm—in coastal North Carolina —attended a one-room schoolhouse, and distinguished himself academically. At Duke University he earned a master's degree in English literature and took an active part in campus life, including theatricals, a fact that would have surprised his colleagues in later life, impressed as they were by Mumford's apparent lack of flair. He was, in the words of the man who had hired him at the New York Public Library, even while young, an excellent judge of character and "in a quiet way . . . a man of forcefulness who gets things done."

Securing an adequate Library appropriation was to be the first test. The Library's recent request had been opposed in Congress, and the nominee was called before a displeased chairman of the House Subcommittee on Appropriations, Walter Horan, as part of an examination of Library expenditures over the previous five years. The chairman wanted codified all laws pertaining to the Library so that its duties would be clear to all, and Mumford agreed to pay attention to this concern.

Questions from other subcommittee members echoed congressional complaints made repeatedly over the years. Why were new people constantly required by the Library? Why did the Library continue to acquire old books and other materials of no apparent practical use? What were the procedures for assigning study rooms and other privileges? And that most persistent of all questions, why couldn't the cataloging ever catch up with the acquisitions?

After letting off steam, Congress approved Mumford's appointment. He moved into his office in September, where he received a message from former Librarian Herbert Putnam: "Welcome, and may good will, good fortune, and good cheer attend you ever." His greeting was appropriate, for Mumford had more in common with Putnam than with his immediate predecessors. Mumford's tenure at the Library of Congress would be marked, as Putnam's had been, by a concentration on internal affairs and a pressing need for more space.

Ironically, some librarians had reservations about Mumford. He had also been made president of the American Library Association, but he was very much a *public* librarian. His doubters within the profession were primarily directors of university libraries in the Association of Research Libraries (ARL), a group that had benefited under the regimes of both MacLeish and Evans and worried about Mumford's commitment to the concept of a national library. Would he support acquisitions and bibliographical projects beyond the means of most universities?

Mumford refrained from automatically offering the services of the Library to members of the ARL, but he listened to their requests. He declined to commit the Library to projects until he had discussed them with his subordinates, but the Library would, if less demonstratively than under his predecessors, provide much the same research support it had offered in the past.

The Library—like L. Quincy Mumford—faced a new, markedly different world. The appropriation provided by Congress in the first year of his tenure was an anemic $9.4 million, and the amount available for buying books, excluding those for the blind and for the Law and Supreme Court libraries, was less than that provided to many university libraries so eager for the Library's help.

In the words of Benjamin E. Powell, writing in *The Librarians of Congress*, the Library had to deal in a serious way not just with the increasingly rapid growth of knowledge, but also with "technological progress and its potential for storage, retrieval, and transmission of information, and equalization of job opportunity."

The Library had some thirty-three million items packed within its collective walls. Mumford began to plan for a third structure to house these and the Library's expanding activities, one whose size would exceed that of the Jefferson Building and whose long, sometimes difficult gestation would recall the earlier times of Ainsworth Spofford.

The position of Assistant Librarian was abolished, and the Librarian's salary raised by Congress to $20,000 annually as part of a bill generally increasing compensation for heads of executive departments in federal agencies. The Library formally committed to publishing, over the course of several decades, more than six hundred volumes of the *National Union Catalog: Pre-1956 Imprints*, including records from other American and Canadian libraries. Such a bibliography would prove invaluable to research libraries all over the world in the finding and cataloging of books.

Congress's close scrutiny of Library affairs persisted during Mumford's early years. He was asked when he envisioned a reduction in its financial needs; he pointed out that all requests for appropriations were legitimate, the implication being that rising costs were inevitable. The Library could not remain static but must by definition grow. It had, he added, "responsibilities for service to the Congress, to government agencies, and to the public."

In 1958, the Library was given the right to acquire books in foreign countries with foreign currency owned by the United States. This enabled it to open acquisition offices abroad, specifically in Cairo and New Delhi, a continuation of the overseas expansion begun by Luther Evans. And the Architect of the Capitol submitted a summary of requirements for the third Library building to the Joint Committee on the Library after a study by Library staff had been completed.

It would take another two years for Congress to pass, and for President Eisenhower to sign, a bill authorizing $75,000 for preliminary plans and cost estimates for the new building. Meanwhile sufficient additional funds had to be found to rent sixty-two thousand feet of indoor space somewhere in Washington to accommodate a Library bursting at the seams.

In 1960 the Library published *A Guide to the Study of the United States of America: Representative Books Reflecting the Development of American Life and Thought*. This 1,193-page compendium identifying and describing more than ten thousand titles had been prepared by the General Reference and Bibliography Division of the Reference Department and represented an important milestone in American bibliography.

President John Kennedy retained Mumford at the Library, but the new chief executive had a fondness for the style of former Librarian Archibald MacLeish and the broad cultural—if controversial—leadership the Library had offered during MacLeish's tenure. Mumford was a career librarian. As such, he exhibited more caution and focused more on the Library's material problems. Primarily these were a need of additional space and incorporation of technological advancements in cataloging and the collecting of information.

Technology was also a prime concern of the Congress. Mumford was questioned more than once by the chairman of the Subcommittee on Appropriations on preparations for the electronic future of the Library, and Mumford assured him that the problem was under consideration.

He used a Council on Library Resources (CLR) grant of $100,000 in 1961 for a study, conducted by a panel of experts, for "the organization, storage, and retrieval of information." The experts came from the fields of computer technology, data processing, systems analysis, and the storage and retrieval of information. Their mandate was to determine the effect of these rapidly developing technologies on the Library and on its relationship with other research institutions.

The study would take years to complete. Meanwhile Mumford's caution did not sit well with some in Congress. They wanted to see the Library exert more leadership nationally—the original concern of the university librarians—and one of them, associate director of the Harvard Library Douglas W. Bryant, was requested by Senator Claiborne Pell of Rhode Island, a member of the Joint Committee on the Library, to prepare a memorandum on the Library's function and potential.

Bryant's report was placed in the *Congressional Record* by Senator Pell, who wished to stimulate discussion. "[W]e have tended to take for granted our Library of Congress—our basic working tool which underlies all our useful scholarship, the responsible work of our Congress, and the very culture of our nation." That succinct statement reaffirmed the original vision of the third president of the United States.

The report reflected the view that the Library lacked sufficient involvement and imagination—and sufficient funds—to fully benefit other libraries and the nation. Specifically, it recommended increased collecting by research libraries with federal assistance, the implementa-

Among the television programs preserved in the Library's collections is a 16mm kinescope copy of a portion of the *Tonight Show*, starring Johnny Carson, that aired on October 5, 1965, and featured Groucho Marx. This guest read aloud from a letter he had received from Librarian of Congress L. Quincy Mumford asking Groucho Marx to consider giving his papers to the Library of Congress. On camera Marx said to Carson: "I was so pleased when I got this [letter] . . . Having not finished public school to find my letters perhaps laying next to the Gettysburg Address I thought was . . . extremely thrilling. . . . I'm very proud of this." Among the papers he subsequently deposited in the Library's Manuscript Division are his letters to many well-known people outside the entertainment profession, such as poet T. S. Eliot and broadcast journalist Edward R. Murrow.

Frame enlargement. Motion Picture, Broadcasting, and Recorded Sound Division, Library of Congress.

tion of new federal programs in research, library technology and preservation, assistance to libraries in developing nations, and grants and fellowships to improve research and train new librarians.

But Bryant's most controversial proposal concerned the center of power in which the Library should reside. He called for its transfer to the executive branch of government, to be directed by someone of national stature, under the tutelage of a Library board composed of a dozen influential members. This was troubling to Mumford and to many in Congress.

Mumford's response, also included in the *Congressional Record*, pointed out that the Library of Congress was in fact already a national library, the result of similar debates held almost from its inception, and that most failings could be traced to a lack of space, a century-long complaint. "[T]he Library of Congress today performs more national library functions than any other national library in the world."

Mumford admitted a need for better communication between the Library of Congress and research libraries and endorsed the notion of an advisory board, but a permanent one composed of other professionals. And he recognized the benefit of the general discussion of the Library's considerable problems. Writing in the 1962 *Annual Report*, he noted that leadership should "strike a delicate balance between domination and encouragement. Those who urge the Library of Congress to greater leadership would be the first to cry out against attempted government dictation."

But the Library had, he admitted, "of late been too careful to remain in the background rather than pushing to the vanguard."

The Librarian's public relations problems persisted. In 1963, an article in the *Saturday Review* suggested that Congress had neglected the Library and proved dilatory in making decisions affecting the new building. This caused some ire among the representatives. The article also criticized the fact that the Library's appropriation came from one committee, directives from another, and building decisions from a third.

Mumford found himself defending a Congress which "has been quite understanding to our needs and has been responsive to the requests," though ambiguous and belated those responses could sometimes be.

The House Committee on Appropriations recommended $20.5 million for the following year. It also formally recognized the fact that a third Library building was urgently needed. "This is a great cultural and research institution," the report noted, "and in the committee's view ought to be brought to a good state of accommodation and efficiency at an early date. Although originally conceived and established as the Library of Congress, it is in fact, by reason of many congressional actions over a long period of years, the national library of the United States and of inestimable value to the nation's library facilities at all levels."

Congress was not sympathetic to changing the name of the Library or to transferring it to the executive branch.

Another contemporary debate at this time involved the Library's employees. In the past, staffing had been a relatively simple matter of acquiring funding from Congress and then hiring qualified people to do the necessary jobs. Now demands arose within Congress and outside it for equal opportunity for minorities and for women.

The Library was in a relatively strong position when considered in relation to the rest of the federal government. Asked about job discrimination by a member of the Senate Appropriations Committee in 1963, Mumford was able to answer that a fair employment practices officer had been appointed the year before. In addition, the Library of Congress had more African Americans on its payroll, in all grades, than was the average for other federal agencies.

In the lowest GS (government service) grades, 1 through 4, the number of African Americans on the payroll was 36.6 percent—twice that in other agencies. Because of educational deficiencies, however, staffers at the lower levels had little opportunity for advancement. The problem was being dealt with incrementally through consultation and training, but it would takes years to for the results to be seen—too late, as developments proved.

A Data Processing Office was created in 1963. Automation received an impetus the next year when the Library received authorization to develop a standard format for processing catalog cards.

Within two years Machine-Readable Cataloging (MARC) tapes were ready for distribution to a few select libraries. Also, the results of the study financed by the Council on Library Resources, Inc., were published as *Automation and the Library of Congress*. An information systems specialist was appointed at the Library charged with developing "machine-readable catalog data in a standardized format not only for use in producing book catalogs but also for distribution to other libraries."

Anticipated was a process for printing catalog cards by using a combination of a computer and photocopying equipment, components in a new technology that would revolutionize the Library's services.

The report concluded that automation was not only possible but desirable in large research libraries for processing, locating, and documenting transactions. Making the content of large collections accessible through automation was considerably more difficult, and as yet computerizing the catalog cards of the Library of Congress and other libraries was impossible. Neither the equipment nor the funds were available for the task.

Mississippi John Hurt recording in the Archive of Folk Song at the Library of Congress in 1964, assisted by staff members Rae Korson and Joe Hickerson. He had lived most of his life in obscurity. Having taught himself to play the guitar, Hurt sang the blues, folk songs, and ballads in occasional performances around Avalon, Mississippi, where he did farm work, until a folk music fan brought him to national attention in 1963. Mississippi John Hurt was then seventy-one years old; he died in 1966.

Photoduplication Service, Library of Congress. LC-USP6-4376C

The annual appropriation to the Library from Congress had risen steadily in Mumford's time there, but a single system of bibliographic control could cost as much as $70 million. The Library, however, was the only institution capable of undertaking such an ambitious, long-range objective.

In 1964, two other things occurred that indicated the breadth and concern of the Library of Congress. The blues musician, Mississippi John Hurt, was recorded singing and playing his guitar by the Archive of Folk Song. And for the first time the Library undertook the use of a computer, an IBM 1401—rented, and used in payroll and other budgetary calculations.

At this time a broadscale effort was under way to preserve what the Library already had in its possession—books and newspapers. It continued to preserve the latter on microfilm and to lead the way in the preservation of books by establishing a Preservation Office to assist libraries all over the United States.

The Library joined with the Association of Research Libraries and the American Library Association in asking Congress to amend the Education Act of 1965 so that the Library might acquire "as far as possible all library materials of value to scholarship that are currently published throughout the world." It might then provide cataloging information for those materials.

Cataloging was of paramount concern to all libraries, but few but the Library of Congress had the means and expertise to deal adequately with books from all over the world. The Library's centralized catalog was not only invaluable to other institutions but use of its cataloging information elsewhere avoided expensive duplication, and Congress responded with instructions "to provide new and unparalleled services for the benefit of other libraries."

Mumford was proving to be a friend to all libraries, public and research. Appropriations rose steadily. The National Program for Acquisitions and Cataloging (NPAC), established in 1966 with modest funding, proceeded with the cooperation of England, France, West Germany, Austria, and Norway to obtain scholarly material from other countries. In less than a decade forty countries would be participating in the program, greatly enhancing acquisitions and avoiding millions of dollars in cataloging costs.

Imagery

The breadth of the Library's collections is without equal in the world. Fascinating materials can be found throughout the Jefferson Building, in well-traveled corridors and hidden alcoves. Beyond the Library's walls are being kept or assembled additional materials relevant to some future inquiry. The purpose of it all, and a contemporary reminder of the statement by Thomas Jefferson that no field of inquiry was beyond the potential interest of Congress, is the preservation of knowledge in its infinite guises.

Just one example of diversity amid hundreds of collections that have found a home in the Library is that of propaganda posters belonging to Gary Yanker. Amassed from some fifty countries, this "prop art" collection, mostly from America, represents sources as varied as the League of Women Voters and the National Association for Irish Freedom. The thirty-five hundred items also include campaign buttons, banners, and bumper stickers considered by Yanker to be "poster substitutes."

All these reside in the Prints and Photographs Division, one of the Library's most extensive custodial divisions, holding at the end of the century some 13.5 million items. Graphic art collections—posters, cartoons, lithographs, magazine illustrations—are one of the division's great strengths. Posters totaling more than seventy thousand included an advertising poster printed in 1856,

works by Toulouse-Lautrec, German posters from both world wars, and news posters from the early years of the Soviet Union.

The Cabinet of American Illustration, containing some four thousand original drawings made between 1850 and 1930, includes political cartoons by Thomas Nast for *Harper's Weekly*. The Swann Collection includes original drawings from the 1930s such as those for the comic strip "Secret Agent X-9," created by the mystery writer Dashiell Hammett. The Art Deco period is represented by, among other items, covers for *The New Yorker* and *Vanity Fair* magazines.

Political prints and cartoons from Revolutionary France and the Napoleonic era are carefully preserved, as are the British Cartoon Collection's twelve thousand items from the seventeenth through the mid-nineteenth century, including works considered subversive by the British royal family and suppressed.

The Prints and Photographs Division houses not only the Brady photographs from the Civil War but also John C. H. Grabill's documentation of frontier life a century ago, Charles Currier's 523 glass negatives of photographs of life in Boston between 1887 and 1910, the photojournalism and architectural photography of the pioneering woman photographer Frances Benjamin Johnston, twenty thousand images by the portraitist Arnold

Genthe from San Francisco, cultural portraits by Carl Van Vechten, and the Depression-era work of Walker Evans, Dorothea Lange, and Carl Mydans.

Among more than eight thousand photographs of Native Americans are twenty-three hundred portraits by Edward S. Curtis. Also strongly represented are the well-known photographs by Alfred Stieglitz, Julia Margaret Cameron, and Ansel Adams, including his unique 1943 documentation of Japanese internment camp life in California.

The Fenton collection holds the earliest known war photography, from the Crimean War. The photographs of Sergei Mikhailovich Prokudin-Gorskii document Czarist Russia, and the Third Reich collection includes Hermann Goering's autobiographical chronicle from 1933 to 1942.

The challenge of safely storing such materials extends to the preservation of fine prints, among them the works of Rembrandt, Goya, and Dürer. The Chadbourne collection, made up of 188 rare Japanese woodblock prints of foreign subjects done in the nineteenth century, presents challenges for preservation, as do the prints of Joseph Pennell, lithographs, etchings, and sketches by James McNeill Whistler, more contemporary works by Roy Lichtenstein, and many others.

In addition, the division maintains a separate file for the images of American presidents—photographs, etchings, reproductions of portrait paintings, and cartoons—and a collection of Washingtoniana from which emerges a continuous portrait of the capital city from its birth into the last half of the twentieth century and the beginning of the next.

The hammer and sickle featured on this poster issued in 1967 was adopted for use on the national flag of the USSR in 1923. Symbolic of worker and peasant, this combination represented the ideals of the Soviet Union. Fifty years after the 1917 revolution, the Soviet state found itself less intent upon ideological uniformity and focused instead on bringing about the industrial transformation of Russia. At this point, the cold war had become a "cold peace."

Yanker Poster Collection, Prints and Photographs Division, Library of Congress.

The Trylon and the Perisphere were symbols of the 1939–40 World's
Fair held in Flushing Meadows, New York, and opened by Franklin
Delano Roosevelt. Television was seen there by many visitors for the
first time. After World War II, the television broadcasting industry
began to flourish, and by mid-century television was a fact of almost
every American's life, an essential part of the modern world.

The New York World's Fair, poster by Nembhard N. Culin,
offset lithograph, 1937. Prints and Photographs Division,
Library of Congress.LC–USZC4-4856

Joseph and Elizabeth Robins Pennell
themselves gave this self-portrait of James
MacNeill Whistler to the Library in 1917.
The drawing was done in pen and ink
about 1898–1900. Whistler was a personal
friend of the Pennells, whose work Joseph
Pennell greatly admired. Pennell was an
artist who experimented with graphic
techniques and book illustration and
included in the bequest that came to the
Library in 1926 much Whistleriana, his
own work, and a fund for the purchase of
work by modern artists.

Pennell Collection, Prints and Photographs
Division, Library of Congress. LC-USC4-4661
(color); LC-USZ62-14689 (black and white)

The Banjo Lesson was created by Mary
Cassatt in color drypoint and aquatint
with hand coloring about 1893 in Paris.
Cassatt had left Pennsylvania to study in
France in 1866 and lived there permanently
after 1874; but she went to Chicago when
commissioned to paint a fifty-eight-foot
mural for the Woman's Building for the
1893 Chicago World's Fair. On the theme
of "Modern Woman," the mural showed
young women pursuing knowledge, science, and fame. She based this image of a
woman playing a banjo on the right panel
of the mural, which had three panels. *The
Banjo Lesson* was purchased through the
Pennell Fund for the acquisition of contemporary prints of the highest quality.

Prints and Photographs Division, Library of
Congress. LC-USC4-4634

Roger Fenton went to Crimea in 1855 to photograph the Balaklava harbor, the battlefields, the British, French, and Turkish commanders, and the men they led against the Russians in the Crimean War. Fenton used a horse-drawn van for a darkroom for the wet collodion process and made his prints after his return to England. His was the earliest documentary war photography, carried out for purposes of British propaganda about the conditions of war of their own soldiers. The battle of Balaklava on the Black Sea was celebrated by Tennyson in "The Charge of the Light Brigade."

Prints and Photographs Division, Library of Congress. LC-USZ62-2319

Arthur Rothstein, working for the Farm Security Administration (FSA) documenting life in America during the Depression, photographed a farmer and his sons in a dust storm in Oklahoma in 1936. The young photographer worked under Roy Stryker, head of the FSA's photographic section, and traveled to Texas and Kansas taking pictures of drought and erosion there as well. Some 77,000 photographs produced by the section became part of the Library's collections in 1946.

Prints and Photographs Division, Library of Congress. LC-USZC4-4840

A sketch for the statue of Abraham Lincoln in the Lincoln Memorial was done in graphite on tracing paper by Henry Bacon in Chicago in 1917 as he worked on its design. Architect for the memorial, Bacon formulated his ideas for the sculptor Daniel Chester French, who actually created the sculpture. It was on the steps of this memorial that Martin Luther King would give the keynote speech for the March on Washington for Jobs and Freedom, known as his "I Have a Dream" speech, on August 28, 1963.

Architecture, Design, and Engineering Collections, Prints and Photographs Division, Library of Congress. LC-USZC4-4709

In November 1919 Felix the Cat, credited to Pat Sullivan but actually drawn by Otto Messmer, began as an animated silent screen cartoon, which lost its audience to Walt Disney's animated films with sound by 1930. The first Felix the Cat comic strip, also drawn by Messmer, appeared in a newspaper in England on August 1, 1923, was syndicated in the United States on August 19, 1923, and ran until 1943. This strip was published in 1932. Contemporary cartoonists make up the strongest part of the Library's Swann Collection of Caricature and Cartoon, which also includes the work of popular Mexican artist José Guadalupe Posada, Thomas Nast, and some eighteenth-century artists.

Caroline and Erwin Swann Collection, Prints and Photographs Division, Library of Congress. LC-USZ62-98608

The most pressing, difficult question for Librarian Mumford remained that of the new building. He had pressed continually for more space, and in 1965 Congress finally authorized the construction of another Library edifice, to be named in honor of James Madison who, in 1783, had drawn up the first list of books for the use of the new American legislators.

Madison as president had pressed for the purchase of Jefferson's personal library for the Congress after the British troops burned the Capitol during the War of 1812. A man of books, Madison had also worked diligently with the first Librarian, John J. Beckley. Now the Library's debt to Madison was being repaid.

The new Library building was to rise across Independence Avenue from the Jefferson Building and cost $75 million. It was not yet a reality—neither was the price—but it had been committed to by Congress in a relatively short time, whereas it had taken Spofford twenty-six years to get the Jefferson Building approved, and Putnam twelve years for the Annex.

In 1966, the Library proposed, at a meeting of librarians from six countries being held at the British Museum, that cataloging procedures be universally shared. Adapting cataloging data of various foreign libraries would be undertaken by the Library of Congress under the new National Program for Acquisitions and Cataloging. That same year, President Lyndon Johnson signed an act establishing the American Revolution Bicentennial Commission, with Librarian Mumford as an ex officio member. Within the Library, projects to commemorate this event—with publications and symposia—were already under way.

The Library's first overseas office for shared cataloging opened in London, and offices in Rio de Janeiro and Belgrade soon followed. Meanwhile, in 1966, the first MARC tapes were ready for distribution. Within two years the service would be under way, affecting cataloging all over the United States. First some sixty subscribers would receive the data on tape from the Library in English, which later would be available in French and German and eventually in almost all the Roman-alphabet languages.

The James Madison Memorial Building moved a step closer to reality with the unveiling by the chairman of the Joint Committee on the Library in the Library's Wilson Room of the scale model of the building and the plans drawn up by the architect, Alfred Easton Poor. The new quarters, when finished, were to be occupied by the Office of the Librarian, the Administrative Department, the Copyright Office, the Law Library, the Legislative Reference Service, and the Processing Department. Special-format collections housed in them would include geography and maps, manuscripts, music, prints and photographs, and serials.

Librarian Mumford pressed Congress for increased appropriations to meet costs of other new initiatives, like the *Legislative Status Report*, issued by the Legislative Reference Service to inform members of Congress and committees about up-coming legislation. Grants were acquired for rendering records machine-readable, as the push toward automation continued.

Gifts extended the Library's ongoing cultural role. One, from Walter C. Louchheim, Jr., and his wife Katie, supported the musical performances and poetry readings at the Library and also provided money for transcribing these on tape and film and disseminating them to the public beyond the Library's physical environs. Another, from anonymous donors, enabled the Library to purchase the Charles Feinberg collection of Walt Whitman material—more than twenty thousand items.

The Library of Congress's traditional duties included overseeing the millions of perishable items already in its possession, many of them brittle with age. A Preservation Research Laboratory was set up in 1970, using another grant from the CLR, to deacidify and strengthen the pages of deteriorating books and otherwise rescue materials damaged in the past by water, fire, or exposure. The Library began storing much of its highly flammable nitrate-film motion picture archive at the Wright-Patterson Air Force Base outside Dayton, Ohio, beginning in the late 1960s. In its effort to care for its own collections, the Library's research contributed significantly to the knowledge of preservation of materials and to curatorship in general.

Developments in that most important ongoing project, the James Madison Memorial Building, troubled Librarian Mumford and members of the joint committee. The estimated cost was rising, and some in Congress spoke of using the new building to provide space for other activities of Congress. Again political overtures had to be made in Congress and to the new president, Richard M. Nixon.

In March, the president signed an act increasing the appropriation for the new building to $90 million and stipulating that it not be used "for general office building purposes." But pressure continued to commit the new building to congressional offices rather than to the Library's pressed administrative and reference sections. Within two years the Library would be forced to shift nine million volumes occupying 600,000 feet of shelves to gain some additional space, harkening back to the crowded aisles of Spofford's time.

The Legislative Reorganization Act of 1970 expanded the crucial Legislative Reference Service, renamed it the Congressional Research Service, and increased its independence. The size of the staff had grown to 438 specialists, including 50 librarians, an indication of the rapid rise in demands made upon it, responsible as it was for the specific edification of elected representatives and senators.

Significantly, the House Committee on Rules rejected a suggestion that the service be separated from the Library of Congress. "In our judgement, the Library

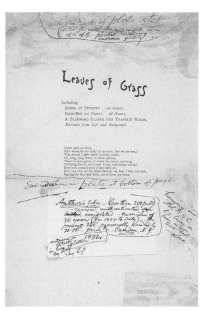

(left) Walt Whitman, who changed the way Americans thought about poetry and about themselves, lived in Brooklyn and New Orleans, where he was a journalist, in Washington, D.C., where he nursed the Civil War wounded, and, after he suffered paralysis in 1873, in Camden, New Jersey, where he continued to wait for his talent to be widely recognized. Charles E. Feinberg assembled an exceptional, comprehensive collection of personal papers and other materials relating to the poet, which was purchased by the Library during the 1970s with the help of funds from anonymous donors.

Photograph by George C. Cox, ca. 1887. Prints and Photographs Division, Library of Congress. LC-USZC4-5181 (color); LC-USZ62-4061 (black and white)

A printer's proof of the title page for *Leaves of Grass* marked in Whitman's own hand, with instructions for typesetting the added lines, exhibited the care with which he prepared the final, 1892 edition of the poem he had worked on for thirty-five or forty years. *Leaves of Grass* was first published on July 4, 1855.

Manuscript Division, Library of Congress. LC-USZC4-5338

serves as a useful mantle for protecting the Service from partisan pressures. Furthermore, the effectiveness of the CRS will be enhanced by its continued instant access to the Library's collections and administrative support services."

Construction on the James Madison Memorial Building began in 1971. The following year, Mumford presented to Congress a detailed report of the Library's myriad duties and asked for an increase of $9 million in the Library's 1973 appropriation. That was almost double what the appropriation had been when he took office. But Mumford and his colleagues at the Library were not thinking solely of the budget.

The United States had undergone a social revolution in the last decade. A president had been assassinated, and so had been the leader of the civil rights movement that had made great strides in the achievement of racial equality.

The concerns and legacy of Martin Luther King, Jr., still gathering strength, became manifest—as all things American must—in the halls and in the concerns of the Library of Congress.

Labor relations had remained uneasy at the Library despite some efforts on behalf of minority staffers. A four-day work stoppage by Library deck attendants in 1971 had resulted in the dismissal of eleven employees. The American Library Association had approved a resolution at its annual conference the same year to look into an allegation that the Library of Congress "discriminates on racial grounds in recruitment, training, and promotion practices."

Subsequently a plan was drawn up that provided for officers to recruit among minorities, and to train and counsel Library employees, to be financed by a supplemental appropriation. The Library's Affirmative Action Plan established a coordinating committee, and a Training, Appraisal, and Promotion (TAP) program was established to provide fifty openings for Library employees to be trained and promoted, if qualified. And tests for those seeking employment were revamped.

The American Revolution Bicentennial was just two years away as 1973 ended, when President Nixon signed a law authorizing the Librarian of Congress, the secretary of the Smithsonian Institution, and the Archivist of the United States to cooperate with the administration in bringing together materials relevant to the Revolutionary War for display in an upcoming celebration which, many hoped, would serve to unify the nation.

Nixon also signed an executive order exempting the Librarian from mandatory retirement until the end of 1974, for Mumford was now seventy years old. He had served the Library of Congress for almost twenty years, under four presidents—soon to be five with the appointment of Gerald Ford—and he was now in poor health.

During the two decades when L. Quincy Mumford was librarian, the number of items in the Library of Congress had grown to seventy-four million, and the staff had more than doubled, from 1,564 to 4,250 people. The most striking indication of the Library's growth and expanded responsibilities, however, lay in the tenfold increase in annual expenditures—from $9.4 million to almost $97 million.

Lawrence Quincy Mumford, the professional librarian, had not escaped criticism by other professionals who thought he had slighted research. His unassuming personality and attention to detail had left him open to charges of ineffectual leadership. But he had traveled as much as any Librarian on behalf of the Library and could list among the countries he had visited on Library affairs England, France, Holland, Belgium, Austria, West Germany, Italy, Russia, Poland,

Yugoslavia, Hungary, Romania, Egypt, India, Pakistan, Japan, and New Zealand.

Few of Mumford's critics knew that at social gatherings, the Librarian continued to entertain friends with imitations of the tobacco auctioneers he had heard as a child or with songs such as "Carolina Moon" that he had sung in college theatricals half a century earlier.

Achievements made during Mumford's time at the Library had been real and ranged broadly, from automation and rapid information retrieval to the preservation on film of the personal papers of twenty-three presidents of the United States. The books for the blind program had been expanded to all people with physical handicaps that made it difficult for them to read. A Near Eastern and North African Law Division had been established, as well as an African Section, a Children's Book Section, a national Referral Center for Science and Technology, and the National Union Catalog of Manuscript Collections.

As 1974 drew to a close there could be seen rising across Independence Avenue from the Library of Congress a vast contemporary structure connected by tunnels to the Library's Main Building, to the Annex, and to the Cannon House Office Building. As the towering steel ribs of the James Madison Memorial Building took on their flesh of polished marble, more than two million square feet inside were being fitted to serve the most extensive library on earth.

The Rare and the Special

The individual divisions within the Library of Congress had already become, before the James Madison Memorial Building was complete, large and complex institutions in their own right—libraries within the Library. And each had its own rationale for best serving Congress, scholars, and posterity.

For instance, the Rare Book and Special Collections Division did not include among its treasures the unique library of Sheikh Maḥmūd al-Imām al-Manṣūrī, of Cairo, some five thousand rare volumes and manuscripts acquired during the time of Librarian Archibald MacLeish. These were kept instead in the Arabic collection, because the Rare Book and Special Collections Division focuses on European and American culture.

By century's end, the division's holdings included such diverse items as Picasso lithographs

and American paperback novels from the 1960s. But probably its rarest collection—and the Library's—is a collection of illustrated books ranging from the genesis of printing to the present coupled with illustrated manuscripts dating from the twelfth century donated by Lessing J. Rosenwald, a private collector who spent much of a lifetime searching for books produced by the earliest printers and presses of distinction. Rosenwald used the illustrated book as his theme, and also sought out books on subjects dear to him: science, calligraphy, botany, and chess.

The bulk of the collection remained in his private Alverthorpe Gallery in Jenkintown, Pennsylvania, until shortly after his death in 1979, although some came to the Library as early as 1943. Exquisite woodcuts from the fifteenth century; one of two known copies of the 1495 edition of *Epistolae et Evangelia*; books by the poet William Blake, containing his drawings and engravings; four complete books printed by William Caxton, England's first printer; and the Giant Bible of Mainz, the manuscript Bible completed about the same time Gutenberg's printed Bible was, were extraordinary treasures.

In all, the Rosenwald Collection provided such a valuable source of research because many of the books were unique, most were in excellent condition, and they were often accompanied by related original drawings, proofs, or letters. The Blake material included fourteen of the twenty illuminated books, in such demand by scholars when first donated that Rosenwald allowed facsimiles to be made.

Particular importance was assigned to the Rosenwald Collection because of its size and unifying themes. It would take decades for scholars to thoroughly investigate what in large part had been unavailable for centuries. One example was the 160 fifteenth- and sixteenth-century Dutch and Flemish books which, before being purchased by Rosenwald, had been in the private library of the Dukes of Arenberg for generations.

The Rare Book and Special Collections Division, also responsible for a large assembly of books relating to the Age of Discovery, holds the published letter from Christopher Columbus describing his first encounters in the New World; a narrative by Cortés; the earliest book printed in America currently in existence, the Bay Psalm Book printed by Matthew Daye of Cambridge, Massachusetts, in 1640; and John Eliot's 1663 Indian Bible, also produced in Cambridge after being painstakingly translated into the language of what were described as "New England Indians."

The division's large collection of early American almanacs includes every edition of Benjamin Franklin's *Poor Richard's Almanac* published after 1735. What survives of Jefferson's personal library, the foundation of the Library of Congress purchased from the former president in 1815, is kept in a separate vault. Housed there also are thousands of broadsides and printed documents issued by the Continental Congress, the Constitutional Convention of 1787, and the first fourteen U.S. Congresses.

The Library's nineteenth-century Americana includes rich material related to westward expansion: exploration narratives and works of natural science and ethnography, among them unbound plates from James Audubon's *Birds of America* and the folio renderings of American Indians by Karl Bodmer in Prince Maximilian von Wied-Neuwied's travel accounts. The Civil War period is represented by slave narratives and, in the Stern Collection of Lincolniana, autographed letters and documents of the president, broadsides that included the Emancipation Proclamation, a scrapbook from the debates with Stephen Douglas, and life masks of Abraham Lincoln.

Among the books relating to early women's rights are the library of Susan B. Anthony and that of Carrie Chapman Catt. Various libraries of other significant individuals offer insight to scholars: the library of the Oliver Wendell Holmes family, Woodrow Wilson's library, and the extensive hunting library of Theodore Roosevelt. Literary Americans are represented by the works of Washington Irving, Walt Whitman, Mark Twain and Henry James, and first editions of more contemporary authors such as Ernest Hemingway, John Steinbeck, and William Faulkner.

In addition, some forty thousand "dime novels" from the nineteenth century and a collection of "Big Little Books" for children deposited for copyright in the 1930s and 1940s surprise some researchers by their presence among the rare books. Little more than four inches square, the 534 Big Little Books contain stories based on comic strips, movies, radio shows and traditional children's stories, including the exploits of such characters as Tom Mix, Little Orphan Annie, Dick Tracy, Flash Gordon, and Mickey Mouse.

The division's extraordinary assembly of books and documents relating to European culture includes fifty-seven hundred rare incunabula. There are books from the genesis of printing with moveable type in the West, made between 1455 and 1501. Early illustrated editions of Chaucer, early works of Martin Luther, a version of Marco Polo's travel account, a collection devoted to Sir Francis Drake—with maps, manuscripts, and memorabilia—and large illustrated books by Vesalius and Helvetius are available for research.

Books on European gastronomy include a fifteenth-century Italian manuscript that may be the first cookbook. There are rare first editions of more recent writers—Hans Christian Andersen, Cervantes, Charles Dickens, Jules Verne, and Rudyard Kipling—all just a mote in the collective eye of the Rare Book and Special Collections Division.

The Wild Turkey, Meleagris gallopavo, engraved by William H. Lizars after the original watercolor by John James Audubon, was the first plate in Audubon's *Birds of America*, an elephant folio edition published in London between 1827 and 1838.

Lessing J. Rosenwald began collecting prints in the early twenties, purchasing his first illustrated book in 1926 on the advice of A. S. W. Rosenbach, a Philadelphia bookdealer. In 1939 he retired from directing Sears, Roebuck & Company, the mail-order firm whose catalog his father had made such a standby in American homes, to devote himself to public service and to collecting rare books and prints.

Quarterly Journal of the Library of Congress,
October 1945.

Dialogus creaturarum (Gouda: Gerard Leeu, 1480), a collection of 122 fables in dialogue, begins with a hand-colored woodcut decorating the title page. Fifteenth-century books (or *incunabula*; that is, the earliest printed books, those completed before 1501) with woodcut illustrations were one of collector Lessing Rosenwald's strongest interests. This woodcut pictures the sun and the moon, the participants in the first dialogue. Others fables involve the swan and the crow, the pheasant and the peacock, the wolf and the lamb, the hills and the valleys, and, finally, man and death.

Rare Book and Special Collections Division,
Library of Congress.

Works by William Blake assembled by Lessing Rosenwald form one of the finest collections of Blake material and are much used by researchers. *The Book of Urizen* was written, illustrated, and printed by William Blake in 1794 to tell the stories of Genesis and Exodus and to explore themes of repression or oppression and liberty. Urizen represents reason, the rational force that limits and shapes creativity.

Rare Book and Special Collections Division, Library of Congress.

Fernand Léger lived and worked in the United States during World War II, teaching at Yale University and Mills College and pursuing a lifelong interest in depicting circus themes and acrobats. When he returned to France his work was dominated by this passion, and in 1950 he created the book *Cirque*, one of the many twentieth-century artist's books or *livres de peintre* collected by Lessing Rosenwald.

Rosenwald Collection, Rare Book and Special Collections Division, Library of Congress.

The New York Cook Book, compiled by Marie Martinelo and published in 1882, illustrates desserts such as "ice pudding" and strawberry trifles. Acquired by Katherine Golden Bitting, a food chemist at the Department of Agriculture, this "complete manual of cookery in all branches" with its helpful hints on how to make soap or ink, how to get rid of ants and spiders, and how to remove rust from cutlery, was given to the Library by her husband in 1937—along with more than four thousand other volumes Bitting had collected on cooking.

Photograph copyright © Roger Foley. Rare Book and Special Collections Division, Library of Congress.

A broadside dated April 20, 1865, from the Library's collections of these ephemeral items includes a photographic portrait of John Wilkes Booth and advertises a $100,000 reward for the capture of the murderer of President Abraham Lincoln. The assassination only weeks after Lee's surrender shocked the nation and quashed hopes for the North taking a generous view toward the South after the war.

Rare Book and Special Collections Division, Library of Congress. LC-USZC4-5341 (color); LC-USZ62-11193 (black and white)

7

A Republic of Letters

(1975–1987)

Read me, do not let me die!

Edna St.Vincent Millay

The ceiling of the Great Hall had never overspread such a concentration of political lights. This, the swearing-in ceremony for the twelfth Librarian, successor to Lawrence Quincy Mumford, was graced not only by the president of the United States, Gerald R. Ford, and his vice president, Nelson Rockefeller, but also by the Speaker of the House of Representatives, Carl Albert. He was a symbol of the institution the Library served, but the president's presence made a larger point. As the chairman of the Joint Committee on the Library, Representative Lucien N. Nedzi, put it to the assembly, "the Library is the Library of Congress. . . . Of equal importance, if not more so, it is a national library that serves all of the people of the United States."

The man being honored, a bespectacled figure in a bow tie, was Daniel J. Boorstin. Formerly director of the National Museum of American History, a Pulitzer Prize-winner and a distinguished professor of history at the University of Chicago for twenty-five years, Boorstin had brought with him, as President Ford put it, "a love of learning and a scholar's appreciation of the importance of libraries and of the unique contribution of the Library of Congress to American life."

Boorstin had also brought as much controversy as any candidate for the post in the Library's history, including Archibald MacLeish. The tenure of Ainsworth Rand Spofford, when books were piled unceremoniously in the Capitol's corridors to remind Congress of its dalliance in dealing with the Library's space shortage, was recalled by the crowded stacks within the Jefferson Building. MacLeish had written books and espoused political causes some congressmen abhorred. Many in Congress had opposed Boorstin's nomination on the same grounds as they opposed MacLeish's.

As President Gerald R. Ford watched, Daniel J. Boorstin placed his hand on the Thomson Bible from the Library of Congress's Thomas Jefferson collection, held by Speaker of the House of Representatives Carl Albert, and took the oath making him the twelfth Librarian of Congress. At this ceremony, held on November 12, 1975, in the Library's Great Hall, Boorstin pledged himself "to try to keep alive and flourishing the tradition of the Book."

The outspoken Daniel Boorstin had also been opposed by the country's professional librarians. Even a faction of the Library's own employees objected to him on political, rather than professional, grounds.

On this cold November day, 1975, Boorstin addressed the question of "the immortal written or printed word" and pledged himself, in a time of rapidly proliferating technology, "to try to keep alive and flourishing the tradition of the Book."

There were problems at the Library, he admitted: bad ventilation, partitions in crowded work areas, the proverbial piles of books, and the sheer volume of material. "The items which our Library receives in a single day," he said, "are more than five times the whole number of volumes purchased from Thomas Jefferson in 1815."

With the use of computers, the Congressional Research Service was responding to the fifteen hundred daily queries, but technology was also posing problems. Boorstin used a metaphor that surprised some by its bluntness and ingenuity: "We meet in unfamiliar form the familiar Parking Problem and the Traffic Jam. Our multiplying vehicles of art and thought create Traffic Jams of the Mind."

Born in Atlanta, Georgia, in 1914, the grandson of Russian Jewish immigrants, Boorstin grew up in Tulsa, Oklahoma, and attended public school there. He went on to Harvard University, studied history and literature, and graduated summa cum laude. A Rhodes Scholar, he studied law at Balliol College, Oxford University, and would later characterize his time abroad as "divided equally between trying to fit into the aristocratic life of Oxford and on vacation enjoying the bohemian vagrancy of the Continental Left Banks."

He attained a double degree in law from the Inner Temple in London, with honors, making him one of the rare Americans qualified to plead cases in England. Back in the United States, he attended Yale Law School as a Sterling Fellow and after receiving a doctorate returned to Harvard to teach American history and literature. His wide-ranging interests included political radicalism popular on campus in the 1930s. "Nearly everybody I knew in these days," he later recalled, "who was interesting humanly or intellectually was 'leftist' and thought they had a duty to 'do' something about the state of the world."

He belonged to the Communist Party for a short time but was disillusioned by the Nazi-Soviet Pact of 1939. In 1944 he joined the faculty of the University of Chicago, which provided him freedom to write. Over the next three decades he wrote a number of books, among them *The Lost World of Thomas Jefferson* and his prize-winning trilogy, *The Americans*.

Boorstin intended to write more books while serving as Librarian of Congress. This, and his political past, had posed problems for some congressmen. Before the Senate Rules Committee, Boorstin had been asked about plans for his proposed history of the world, and whether or not such a project might not impinge upon his duties.

"Writing is a kind of disease you cannot cure so easily," Boorstin responded. "If I continue to write it will be because the Committee would like to have a scholar and historian in the position . . . not a posthumous scholar but a living scholar."

Senator Claiborne Pell of Rhode Island asked about the possibility of setting up a task force to study the Library's many functions and responsibilities and making recommendations for a more efficient operation in the future. Boorstin endorsed the idea without committing himself to specific objectives; he did favor sharing the findings of any such task force with Congress.

That did not satisfy his critics in the American Library Association, always opposed to nominees who were not professional librarians. The association objected to Boorstin for the same reasons it had objected to MacLeish: Boorstin's background might be distinguished but it did "not include demonstrated leadership and administrative qualities which constitute basic and essential characteristics necessary in the Librarian of Congress."

One of the administrative hurdles involved minority representation at the

Library. Members of the Capital Area Council of Federal Employees of the AFL-CIO and two smaller organizations of Library employees opposed Boorstin on grounds that his writings had supposedly shown lack of sympathy for the efforts of minorities in America. The nominee responded: "I believe in equality and civil rights for all Americans. I do not think that includes quotas—in fact, I think it excludes them."

Support for Boorstin came from the Authors League of America, and from the Association of American Publishers, which praised the president for nominating "a man of broad intellect and humane sensibilities, as distinguished from a more narrowly experienced technician." Speaker Albert endorsed the nominee, as did the minority leader and a bipartisan group of senators that included both from Illinois. Boorstin was approved without debate in September 1975, the opposition having proven ineffective.

The new Librarian took command of some 17.5 million books, forty-six hundred employees, and an annual budget of $116 million. He immediately followed through on the suggestion made earlier by Senator Pell, and in January created the Task Force on Goals, Organization, and Planning. It was to conduct "a full-scale review of the Library and its activities" and to be advised by representatives of the Library's main constituencies. Recommendations from the task force were expected within one year.

"A third of a century has passed since the Library last undertook a full-scale, comprehensive review," Boorstin informed the staff. "These decades have been full of momentous change." This included a technological revolution "more intimate and more pervasive than any before" and new statutory responsibilities. "The arrival of a new Librarian and the near completion of the Madison Building make such a study especially appropriate now."

During Boorstin's first year at the Library a ferment of new ideas and activities was discernible. "We seem to be constantly in an uproar about something in a way we never were before," observed a member of the Library's Professional Guild. Boorstin's avowed opponents withheld their judgment as he brought the staff more into decision making and publicly stated the need for Library employees to have "not merely a career of service, but . . . of self-fulfillment."

The executive director of the American Library Association, made head of the Library advisory group, attested to Boorstin's intention to be a full-time Librarian. To prove this, Boorstin ordered the typewriter removed from his office. He used Library books "like any other American citizen," he said, but his writing was done at home, where he rose at five every morning and worked on his history of the world before going in to Capitol Hill.

Boorstin reorganized the Library's Reference Department and, aware of the need of good public relations, ordered the doors of the main entrance opened

again. For some time scholars and tourists had been entering from the ground level. "What kind of hospitality is that?" Boorstin asked rhetorically; the Library would in future be a more accessible, open institution.

He also ordered the plumbing repaired in the fountain in front of the Jefferson Building and picnic tables, umbrellas, and planters set up on the terrace. This assumed the informal designation "Neptune Plaza." After crossing it and passing through the massive doorway, visitors were greeted by more innovation: velvet settees, gold drapes pulled back from the towering windows, potted plants. The Great Hall reminded some of a vast drawing room with an information desk for easing the public's transition into the world of books.

The Librarian no longer conducted regular luncheons as Putnam had done at the Round Table, but he met often with congressmen over breakfast. He seemed to enjoy the public role, unusual for a Librarian and a noted scholar. "It gives me a lift to be in a place I can admire," he told a visiting journalist, an enthusiasm that carried over to the Library staff and to many of his critics in and out of Congress.

Intent on making the Nation's Library more accessible to the nation's citizens—and to visitors from abroad—Librarian Boorstin ordered the massive main doors of the Thomas Jefferson Building reopened. Picnic tables were set on the terrace in front of those doors, just behind the newly repaired Neptune Fountain and, inside the building's Great Hall, potted plants and other furnishings were added to draw visitors more comfortably into the sometimes daunting world of the Library's huge multimedia collections. "I'm hopeful," Boorstin said to an interviewer, "this library can be one of the great resources of American civilization."

Photograph by Stephen Shore. Publishing Office, Library of Congress..

The "place" in question now contained, in addition to the millions of books, thirty million manuscripts, a quarter of a million phonograph records, one hundred thousand reels of film, and a collection of intellectually related materials unequaled in the world: books printed in Braille and on papyrus, magnetic tape, rolls of microfilm. So great was the collection that it occupied 336 miles of shelving and overflowed into twelve different rented spaces nearby, waiting for the move into the Madison Building.

Master drummer Yacub Addy led the Oboade Drumming and Dance Company down the steps of the Library's Thomas Jefferson Building during a concert on the Neptune Plaza, May 20, 1982, part of the American Folklife Center's Neptune Plaza Concert Series, which began in 1977.

Photograph by John T. Gibbs. American Folklife Center, Library of Congress.

The task force's report was seventy-three pages long when released and contained the distilled suggestions of many users and observers of the Library, among them five hundred Library employees. The general belief was "that the fundamental question before the Library of Congress at this stage in its history is one of organizational unity. How can the Library as a whole better serve both Congress and the nation?"

The report recommended, among other things, a codification of laws relating to the Library that included a formal statement of "purposes, privileges and responsibilities" and an insistence upon retaining the Library's standing as the most comprehensive library on earth. A board of advisers could help formulate the Library's national responsibilities, the report added. Specific suggestions were made for improving services, among them book delivery, reference, and research.

The establishment of a collection development office was recommended, a revitalization of the Library's preservation efforts, and the creation of a national bibliographic control system. The augmentation of cultural and educational programs at the Library was called for, to be placed within the purview of a single committee, and so were more efficient career development efforts for Library employees.

A planning office, the report concluded, should be created "concerned not only with the long-range planning and program development, but also with appraising the Library's major on-going programs and their management."

The planning office quickly became a reality, placed in the charge of a veteran of Library affairs. A free tuition program for employees seeking more education and consequently better jobs was instigated. In an interview, Boorstin compared the Library to "a supermarket of ideas. There are

nearly 80 million items here. Yes, I realize there are very unrewarding jobs. But we're trying to reduce these through [use of] the computer."

He added, "I'm hopeful this library can be one of the great resources of American civilization. It should become a center for study, for more research on American history, all areas of social history. It's hard to predict what areas of knowledge are more important [and] I don't want to second-guess posterity."

Meanwhile, outside donations were serving posterity, making possible the expansion of the Library's cultural capabilities. Funds from the National Endowment for the Humanities, for instance, were eventually applied to the establishment of an important serials data base in the humanities in machine-readable form and for a computer-based catalog of the early motion pictures collected by George Kleine and Theodore Roosevelt.

President Ronald Reagan at the 1983 exhibition *The American Cowboy*, with (*left to right*) Library of Congress exhibits officer William Miner, Librarian of Congress Daniel J. Boorstin, and First Lady Nancy Reagan. Based on material from the Paradise Valley Folklife Project, from the Library's special collections divisions, and from outside collections and institutions, the exhibition presented images from the movies and popular culture as well as from the everyday lives of working cowboys documented by the Library's American Folklife Center in Paradise Valley, Nevada, and elsewhere in the West.

American Folklife Center, Library of Congress.

The Library's commitment to American culture was reflected in the creation of the American Folklife Center by Congress in 1976, "to preserve and present American folklife." Destined to become a focus of national folklore research, the center had been championed early by professor of folklore and former shipwright Archie Green, and by the chairman of the National Endowment for the Arts, Nancy Hanks. Included in its mandate were public performances by practitioners of folk music.

The Folklife Center was placed under the general supervision of the Librarian and provided the support of a board of trustees appointed to help the Library discover, open, and widen its resources. The Library had in its possession thousands of wax cylinder recordings of Indian songs acquired in the 1940s. To these the Archive of Folk Song had added field recordings of American music from various parts of the United States, which it had begun collecting in 1928. Two years after the creation of the Folklife Center, it assumed control of the archive from the Music Division.

The archive's name would later be changed to the Archive of Folk Culture to encompass a broadened definition of what made up traditional folkways in America. The American Folklife Center would seek to preserve manifestations of that culture and to present it to as many Americans as possible.

The Center for the Book

Two years before his confirmation, Boorstin had written in *Harper's* magazine an essay, "A Design for an Anytime, Do-It-Yourself, Energy-Free Communication Device." The device he wrote about was the book, and the Librarian discussed its "wonderful . . . uncanny . . . mystic simplicity." Now an idea arose at the Library for promoting in the American mind this most basic of intellectual commodities.

The idea received support from Lucien N. Nedzi of Michigan in the House of Representatives and from Senator Howard Cannon of Nevada. Congress subsequently backed a program at the Library to "stimulate public interest and research in the role of the book in the diffusion of knowledge," and President Jimmy Carter approved it to show "his commitment to scholarly research and to the development of public interest in books and reading." In October 1977, he signed legislation creating at the Library of Congress a unique place known as the Center for the Book.

To some the name seemed redundant, the Library of Congress being the ultimate center for the book. But the Library's latest creation had a specific mission—in the words of Librarian Boorstin, "to organize, focus, and dramatize our nation's interest and attention on the book."

In addition, the center was publicly endorsed by the Publishers Advisory Group, one of the eight advisory groups to Boorstin's Task Force on Goals,

Librarian of Congress Daniel J. Boorstin's belief in the importance of the "anytime, do-it-yourself, energy-free communication device," otherwise known as "the book," was a basis for the creation of the Center for the Book in the Library of Congress in 1977. This poster advertised 1989 as "The Year of the Young Reader." It was based on a photograph by William Kuntzman of Powell, Wyoming, a prize-winner in the photography contest "A Nation of Readers," sponsored by the American Library Association and the Center for the Book in the Library of Congress during National Library Week, 1985.

Center for the Book, Library of Congress.

Organization, and Planning. The publishers had from 1954 to 1974 supported the National Book Committee to promote books, reading, and libraries, but the Publishers Advisory Group urged the creation at the Library of "a new body to fill and greatly to enlarge the role" earlier played by the committee. Now that prospect had been realized.

The Librarian had to raise money outside the Library to finance the center's activities, one of the stipulations of Congress. The first contribution came from McGraw-Hill—$20,000—used to convene four meetings of interested parties to plan activities and set up an advisory structure. Contributions were also made by Time-Life Books, Mrs. Charles W. Engelhard, Jr., the Engelhard-Hanovia Foundation, Franklin Book Programs, Inc.—in all, more than 130 corporations and individuals over the years. The former ambassador to Great Britain, the publisher and philanthropist Walter Annenberg, would announce in 1994 a $1 million donation through the Annenberg Foundation to the Center for the Book to honor his friend who was then the Librarian of Congress Emeritus, Daniel Boorstin.

The center helped arrange projects, lectures, and traveling exhibits about books and their role in the culture and a public service campaign on commercial television. Its slogan "Books change lives" became a familiar refrain in American schools, printed on posters and otherwise widely distributed.

Librarian Boorstin addressed the question of location for the center and why the Library remained its best home. "This institution has a greater vested interest in the book than any other place on earth. For us, the book is not only a vested interest but a vested idea. As the national library of a great free republic, we have a special interest to see that books do not go unread, that they are read by all ages and conditions, [and] . . . not lost from neglect or obscured from us by specious alternatives and synthetic substitutes. We have a special duty, too, to see that the book is the useful,

illuminating servant of all other technologies, and that all other technologies become the effective, illuminating acolytes of the book."

Another former ambassador, George C. McGhee, became chairman of the National Advisory Board, its members to serve as "channels" between educational and other communities. Four subcommittees were established: television; education and reading; the international role of the book; and publications.

A national seminar on "Television, the Book, and the Classroom" was held in April 1978, and a volume based on the discussions published the next year. The following year the center launched a joint project with CBS Television to encourage television viewers to "Read More About It."

Additional convocations addressed the questions of book reading in America, the audience for children's books, and the international role of books and printed materials. In conjunction with the Library's Rare Book and Special Collections Division, the center sponsored programs about the role of the book in history.

Within twenty years, the Center for the Book had encouraged partnerships with more than thirty-five affiliated centers for the book in individual states and had published dozens of its own books, including *The Community of the Book*, a directory of reading and literacy programs.

First Lady Barbara Bush, flanked by Librarian of Congress James H. Billington and John Y. Cole, director of the Center for the Book. A champion of literacy, Mrs. Bush supported the center by serving as national chairperson for the Year of the Young Reader in 1989.

Center for the Book, Library of Congress.

"Read More About It" has been an ongoing theme of the Center for the Book since its founding. In conjunction with the CBS television network, the center launched a series of public service spots that aired after selected television programs. Actors who had appeared in the programs afterward provided the audience with a short reading list of books that could shed further light on the subject of the program or on an author or a literary work that had been dramatized. Here, Danny Kaye prepared to film a "Read More About It" spot to air after the television broadcast of *Skokie*, a program that depicted the legal, moral, and emotional furor that surrounded the American Nazi Party's declaration of their intent to stage a march in that predominantly Jewish town in Illinois, home to some seven thousand survivors of World War II concentration camps.

Center for the Book, Library of Congress.

In 1979, the Library opened the Performing Arts Library at the John F. Kennedy Center for the Performing Arts in Washington, a joint project. Boorstin had plans for expanding other Library functions and instituting a fifteen-member Council of Scholars, supported with private donations, to meet twice a year and evaluate the Library's collections and services. And he envisioned organizing the Library's collections into the "Multi-media Encyclopedia" with an index, located in the Main Reading Room, to direct visitors and scholars to reading material as well as to films, maps, and music.

In remarks made at the White House Conference on Library and Information Services, Boorstin warned against the "fashionable chronologic myopia of our time" that led people to forget "the main and proper mission of our libraries. 'Libraries have been selling the wrong product for years,' one such faddist explains. 'They have been emphasizing reading. The product that we have is information.' But these are false messiahs," said Boorstin, who distinguished between "information" and the knowledge that grew from serious reading.

The interlibrary loan program was expanded as part of what Boorstin termed the Library of Congress's "special role" in American life. This came at a time, he believed, when "the libraries of the country are in a very sad state as a whole" owing to budgetary restraints.

But first came the move into the Madison Building, anticipated for more than a decade when, in 1980, the single largest library building in the world was opened to the public. It was to contain most of the Library's administrative offices, including the 889-person Congressional Research Service, and many other capabilities, among them special reading rooms for maps, manuscripts, motion pictures, sound recordings, and music.

The building, Boorstin noted in the opening ceremony, represented the "faith on which this nation was built. Not only a faith in freedom, [but] also a faith in knowledge and a belief in our human duty to encompass the resources of literature and the arts, of science and technology, to widen the oceans of knowledge and help us voyage together."

The transfer of staff and special collections required many months. Meanwhile, in the Jefferson Building, free at last of the clutter that had come to characterize the Library in the minds of many, was an exhibit celebrating the building's Italian Renaissance architecture. And discussions were under way with the Architect of the Capitol for restoring the older Library buildings.

Exhibits were becoming standard fare at the Library, the subjects as various as the *Apollo* mission, the American cowboy, and a retrospective show on Disney's animation, *Building a Better Mouse.* The Main Reading Room served now as the center of what Boorstin called the "Circle of Knowledge." The ordering

The third Library of Congress building on Capitol Hill, the James Madison Memorial Building was opened to the public in 1980. The official national memorial to James Madison, principal architect of the U.S. Constitution and fourth president of the United States, it celebrates his belief that "a people who mean to be their own governours, must arm themselves with the power which knowledge gives." The largest library building in the world, the Madison Building houses the U.S. Copyright Office, the Congressional Research Service, a host of special-format collections, facilities for preservation and for public events, and a cafeteria popular with researchers and tourists as well as Library staff.

Photograph by Jim Higgins. Photoduplication Service, Library of Congress.

of information was the objective of many of his projects, and making sure the information was available and relevant.

"How to relate the Library's materials to the world of learning?" Boorstin asked rhetorically during an interview in 1981. "This, after all, is a learning institution. The Council of Scholars is the answer. In the past, scholars doing research at the Library have often been unaware of what others were doing, within their fields or outside. The Council will have twenty-five members, representing all fields of knowledge, who will deliberate twice a year. . . . [T]he members will be in a position to inventory the state of mankind's knowledge and ignorance."

The concept of the multimedia encyclopedia, Boorstin hoped, would make the infinite variety of the collections available, and appealing, to all—scholars and browsers. The Library was receiving about sixty-five hundred books a day, adding to a collection that included books in 468 languages. Only about a third of the books were in English.

The Library's overall volume had reached seventy-six million items in 1981, its staff numbered fifty-two hundred, and the annual budget was $212 million. More than one thousand requests arrived daily from Congress.

In the 1970s and 1980s, Library of Congress exhibitions became more numerous and complex and covered a range of topics that reflected the breadth of the Library's collections. This exhibition catalog accompanied an exhibit celebrating fifty years of Walt Disney's animated films. *Building a Better Mouse* was on display in the Jefferson Building from November 1978 through January 1979 and featured examples from the Copyright Office and Motion Picture, Broadcasting, and Recorded Sound Division collections.

Interpretive Programs Office, Library of Congress.

The Madison Building was not dedicated until November 1981, a ceremony attended by the new president of the United States, Ronald Reagan. Before the president spoke, Boorstin recalled the words of James Madison—"Liberty and learning, each leaning on the other for the mutual and surest support"—and suggested that Madison "would be exhilarated to see, besides our great collection of books, the manuscripts of 23 of our presidents, of many Justices of our Supreme Court, and of a host of literary Americans, from Benjamin Franklin to Walt Whitman and Edna St. Vincent Millay … [and] by forms he never imagined—photography, motion pictures, musical recordings—offered in this very building in unexcelled quality and quantity which themselves attest to the vitality and ingenuity of the nation they celebrate."

Boorstin's personal style, like his bow ties, had become familiar both to Congress and to the public during his six years in office. Voluble and enthusiastic—a writer for *The New Yorker* suggested that if Boorstin's words "came out in Teletype, there would be no spaces between them"—he often brandished a cigar when discussing his ambitions for the Library.

Boorstin sometimes arrived at his office as early as six in the morning, and

regularly attended luncheons and black tie dinners with congressmen, dignitaries, and ranking
Washington intellectuals. His critics sometimes
referred to Boorstin as "His Librarianship," but
none denied his energy and commitment.

Asked how long he planned to remain in his
job, Boorstin said, "I don't see a ratio between the
length of a Librarian's tenure and his contribution. I don't know of any institution that has
suffered because an able leader stayed too short a
time. I will leave when the shine is off."

The third floor of the James Madison
Memorial Building, home to the Prints
and Photographs Division and the Motion
Picture, Broadcasting, and Recorded
Sound Division, in 1983 became the location, as well, of the Mary Pickford Theater, devoted to increasing public access to
the Library's film collections. At the ceremony inaugurating this intimate theater,
Librarian Boorstin addressed an audience
that included *(from left)* Lillian Gish,
Senator Barry Goldwater, Buddy Rogers,
and Douglas Fairbanks, Jr.

Photoduplication Service, Library of Congress.

The move to the Madison Building complete, the Mary Pickford Theater was
opened there in 1983 with grant money from the Mary Pickford Foundation to
provide greater access to the Library's vast film collections. An orientation theater
to acquaint visitors with the Library's collections and services was also opened.
The following year, Congress appropriated $81.5 million for the renovation of
both the Jefferson and the Adams Buildings, a tribute to the role of the Library in
congressional and national affairs—and to the role of the current Librarian.

Less visible were efforts under way to preserve books and manuscripts.
Experimentation was carried on with diethyl zinc for deacidifying paper, and
an optical disk pilot project was undertaken to see if such disks could be used
for preservation of materials. Congress would appropriate more than $11 mil-

lion for the project. By now the staff depended upon the machine-readable cataloging data available on terminals throughout the Library.

Answering a journalist's question about his personal favorites among the millions of items contained by the Library of Congress, the Librarian revealed his preferences. The list offered an insight into the man and the institution.

Favored on it were: the Giant Bible of Mainz, the staff of the Library of Congress, the view of the Capitol from his office in the Madison Building, the Swann Collection of political caricatures, the Hans P. Kraus Sir Francis Drake Collection, the collection of bird's-eye views, the Geography and Map Division, the Great Hall in the Thomas Jefferson Building, and listening to music played on the Library's Stradivari instruments.

Boorstin assisted in the acquisition of the papers of the statesmen W. Averell Harriman and Henry Kissinger. His "hero luncheons" for the friends and families of deceased notable Americans with special connections to the Library honored such people as Charles Lind-

The Library's burgeoning film collection encompassed not only major studio pro-ductions but many fine examples of work by independent filmmakers with an activist view of cinema. Gregory Nava's *El Norte*, produced by Independent Productions/ American Playhouse in New York and released in 1983, told the story of a broth-er and sister who emigrated illegally from war-torn Guatemala to find a better life "up north."

Frame enlargements. Motion Picture, Broadcasting, and Recorded Sound Division, Library of Congress.

bergh, Margaret Mead, Samuel Eliot Morison, and Richard Rodgers. These were recorded and added to the collections.

Likewise, Boorstin encouraged the development of the Archive of World Literature on Tape on his many trips abroad. In 1986 in Japan, he was recognized by the Japan-ese government for assisting in the development of the National Diet Library with one of that country's most pres-tigious decorations, "The Order of the Sacred Treasure."

Back in America, Boorstin appointed Robert Penn Warren as the nation's first poet laureate and consultant in poetry to the Library.

That same year he loudly protested cuts in the Library's appropriation for fiscal 1986. Though $11.5 million was dedicated to building a book-preserva-tion facility in Fort Detrick, Maryland, the overall cuts amounted to 3.4 per-cent, or $8.4 million.

Testifying before the Joint Committee on the Library, he pointed out that the first responsibility of the Library was Congress, but that there were "two other invisible constituencies. One is the community of all past Americans who have built our nation and enriched our culture."

He cited the writers of the letters of the Continental Congress, the drafter of the Gettysburg Address, the members of the National American Woman Suffrage Association, the great composers, writers, mapmakers, and photographers.

"There is also the constituency," he added, "of our children and grandchildren."

Though called "an intellectual Paul Revere," Daniel Boorstin decided at the end of the year to retire. In making his announcement, he told the assembled senior staff that his time at the Library was "the great experience and the great opportunity of my life—to work with the Congress, with you and our other colleagues at the Library, and with librarians of the nation and the world, and to help build this institution."

He intended to leave the following June, he said, to "become a full-time citizen of the Republic of Letters." He would no longer have to worry about separating his administrative duties from his writing.

Boorstin and his wife, Ruth, left behind their own legacy: a $100,000 gift to establish a publication fund in their names to be administered by the Center for the Book.

The Librarian's other legacy was a continuing emphasis upon knowledge and the role of books. After retirement he spoke out about the Jeffersonian ideal of a well-educated, innovative society: "The most important lesson of American history is the promise of the unexpected. None of our ancestors would have imagined settling way over here on this unknown continent. So we must continue to have a society that is hospitable to the unexpected, which allows possibilities to develop beyond our own imaginings."

Maps and Atlases

A comprehensive view of the world throughout history is available in the Library's Geography and Map Division. Within it rests the world's largest collection of maps—more than four million of them—which embody successive perceptions of geographic reality, from the age of discovery to the present, from the fanciful art of early cartographers to the precise Landsat photographs of the remotest parts of the globe.

The oldest, rarest, and most valuable maps are the portolan charts created as visual guides for sailors. The oldest of these to be found in the Library's collections is a map drawn on vellum in the early fourteenth century of the Mediterranean and Black Seas, from what is now Israel to Spain, showing ports in remarkably detailed coastline renderings. A broader perspective is offered by a 1482 Ptolemaic atlas of the world as the Romans saw it, in color, a vision that endured until well after the voyage of Columbus.

The division possesses Caspar Vopell's globe and armillary sphere composed of metal bands, made in 1543, tracing the paths of planets as they were envisioned by Ptolemy. And a pair of great

Venetian globes from the late seventeenth century, displayed in the sixth-floor lobby of the Madison Building, show both the continents of the earth and the celestial constellations.

The first circumnavigation of the globe, accomplished by Magellan, was depicted graphically in the 1544 manuscript atlas by Battista Agnese that came to rest in the Library. Other valuable, evocative maps relating to early America include Samuel de Champlain's 1606–7 visual record of his journeys along the coast of New England and Nova Scotia, complete with Indian settlements.

At the same time, Captain John Smith was preparing the map of Virginia now in the Geography and Map Division, a 1612 representation complete with symbolic representations of trees and land forms, of the three thousand-mile journey along the shores of the Chesapeake Bay that he made when he was twenty-eight years old.

The first existing depiction of Manhattan Island by the Dutch in 1633 found a home in the division's vaults. Other rarities that document the formation of the American nation are sixty-seven maps that belonged to the French commander in North America, the marquis de Rochambeau, and the military maps of the commander of the British fleet sent to America in 1776, Admiral Sir Richard Howe.

One of the most valuable is the large original 1791 drawing by Pierre Charles L'Enfant for the city of Washington, D.C. On the plan are hand-written comments by L'Enfant and some of his advisers, among them Thomas Jefferson.

The collection of Civil War material includes the highly detailed military maps produced by Jedediah Hotchkiss, the Confederate engineer whose work was used in preparation for specific battles and territorial campaigns. Maps used by General William Tecumseh Sherman and hundreds more prepared to inform the public about the progress of the war, complemented by lithographs of forts and individual battlefields, combine to document the conflict.

The historically rich collection of fire insurance maps produced during the century after the Civil War reveals the intricacies of a burgeoning urban America. Hand-colored and richly detailed, the maps were produced to provide information to insurance underwriters of the layouts, structures, and economic activities of towns and cites, giving an unprecedented glimpse of the changing face of the nation. The fire insurance maps themselves are buttressed by the Library's extensive collection of county maps showing land ownership over many years, panoramic city plans from 1865 to the 1920s, and early aerial views of population clusters.

Foremost among maps relating to World War II are a German military atlas prepared for the invasion of Russia in 1942, emblazoned with a swastika, and Nazi architect Albert Speer's renderings of the streets of Berlin. Three-dimensional molded rubber renditions of Pacific islands produced by the Japanese also reside in the Geography and Map Division.

One of the most intriguing, and touching, maps in the Geography and Map Division is one on sealskin depicting the Arctic regions. It was produced by an Inuit, commissioned by the Library through the explorer Admiral Richard E. Byrd. Ice flows, sea channels, and islands have been represented on it by bits of driftwood that were sewed to the skin, creating an object of great beauty, immediacy, and imaginative power.

Among the most venerable treasures in the Geography and Map Division's collections is "universalior cogniti orbis tabula," an engraving with watercolor by Johan Ruysch from a 1507 edition of Ptolemy's classic work *Geographia*. In this map, prepared after Columbus's first voyage, Ruysch adjusted the second-century three-part worldview to include what Europeans called the "new" fourth part, America, though the true boundaries and extent of the newly discovered land were yet to be determined.

Geography and Map Division, Library of Congress.

The course, strategies, and tactics of the U.S. Civil War can be traced through a collection of more than twenty-two hundred Civil War maps—including an outstanding group of materials created, compiled, and collected by Confederate States Army topographic engineer Jedediah Hotchkiss. A provider of indispensable geographic intelligence for Stonewall Jackson, Robert E. Lee, Richard Ewell, Jubal Early, and John B. Gordon, Hotchkiss would note, often hurriedly on horseback, features of terrain and vegetation that would later adorn his very detailed, often beautiful maps. Three items from the Hotchkiss collection are shown here: (*top*) A field notebook, open to a page of rough sketch notes, in which Hotchkiss recorded the positions of the Second Corps of the Army of Northern Virginia during 1864–65 engagements; (*center*) a finished manuscript map covering the area from the southern Shenandoah Valley to Washington, D.C.; (*bottom*) a closed notebook with inscribed cover.

Geography and Map Division, Library of Congress.
Photograph copyright © by Roger Foley.

Cartography is not always about geography alone. Maps have depicted fairylands and other fictional places, shown the names of writers associated with particular places, detailed information necessary for insurance coverage, shown celestial diagrams, or provided puzzles or a humorous view of geography. The all-American game of football, derived from the nineteenth-century English games of soccer and rugby, is celebrated in this pictorial map published in Milwaukee in 1941. Though it mentions the ten major professional teams playing at the time, "The Albert Richard All-American Football Map" emphasizes the collegiate side of the sport, providing team nick-names, 1940 season records, and major conference championships.

Geography and Map Division,
Library of Congress.

The residents of St. Louis, Missouri, and vicinity, were not saying "cheese" when this photograph was taken on July 4, 1988—since they were undoubtedly unaware that this image was being captured by the Earth Observation Satellite Company (EOSAT) of Lanham, Maryland. One of 1.6 million aerial photographs and remote-sensing images in the Geography and Map Division collections, this photograph shows the confluence of the Missouri and Mississippi Rivers just north of St. Louis in a year plagued by drought.

Geography and Map Division, Library of Congress.
Courtesy of Space imaging EOSAT.

8

Accessible _____

(1987–2000)

*A public institution alone can
supply those sciences which . . . are yet necessary to
complete the circle, all the parts of which contribute
to the improvement of the country.*

Thomas Jefferson

The task of choosing the thirteenth Librarian of Congress fell to President
Ronald Reagan. As the end of a century—and a millennium—approached, the
line of succession at Independence Avenue and First Street was complicated by
the Library's efforts to respond to an increasingly diverse, outspoken American
public. In the past, the demands of professional librarians had been heard first and
most insistently, but now to that chorus were added those of women and minorities for representation at the top of the country's foremost intellectual institution.

After due deliberation, the president choose as Daniel Boorstin's successor
the director of the Woodrow Wilson International Center for Scholars at the
Smithsonian Institution and a noted historian, James Hadley Billington. Previously a Rhodes Scholar and a professor at Princeton, Billington, fifty-seven, was
an authority on Russian society and the revolutionary spirit throughout history. He had integrated the components of various cultures into his academic
lectures, an indication of wide-ranging interests in keeping with the Library's
contents and its mandate.

A member of the Council on Foreign Relations, Billington also sat on the
editorial advisory boards of *Foreign Affairs* and *Theology Today*. He had written
several books, among them *The Icon and the Axe: An Interpretive History of Russian Culture* and *Fire in the Minds of Men: Origins of the Revolutionary Faith*. At the
Wilson Center, he had created eight new programs, increased the number of
conferences, and founded the *Wilson Quarterly*, a journal devoted to scholarship and the promulgation of ideas. Billington was considered a strong propo-
nent of the global perspective and a leader particularly well suited for grappling
with the Library's almost infinite cultural and technological complexities.

He also served as an unofficial adviser to President Reagan on matters relating

James H. Billington was sworn in as the thirteenth Librarian of Congress in a ceremony in the Library's Great Hall on September 14, 1987. An authority on Russian history, Billington applied his global perspective to the challenges of preserving and protecting the Library's collections while at the same time finding new ways of broadening access to them.

Publishing Office, Library of Congress. Photograph copyright © Roger Foley.

to Russia. Billington had conversed in Russian with the Soviet premier, Mikhail Gorbachev, and generally given support to the Reagan administration's cold war policies. His knowledge of international affairs had further strengthened his candidacy with those in Congress who thought this a more important qualification in a potential Librarian than formal training in Library management.

Billington had grown up in a house in suburban Philadelphia filled with second-hand volumes that had been bought by his father, a book-lover who had never attended college. At an early age the young Billington read many of the books and was impressed by the underlining in them. He later attributed his interest in scholarship to the curiosity the underlining aroused, making him question various texts and wonder why a previous reader had found them significant. Consequently, Billington came to believe in the importance of all books.

This fact was noted by Boorstin when he publicly endorsed President Reagan's choice of a new Librarian of Congress. "James Billington has a unique set of qualifications. He is a man of letters, a spokesman and an advocate of the great tradition of the book, a man of broad culture and sympathies, and a proven successful administrator who knows the needs and interests of Congress. He is well qualified to serve the library profession and the nation's libraries."

All this did not forestall objections from some professional librarians, who put forward the familiar argument that Congress and the Library would be better served by one of their own. To augment the more than twenty-five million volumes on 532 miles of shelves at the Library were some seven thousand items added daily.

Some of the books were being transferred to digital disks, the first of the musical compact disks had been released, and part of the photographic collections were being put on analog disks that held as many as fifty-four thousand photos on a side. Never had a Librarian been responsible for so much.

The nomination of Billington was widely praised outside the library profession. The *Washington Post* called him "a fine choice" and pointed out that in a time of budgetary restraints, Billington's experience at the Wilson Center and his awareness of the needs of Congress would serve him well. "Every congressional district and every state has an equal call on the Library through the research service," Billington said at the time. "When constituents write their representative in Washington, there's a good chance the response they get comes in part from information the research service provided."

Officials of the American Library Association did meet with Billington to discuss the relationship between the Library and the ALA. They offered their services to the nominee, but not their endorsement.

At the confirmation hearing before the Senate Rules and Administration Committee in July 1987, Billington spoke of the Library as "a place where the free, hard-working individual rules in the exercise of that which makes him or her most majestically human: a ranging, restless God-given intellect." He characterized the Library as part of the American dream, "a living witness to our abiding hope that each new generation will surpass the preceding one by increasing knowledge, ripening it into wisdom, and creatively applying it for human betterment." It must, he added, "above all, remain true to its basic mission as a catalyst of freedom: conserving, creating, and celebrating human knowledge."

Specifically, the Library of Congress under Billington's leadership would seek to conserve the national memory using modern electronic technology. And, he said, it would celebrate the life of the mind as represented in all media. It would also "bring out the music that is already there"—in other words, improve the vast, invaluable collections in place and make them more widely available.

"I would further hope that Americans of the twenty-first century might look back and conclude that this unmatched storehouse of knowledge had found ways in the late years of the twentieth to help both toughen and enrich education in America."

Billington was confirmed as the thirteenth Librarian and sworn in that year in the Great Hall of the Thomas Jefferson Building. President Reagan spoke of Billington's "life-long love of books," and the new Librarian described the task now at hand as moving simultaneously in two directions, "despite the seeming contradiction between the two: out more broadly and in more deeply."

The new Librarian felt that there were two pressing problems at the institution for which he was now responsible: maintaining the genius of the universal

Librarian of Congress James H. Billington (*left*) chatted with Jerry Garcia and Mickey Hart of the Grateful Dead at a reception in the Library's Great Hall in March 1993 celebrating publication of *The Spirit Cries: Music from the Rainforests of South America & the Caribbean*, a compact disk produced by Hart in conjunction with the American Folklife Center. The CD was the first in a series called the Endangered Music Project, designed to use new technologies to share with a wide audience some of the little-known documentary field recordings from around the world that were housed in the Archive of Folk Culture.

Photograph by Yusef El-Amin. American Folklife Center, Library of Congress.

collections, and getting more people to make use of the Library of Congress in the new age.

Inherent in the second problem was the Library's vast, varied contents and what he saw as its untapped potential for enlightening potential users. Getting out the music already there meant turning passive Library resources into dynamic ones through electronics. The Library, he said repeatedly, had the potential to deliver to a larger audience and to make its services to Congress more efficient.

The first problem involved basic maintenance, deferred for years and, in some cases, for decades. The year Billington was confirmed, 2.3 million people visited the Library, but its management structure remained antiquated. Furthermore, the three Library buildings harbored forty million still uncataloged items. There was misplacement of books and other materials, lax security, vandalism—primarily the removal of art work and other valuable illustrations from books—and outright theft of volumes. Reports of the damage were sometimes exaggerated, but the situation clearly needed rectifying by means other than the traditional monitoring of activities in the stacks and reading rooms.

And the Library's constituency needed expanding and enhancing. Rather than broadly based, it was concentrated in small groups of professionals passionate about different issues but less so about the whole Library of Congress.

Billington wanted the Library to be recognized as performing basic services for the taxpayer who supported it. In his view, providing services to the individual citizen was both a moral responsibility and a practical necessity.

The Library had all the problems of both an academic bureaucracy and a governmental agency. The task before Billington included reshaping the institution for the modern era. He initiated the first audit in the Library's history and began a thorough, yearlong review of the Library to see how the Library might "intensify and energize the intellectual life" and "reach out more broadly by sharing its richness with the Congress and the people of the United States."

Specifically, the review, undertaken by Arthur Young and Company, was to assess selected Library operations and suggest ways of improving them; it was also to facilitate strategic planning. Library personnel was to be the first area of inquiry, with special attention to Equal Opportunity and Affirmative Action. Lingering complaints by the staff about promotion were to be addressed.

Previous efforts to put the catalog into electronic form were intensified. The new Librarian made book cataloging a more collective effort, to bring together some of the Library's various functions and disciplines that were often pursued in isolation from one another. Arrearages, found most often in the special collections, were also addressed. Dealing with this problem would be made easier when Congress voted additional funds for the purpose.

Billington ordered the formation of an internal management and planning committee made up of twenty-seven of the Library's middle managers and excluding those at the top. Its open meetings were attended by as many as one thousand Library employees, and often by the Librarian himself. He encouraged employees and users to make suggestions about improving services and conditions at the Library, and more than nine hundred responded.

The result was a more efficient management team for the Library in general and a more open discussion of personnel problems that had existed since the 1960s.

And a national advisory committee was formed to represent diverse Library users around the country. The committee was made up of twenty-nine leaders from universities, foundations, corporations, and the realms of literature and publishing. Among them were a Supreme Court justice and two former members of Congress.

Reaching out to the professional librarians who had been cool to his stewardship, Billington spoke at national gatherings of members of the American Library Association and the Association of Research Libraries. He acted to increase and deepen direct use of the Library by scholars and took steps to make it easier for the Library to acquire books for copyright deposit.

The Center for the Book received additional support from Billington, who saw it as an effective force for promoting books, reading, and the Library of Congress itself. The Librarian of Congress encouraged the creation of additional state centers for the book, each expected to promote its own literary heritage. Educational and civic organizations became "reading promotion partners" of the Library of Congress, and a program to emphasize book and library history found support in academic and research institutions.

Billington's ideas about the gravity of books raised hackles among some publishers outside of Washington. He encouraged them to publish manuscripts dealing with large, important subjects, rather than "titillating answers to highly ephemeral contemporary questions." He initiated copublishing efforts involving the Library, to make his point. Among them were *Documenting America, 1935–1943*, a photographic essay on America in the 1930s published in association with the University of California Press, and *The North American Indian Portfolios from the Library of Congress*, published by Abbeville Press.

An office was created at the Library to coordinate special programs, such as its participation in the Bicentennial of Congress, educational programs for the public, and preparations for the celebration of the Library's own Bicentennial in 2000. Plans for the Development Office, formally created in 1990, were set in motion, as another initiative on the part of James Billington. But such an initiative would take more time than was available to raise necessary funds, and the Librarian already had grander plans.

Coincidental with the yearlong review of the Library's activities were forums held in eleven different locations—in Pennsylvania, Wisconsin, Florida, California, Illinois, Louisiana, Colorado, Rhode Island, Wyoming, and Nebraska—to acquaint Americans with the Library.

Emerging forcefully from these forums was the compelling idea of digitalization, among other developments in communications. Another was the realization that access to books was not enjoyed by all young Americans. As Billington would later remark, "When I took this job I remember coming across the fact that a convict in California's prison system is more likely to have access to a library than a student in its public schools." The forums indicated the ongoing interest of children in books.

The Librarian wanted to make more of the Library's treasures available to all Americans. One means was the American Memory project at the Library. It would disseminate Library material to libraries all over the country, beginning with a pilot optical disk about Congress and the governing of America. Included would be broadsides from the time of the Continental Congress, portraits of early statesmen, manuscripts, and other items. Subsequent electronically transmitted treasures would apply more specifically to a wide range of subjects.

From the tens of thousands of pictures taken by Dorothea Lange, Walker Evans, Gordon Parks, Esther Bubley, and other Depression-era photographers employed by the Farm Security Administration and later the Office of War Information, a selection was examined in a book published by the University of California Press in 1988 in association with the Library entitled *Documenting America, 1935–1943.* In her photograph of an employment agency, Marion Post Wolcott captured a moment in Miami, Florida, in 1939.

Prints and Photographs Division, Library of Congress. LC-USF34T01-50772-E

American
Memory

memory.loc.gov

Historical Collections
for the
National Digital Library

Library of Congress

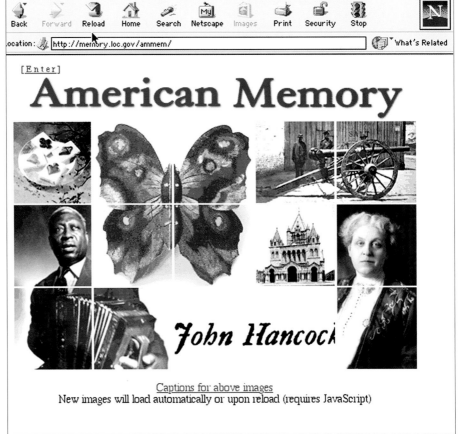

The American Memory project began as an effort to distribute electronic reproductions of Library of Congress materials to other libraries on optical disks and grew to be an important feature of its Web site. Civil War photographs, documents from the Continental Congress, early radio recordings and motion pictures, and portraits of statesmen were added to an ever-growing list of historical materials easily accessible on-line to people around the world.

Screen captures by Glenn Ricci. National Digital Library, Library of Congress.

To finance American Memory, Billington had to raise substantial private money besides the $1 million that Congress appropriated for each of five consecutive years to put 210,000 digitized items on compact disks (CD-ROMs) to be distributed to forty-four different sites in the United States. The Library, in Billington's words, was "doing more things for more Americans," building a new, younger constituency for its special collections, and contributing to education in a new and imaginative way.

The effort would prove particularly effective with grammar school students. From the beginning, they reacted with enthusiasm to audio and visual renditions of documents relating to milestones in American history like the Civil War and the Great Depression. Included were some of the many photographs in the Mathew Brady collection and others collected by the Detroit Publishing Company portraying life in America at the turn of the century. The American Memory project drew adults to local libraries who might not otherwise have visited them, and it demonstrated a new medium for the preservation of valuable national heirlooms that would live on in electronic form. The American Memory project also attracted a large and ever-growing foreign audience.

The review of the Library had been paid for almost entirely by privately raised monies. On its completion, the Librarian spoke to Congress of its "one overriding conclusion—that a radically different concept of operation and management philosophy is necessary for the Library to carry out its mission successfully in the changing environment of the 1990s."

Four "objects of service" had been identified: the collections, Congress, its constituents, and what the Librarian termed "the creative community." Each of the new management units created under Billington would focus on these areas, and an office for special projects was to concentrate on critical issues cutting across organizational lines within the Library. These included Affirmative Action, the cataloging backlog, communications within and outside the Library, acquisitions, and personnel practices.

People working at the Library remained a prime consideration. When Billington requested $289.3 million for fiscal 1990, an increase of $31.8 million—almost 13 percent—he pointed out that "the key element in the . . . request is the need to remedy the central, crippling fact that one of every ten of the Library's authorized positions is currently vacant for lack of funding."

The Library could not depend upon Congress to finance many of the projects the Librarian had started. And he had many more yet in mind. The problem of fund-raising had to be answered in a new and more imaginative way.

Budget restraints were being felt throughout the government. Congress encouraged various agencies to seek outside funding. But Billington didn't want to raise money for the Library in a commercial manner. In his opinion, providing products, or accepting sponsorship that would have to be associated with some artifact, might compromise the Library's dignity and credibility. Consequently he turned to individual Americans who shared his views about the Library's potential and the absolute need for maintaining integrity and independence.

"Get the champagne out of the bottle and onto the picnic table" became a familiar refrain at the Library of Congress. The Librarian's words reflected a desire to thoroughly democratize knowledge. He wanted to effect greater use of the Library's vast foreign-language collections and to renew the Library's staff as its invaluable members went into retirement. He also saw the need for ambitious, external programs and sought a way to provide the necessary additional funds, perhaps with revenues donated by corporations and wealthy individuals.

First Billington encouraged Congress to expand the Library's Trust Fund Board beyond the current members, which were the secretary of the treasury, the chairman of the Joint Committee on the Library, the Librarian of Congress, and two citizens appointed by the president. But he had another idea: a national, private sector advisory body, the first in the 190-year history of the Library of Congress, to help raise funds and increase the Library's visibility among all Americans.

Such a body might prove a testing ground for new ideas. In January 1990, Billington brought together for the first time forty founding members of the newly created national James Madison Council, named for the fourth president of the United States, a man responsible for many of the basic rights of Americans and one of the great founders of the republic. The Librarian thought that Madison, a champion of intellectual endeavor and of books, deserved special recognition. The Library's latest building bore his name and had been designated as the nation's official monument to him.

Relatively few members of the new council were from Washington. Billington wanted instead a broad representation of the America's entrepreneurial talent. Among those attending the first meeting of the Madison Council were not only the Senate Majority Leader, George Mitchell of Maine, but also John W. Kluge, a media magnate

and the council's first chairman. The group, among them some of the country's most successful business leaders, spent a day at the Library being informed about its operations and viewing some of the national heirlooms in the special collections. The members were expected to contribute their own ideas about increasing the Library's intellectual reach, draw upon their broad range of expertise, and offer financial support—either personally, or through the efforts of institutions with which they were affiliated.

Eventually there were about one hundred members with agreed-upon objectives and good rapport. Billington envisioned the council members as links between the Library and other libraries and educational institutions, and he charged them with building the Library's national constituency and improving the condition and the accessibility of the collections.

The council met two more times that year and was apprised of various Library initiatives, among them the Global Library Project and the exhibition of Vatican treasures scheduled for 1992–93.

Billington received what he considered good advice from council members, whose ranks came to include such varied personalities as Trammell Crow, real estate investor, Jerry Jones, owner of the Dallas Cowboys football team, Katharine Graham, chairman of the *Washington Post*, and a former Miss America, Phyllis George.

Over the course of several years the Madison Council would make $100 million available to the Library for special projects, exhibits, and acquisitions. The special funding also enabled the Library to broadly influence the quality of the information that it was to make available through the rapidly developing Internet.

And the council, looking to the Library's immediate future and the recognition of its two-hundred-year history, assumed the main funding responsibility for supporting its upcoming year 2000 Bicentennial celebration.

U.S. President Bill Clinton (*center*) and President Boris Yeltsin
of Russia (*right*) opened the exhibition *In the Beginning Was the
Word: The Russian Orthodox Church and Native Alaskan Cultures*, on
September 28, 1994, in the James Madison Building. While on a
state visit to Washington, Mr. Yeltsin had expressed an interest in the
Library's Russian holdings, which included materials written by Russian
missionaries documenting the encounter between the Russian Orthodox Church and native peoples of Alaska between 1794 and about
1915. Both world leaders joined Librarian James Billington (*behind
Yeltsin*) in greeting members of the Madison Council, which had
helped to fund the exhibition, including members Esther Cooper-
smith (*front left*) and Buffy Cafritz (*left center*).

Development Office, Library of Congress.

In 1990, John W. Kluge was named the first chairman of the Madison Council and by 1999 headed a group of more than a hundred leaders in philanthropy, business, and cultural affairs. Encyclopedia Britannica had established the James Madison National Council Fund by its gift to the Library in 1989. The council gives the Library the advantage of the various members' leadership, professional expertise, contacts, and financial support in advancing its many initiatives.

Development Office, Library of Congress.

At yearly meetings at the Library, Madison Council members are made aware of every aspect of the Library's workings and resources so that they can fully appreciate and better assist in the Library's missions. Madison Council Members Joan Wegner (*left*) and Julienne Krasnoff (*right*) felt the raised dots on pages of a braille magazine during their tour of the National Service for the Blind and Physically Handicapped at the council's October 1998 meeting. The Library's initiative for the visually handicapped began in 1897 when Librarian Young opened a reading room for the blind in the newly constructed Thomas Jefferson Building.

Development Office, Library of Congress.

Standing beneath photographs of some of the inaugural items on display, Madison Council member Paul A. Allaire spoke at the opening of *American Treasures of the Library of Congress*, a permanent rotating exhibition of the most highly prized pieces in the varied collections of the Library. Sponsoring the exhibit was the Xerox Corporation, of which Allaire was chairman and chief executive officer. Housed in one of the galleries in the Thomas Jefferson Building, the varied exhibits included such treasures as (*from left*) an eighteenth-century American powder horn inscribed with a map of the Hudson and Mohawk River Valleys, a first edition of American Frank Baum's *The Wizard of Oz*, and the contents of Lincoln's pockets on the night he died, paired with a newspaper account of the assassination.

Development Office, Library of Congress.

For fiscal 1991, the Library received $7.6 million in new money from Congress to hire 164 people to more effectively deal with the arrearage problem. The number of uncataloged items was quickly reduced by one million, but there were still thirty-eight million left. The Librarian intended to cut arrearages by 80 percent before the end of the decade.

In June 1991, the Main Reading Room in the Thomas Jefferson Building, previously closed for renovations, was reopened to the public. It retained both its historic architectural distinction and traditional decor, but in it were the products of the latest technological developments, giving new on-line access to the Library's computerized files. Changes in the Main Reading Room and those planned for the Science Reading Room would result in an additional 787 seats for scholars and other readers.

For the following year, Billington requested $361 million from Congress, an increase of 18 percent. This was to meet mandatory pay and price increases and to better prepare the Library for what was termed "the information explosion." Almost $8 million was to go for new automation systems for better dealing with the Library's ninety-one million items, but this was almost matched—about $6 million—by funds requested for the preservation of books, always the Library's foundation.

Automation at the Library had grown from 75 systems in 1980 to 123 a decade or so later, a growth of 64 percent. But funding for it had grown by a fraction of that. About $5.5 million of the requested funds would go for computer work stations and 800 million bytes of storage and optical disk capability. An automated system was also being installed to provide more comprehensive control of acquisitions.

"We are trying to accomplish in our time what Thomas Jefferson wanted to do when this place was founded," Billington told an interviewer for the *Los Angeles Times*. "Jefferson believed that in order for an open society to function as it should, you have to have an ever increasing knowledge base."

In the realm of books, plans were already in place for deacidifying 300,000 books in 1992 and a million books annually after that. The cost was $7.50 a copy. Those books too brittle to be deacidified were to be microfilmed.

The special collections had also increased rapidly in the last decade. The manuscript collection, for instance, was twice as numerous as it had been in 1982, whereas the reference staff dealing with it had not grown at all. And demand for access was much greater. The Chinese collection alone was growing by fourteen thousand volumes annually, and readership had increased 85 percent.

The following year, 1993, with the approval of Congress, the Library's bibliographic records were made available on the Internet. Users were able to tap

into the Library's computerized trove, some from the privacy of their own homes. This made the process of electronically distributing Library material generally much easier; once the conversions were put into effect around the country, expensive technology would not be necessary for the user to receive more and more information about the Library's books, manuscripts, and other treasures.

For universal access to be achieved, Congress had contributed $3 million to assist in the effort. Billington had helped raise an additional $9 million.

Invaluable Library holdings were not the only ones made available on computer screens. The Library displayed items from exhibits of treasures from the Vatican Library and the Bibliothèque nationale de France; it served as an example of global cooperation in disseminating knowledge. In addition to interns brought to the Library as part of the program to attract qualified graduates of American library schools were interns from foreign libraries, part of the effort to build a worldwide communications network.

Billington felt that the Library—and all libraries—had a moral responsibility to counter the preponderance of unfiltered, valueless, and sometimes dam-

Henri d'Albret, king of Navarre, holding a daisy (*marguerite*) in this miniature from a book presented to his bride, Marguerite d'Angoulême, in 1527. One of the treasures from the Bibliothèque nationale de France included in a Library of Congress exhibition in 1995, the book is an artistic treasure as well as a valuable artifact reflecting the personal history of Marguerite—the "pearl" of princesses, a poetess, a storyteller, and a serious reader—and the history of France itself, for Marguerite played an important role in the beginnings of the Reformation there. The Library of Congress extended the reach of this important exhibit by reproducing many of the treasures on its Web site.

Courtesy Bibliothèque nationale de France.

Thurgood Marshall (1908–1993) (*left*) and Roy Wilkins at work in the 1940s during the long, slow campaign to achieve equal rights for African Americans. Marshall, a crusading attorney whose civil rights cases included the landmark Supreme Court victory in *Brown v. Board of Education of Topeka, Kansas* (1954), was appointed to a federal judgeship in 1962. He was appointed to the U.S. Supreme Court in 1967, becoming the first African American justice on the nation's highest judicial body. Marshall gave his papers to the Library of Congress, to be held in the Manuscript Division, with explicit instructions that they be opened for the use of researchers at his death.

Prints and Photographs Division, Library of Congress. LC-USZ62-36621

aging material found on the Internet, and to struggle against the general degradation of language. "Without the integrity of language," he would later say, "you don't have civilization, because the inability to communicate undermines all else."

As a national library, the Library of Congress was an institution that could set a standard for quality, for continuity, and for constitutional rights. When sentiment surfaced to withhold certain information from the public, Billington resisted. The release of the private papers of the deceased associate justice of the Supreme Court, Thurgood Marshall, a leading figure in the civil rights movement, was opposed by some, but Billington decided to abide by Marshall's wishes as Marshall had expressed them before his death, and released the papers. "In so doing," he announced, "we have followed traditional library practice of strict adherence to the donor's explicit instructions."

Members of Marshall's family and the current chief justice had objected to the fact that journalists would have access to the papers, but the Librarian pointed out that the term "researchers," used by Marshall, "has always referred to adults working on specific research projects, be they authors, journalists, or lawyers." There was another potent objection: that the release would threaten the privacy of the Supreme Court's current deliberations. "The Library does not hold itself above the law," Billington said. "It obeys federal document classification edicts and follows the restrictions imposed by donors of papers. [We] cannot serve as the Court's watchdog."

The Librarian's view of the future of libraries everywhere could be dour. He warned in 1994 of a protracted collapse of such institutions of knowledge brought about by a combination of neglect, vandalism, and censorship. "Our modern Alexandria," Billington told the Century Association in New York, referring to the library of ancient Egypt that was consumed by flames, "—the Library of Congress, the largest and most diverse collection of human knowledge and creativity ever assembled on this planet, with 104 million items and all its infinite potential for human use—is in fact burning."

Seventy thousand books in the Library were still becoming embrittled every year. "And almost every other medium in our immense copyright deposit record of American creativity comes to us in highly perishable forms: film, videotape, recorded sound. In addition to the slow fires by which the records of our throw-away society are being consumed, there are the growing threats of selective torching by both vandalism and censorship." Theft and defacing of books had led to the recent closing of the stacks at the Library, a highly controversial move.

"The historic support and protection of a pluralistic and democratic Congress have made the Library of Congress less susceptible than most institutions to the pressures for selective censorship which are again growing in the nation. Of course," he went on, "by far the biggest threat to the future of the Library of Congress lies in our version of the budget crisis which affects all libraries."

Mandated but unfunded pay raises had cut into available resources of the Library, which had fewer employees than it had had fifteen years before, and greatly expanded duties. There were now twenty-two reading rooms, services provided to 750,000 homes of the blind around the country, and a cataloging service that saved the nation's libraries about $350 million annually. And efforts were under way to electronically make available to the world what Billington called "the American creative spirit." He wanted to "entice more people into gratification of their curiosity. The Library should be part of the whole life of the country."

Those physical monuments housing so much of the Library and its history, the Jefferson and Adams Buildings, were being renovated. Eight hundred workers were to be relocated over the next two years, and plans were afoot for celebrating the 100th anniversary of the Jefferson Building in 1997 and the Library's Bicentennial in 2000.

Some forty million computerized records of books, legislation, and copyright deposits became accessible electronically, a milestone. Billington saw the electronic revolution as both a problem and an opportunity. The Library of Congress was the living body and testament to democracy, Billington thought, and it was the duty of those who worked there to get more of its contents out to the people.

This was easier said than done. One major problem had been the expense of equipment required to receive much of the bounty residing in the various collections, but the price of personal computers was falling, and with it barriers to a wider dissemination of knowledge by way of the Internet.

The Library's nascent National Digital Library was created at a cost of $60 million to digitalize five million items from the American history collections: unpublished literature, maps, periodicals, films, television programs, photographs, cartoons, posters, and sheet music. "The library was riding the crest of two waves," as Billington said later. Digitalization "made it possible for people to search across the collections, and it made a more effective teaching device."

The $15 million pledged by Congress to help meet the cost had to be supplemented by $45 million raised by the Librarian among private individuals and organizations, with the help of the Madison Council. John Kluge donated $5 million and the David and Lucile Packard Foundation pledged another $5 million to launch the National Digital Library, and by 1998 the full amount of private funding was raised.

Joining many American Memory materials that went on-line were thousands of other items, including items from the Library's special exhibitions on the Vatican Library and the Dead Sea Scrolls. Glimpses of American life in the 1930s were provided by digitized documents from the Federal Writers' Project. The Library's Global Legal Information Network provided an electronic database of the laws of the United States and fourteen other countries.

Curators throughout the Library labored to get their most important and interesting materials on-line. In the Manuscript Division, selections from those collections used most often were digitized: the papers of Presidents Washington, Jefferson, Madison, Monroe, Jackson, Van Buren, Lincoln, Grant, Theodore Roosevelt, and Wilson.

The on-line version of the *Congressional Record* that included the text of all recent congressional bills was launched in 1995. It was called "THOMAS," after the third president of the United States, who had contributed so much to the Library in its early years. It was Thomas Jefferson who had stated, two centuries before, that nothing lay outside the potential interest of a member of Congress.

At the end of the fiscal year, the Library was recording about twenty million electronic transactions a month, half of them on the Internet. Electronics had

proved to be more of an opportunity than a problem; in the future, the Librarian felt, it could well represent salvation. "The Library exemplifies the country's diversity. The inherent tensions in a highly pluralistic society mean that a country can break apart, but the pursuit of truth keeps us from the pursuit of one another."

In a modern society there were physical limits on freedom, "but not on the intellect. By going out more broadly and in more deeply, we have more opportunities to ameliorate the human condition."

Despite the general budgetary restraints experienced by most government institutions at the time, acquisitions continued at the Library, many of them bequeathed. Among those were the Charles and Ray Eames collection of design and the Leonard Bernstein archives. The Library's book collection reached the twenty-two million mark; the book shelves, if laid end-to-end, would now have stretched from Washington, D.C., to Chicago.

Among the growing number of special collections that have been digitized and stored in electronic format, in whole or in part—and thereby made accessible to researchers unable to visit the Library in person—is the Leonard Bernstein collection housed in the Music Division. A prodigiously gifted conductor, composer, and teacher, Bernstein (1918–1990) used the power of television to communicate the joy of music to vast audiences. "So it seems entirely in keeping with Bernstein's generosity of spirit," Jamie Bernstein Thomas noted in a message on the Bernstein Web site, "to make materials from his archives available to the greatest number of people—which is the essential purpose of the National Digital Library Program." Bernstein was photographed by Victor Kraft in September 1947 working in his apartment at 32 West Tenth Street, New York, New York.

Music Division, Library of Congress.

Billington had raised the electronic threshold at the Library and insisted upon incorporating the latest technological advances, but his favorite items in the Library were thoroughly traditional. These did not include some of the more commonly recognized treasures, such as the seventh-century Buddhist sutra, or the oldest printed artifact, the Gutenberg Bible, or Abraham Lincoln's handwritten drafts of the Gettysburg Address. Nor did they include unusual copyright deposits such as the first Barbie doll.

His favorites were the Bay Psalm Book, which was in his opinion a celebration of the root values of America, and the draft of the Declaration of Independence that bore the markings and corrections of the drafters, an indication that ordinary men could achieve extraordinary things. The Rosenwald Collection of rare books from the fifteenth through the twentieth century was prized, but so was the proof of Walt Whitman's poem "O Captain! My Captain!," the Farm Security Administration archives showing a lost way of American life, and the Sergei Mikhailovich Prokudin-Gorskii collection of photographs of Imperial Russia.

These examples of the work of one of the first Russians to experiment with color photography had been acquired by the Library in 1948. Prokudin-Gorskii traveled with a railroad car dark room provided by Czar Nicholas II in the early years of the twentieth century and photographed a broad array of aspects of Russian culture: art works, architecture, industrial and agricultural sites, and the daily life of Russians. At the outset of the Russian Revolution, Prokudin-Gorskii escaped to Paris with nineteen hundred glass plate negatives.

The Library gradually became aware of all that it had in other collections relating to that country, including law and music. Among the discoveries made was that of a child's picture book from which Czar Nicholas II read to his children shortly before he and his family were executed in 1917.

A new and substantial archive was created on the Soviet period, including papers from various ambassadors. Billington himself was in Russia during the collapse of the Soviet regime and was able to negotiate a loan of five hundred documents from secret Soviet files for a special exhibit at the Library of Congress. The Library also established a representative in Moscow to collect ephemera including political broadsides, manifestos, brochures, and other relevant material to bring back to Washington.

Billington generally praised the dedicated people at the Library of Congress in charge of various aspects of the Library's infinite storehouse of knowledge and objects relating to its acquisition. He praised what he called "the loving curator in whose hands dead material comes alive."

In 1999, sixty-eight American history collections designated for the Library's Web site had been put on-line. Digital files that were already available either on-line or in the digital archives totaled just under 2.5 million, and almost that number were in production. Twelve Library exhibits —among them *Oliphant's Anthem: Pat Oliphant at the Library of Congress*, a sampling of the artist's editorial cartoons, and *Sigmund Freud: Conflict and Culture*—were accessible electronically, and the Library was averaging twenty million electronic transactions every month.

The arrearages that Billington had addressed at the outset of his tenure had been reduced by almost 50 percent, to twenty million. Plans were under way to develop a storage facility for Library books at Fort Meade, Maryland, and a new national audio-visual conservation center near Culpeper, Virginia, at a property purchased for the Library by the David and Lucile Packard Foundation. New collections continued to grace the Library. Among these was per-

The deep unrest which, exacerbated by the trials of World War I, led to the fall of Russia's Romanov dynasty was suggested in the poster *1905 Workers' Revolution*, published in 1918 to illustrate the confrontation between workers and soldiers that had occurred on January 22, 1905. Nicholas II was forced by the growing wave of strikes and demonstrations and demand for political reform and social change to sign the October Manifesto of 1905. The manifesto promised such reforms as the establishment of a *duma*, or legislature, elected by the people.

Poster by A. Bient. Russian Central Committee, St. Petersburg. Prints and Photographs Division, Library of Congress.

By means of this "Skippet and Document,"
Czar Alexander I (1777–1825), grandson
of Catherine the Great, granted certain
rights to the recipient. Though Alexander
began his reign with ideas for sweeping
reforms and encouraged education and
science, he became increasingly reactionary
as time went on.

Law Library, Library of Congress.

haps the largest private assembly of Americana—ten thousand manuscripts,
rare books, prints, and documents—which had belonged to Marian S. Carson.
The Library also acquired the papers of the architect of the East Wing of the
National Gallery of Art, I. M. Pei; eight thousand films and videotapes from
the Public Broadcasting System; and the Morton Gould collection of twenty
thousand musical scores and personal papers.

The decade of renovation came to an end the following year, when the
Thomas Jefferson Building was formally reopened to the public on May 1,
1997. A stellar collection of political figures and dignitaries gathered to celebrate: President Bill Clinton, Speaker of the House Newt Gingrich of Georgia, Senate Minority Leader Thomas Daschle of South Dakota, Chief Justice
William H. Rehnquist, and the chairman of the Joint Committee on the
Library, Representative William M. Thomas of California.

At this time the new permanent, rotating exhibit *American Treasures of the
Library of Congress* opened. It reflected the breadth and complexity of the
Library's collections and met the expectations of those working at the Library
itself, of Congress, and of the nation. Notable exhibitions exploring specific
aspects of American history were *To Make All Laws*, celebrating the first 200

In a coded cable dated April 23, 1961, the Soviet ambassador reported on his talks with William O. Douglas concerning relations with Cuba and quoted the Supreme Court Justice as saying that the director of the CIA, Allen Dulles, "pulled a fast one on Eisenhower with the U-2 flight and now nudged Kennedy into this risky step with Cuba." This photograph from Soviet archives showed weapons captured when Cuban exiles made an aborted attempt to wrest control of the country from Premier Fidel Castro by invading the Bay of Pigs from the United States in April 1961, a prelude to the "Cuban Missile Crisis" that threatened nuclear war in 1962. The photograph itself was one of many documents from Soviet archives that came to the Library in 1992, after an August 1991 coup failed to restore authoritarian rule in the USSR and the Communist Party was dissolved. Russian archivists were determined to preserve the historical record and open to the view of scholars and the public the inner workings of the world's longest-lived totalitarian state.

From *Revelations from the Russian Archives* (Library of Congress, 1997). European Division, Library of Congress.

"Frontiers of the Mind in the Twenty-first Century" was the theme of a symposium that brought together fifty scholars to discuss achievements of the past century and speculate about developments in the next. Experts in fields from cosmology to the behavioral sciences gathered at the Library on June 15–17, 1999. Mary Douglas, a scholar in cultural analysis, talked with James Billington and her husband, James Douglas (*left*). Douglas, whose books range from *Purity and Danger: An Analysis of Concepts of Pollution and Taboo* to *Leviticus as Literature*, commented about "canons"—in religious belief, in literature, in science—and about how they help mediate the ongoing tension between control and growth. The past, she remarked, is always being refurbished.

Public Affairs Office, Library of Congress.

years of the Congress of the United States, *The African American Odyssey*, starting with the slave trade and advancing through the civil rights movement, and *Religion and the Founding of the American Republic*.

The centennial celebration of the Jefferson Building came at the end of a year that saw the acquisition of new and historically significant collections, and a single item of great symbolic importance: a 1745 edition of the works of Horace that had belonged to Thomas Jefferson. On the inside cover was Jefferson's handwriting, marking out the meter of the individual poems.

The Library's Bicentennial in the year 2000 would recognize the Library as the oldest federal cultural institution in the nation, and a fitting theme was chosen: "Libraries, Creativity, and Liberty." The goal was greater use of the Library, inspired in part by what had become its vastly increased accessibility through electronics.

James H. Billington had come to see the Library of Congress as "the memory for an inherently memory-less society" that was swiftly becoming international in character, he said in interviews conducted at the end of 1998. Many of the mediums for knowledge would self-destruct if not maintained, and in this regard the repository of cultural artifacts and tributes to the imagination at the Library was invaluable. "We are not going to have creativity unless the individual is free to roam among these many resources," he said.

Just as Herbert Putnam had taken steps to standardize cataloging at the outset of the century, Billington acted toward century's end to establish standards for quality and electronic access to Library holdings. He saw the Library's primary responsibility as that of neutral provider of information from which knowledge is derived, at no charge, so that people would be free to make up their own minds in matters small and momentous.

Billington's Library of Congress had been reshaped for the next century, with managerial adaptations, clean audits, arrearage reductions, secure stacks, excellent relations with the literary community, and universal access to its treasures. In the midst of the computer revolution, while institutions around the United States, both public and private, spoke of expanding access to knowledge in the flash of an electron, the Library of Congress was actually effecting these changes, with less money and a much smaller, dedicated staff.

On the eve of the 200th anniversary, the Librarian spoke of the "uplifting, symbolic, and psychological ambience of the Library in a culture where everything is disaggregated, everything taken apart and nothing put back together." The Library was countering that impulse by providing a haven for intercultural, interlinguistic, interdisciplinary scholarship "similar to the unifying efforts of the Renaissance and the Enlightenment. We have to keep it going for the next generation."

Renovation, Restoration, and Renewal

The newly renovated Thomas Jefferson Building binds past and future in an unbroken narrative older than the first books purchased in England by the Continental Congress in 1800, shipped aboard the frigate *The American*, and lost in the United States Capitol fire during the War of 1812.

The story goes back to the dawn of knowledge, the classical motifs celebrated in the Great Hall where the colors have been restored, dominated by the warm, lucid hue of sunlight, and continues up the grand staircases and down hallways, past heroic murals, sculpture, mosaics, and other formal artistic tributes to learning and the freedom that flowed from it.

The Main Reading Room's resplendent dome reemerged from its cocoon of scaffolding and drop cloths, French in design and Italian in ornamentation but, wrote an architectural critic for the *New York Times*, "purely American in the exuberance with which it sponges up the best of all earlier civilizations as a young and muscular country's birthright." Now "the best"—books, and more— is available in the flash of an electron in every state in the nation and around the globe.

The renovation required of Congress and the American people some $70 million, many times the cost of the building's original construction, as well as the determination of the members of the Joint Committee on the Library, and especially Senator Mark O. Hatfield of Oregon, to secure the appropriation. Within the renovated building, the opening of the Library's four area studies reading rooms—African and Middle Eastern, Asian, European, and Hispanic—makes available to scholars from all countries the intellectual resources of the earth, without qualification or restriction, an embrace of universal knowledge that would have gladdened the man for whom the building is named.

Jefferson wrote in 1823, "It is the duty of every good citizen to use all the opportunities which occur to him, for preserving documents relating to the history of our country." A tribute to his wisdom, and a physical embodiment of the nation, lies in the *American Treasures of the Library of Congress* exhibit, spread before the thousands who come to learn, a diverse, precious, highly anecdotal view of the past.

It includes the Declaration of Independence, the Gettysburg Address, and the contents of Abraham Lincoln's pockets on his last night alive, a design of the Capitol, a letter from Theodore Roosevelt to his son, comic books, Indian flute music, jazz scores—a near-infinitude of examples of the infinite, triumphant American imagination.

(left) A dramatic before-and-after contrast was evident in one of the panels in the north corridor of the Great Hall, part of the series The Family by Charles Sprague Pearce. The graceful red-headed figures carrying a scroll with an inscription from Confucius were so blackened over the years that their brilliant colors, which became vibrant again as conservators carefully cleaned each small section, had been totally obscured.

Courtesy of the Architect of the Capitol.

(above) In the course of the Jefferson Building renovation, conservators painstakingly removed grime that had accumulated over the course of a century from Robert Leftwich Dodge's mural Water in the southeast pavilion. In addition to grime, the mural had endured some crude repainting, and leaks had caused the paint to flake. The contrast between the cleaned and uncleaned areas of the painting is dramatic.

Photograph by Reid Baker. Publishing Office, Library of Congress.

The Main Reading Room of the Library of Congress, the heart of the Thomas Jefferson Building—and of the Library itself—emerged from under renovation scaffolding with the brilliance of its decoration restored and its facilities for researchers updated to accommodate personal computers. The card catalog, which had been a central feature of the Main Reading Room for many years, was removed from the room itself but placed in an area that was still accessible to readers.

Photograph copyright © by Michael Dersin.

Bibliography

Adams, William Howard. *Jefferson's Monticello*. New York: Abbeville Press, 1983.

American Treasures of the Library of Congress. New York: Harry N. Abrams, Inc., in association with the Library of Congress, 1997.

Ammon Harry. *James Monroe: The Quest for National Identity*. New York: McGraw-Hill Book Co., 1971.

Angle, Paul M. *The Library of Congress: An Account, Historical and Descriptive*. Kingsport, Tenn.: Kingsport Press, 1958.

Annual Report of the Librarian of Congress. Washington: Library of Congress, various years.

Armbruster, Carol. "The Origins of International Literary Exchanges: Alexandre Vattemare's Adventures in America." *Biblion: The Bulletin of the New York Public Library* 5, no. 2 (Spring 1997): 128–47.

Arnold, Matthew. *Civilization in the United States: First and Last Impressions of America*. 1888; reprinted, Freeport, N.Y.: Books for Libraries Press, 1972.

Ashworth, John. *"Agrarians" & "Aristocrats": Party Political Ideology in the United States, 1837–1846*. London: Royal Historical Society; Atlantic Highlands, N. J.: Humanities Press Inc., 1983.

Atwater, Maxine. *Capital Tales: True Stories about Washington's Heroes, Villains & Belles*. Bethesda, Md.: Mercury Press, 1996.

Bard, Mitchell G. "The Custodian of Knowledge." *The World & I,* March 1996: 125–31.

"The Best Librarian of Congress: American Librarians Speak Out." *Library Journal*, April 1, 1987: 23–34.

Billington, James H. "The Case for Orthodoxy." *New Republic*, May 30, 1994: 24–27.

————. "Is Alexandria Burning?" Typescript for talk before the Century Association, New York, N.Y., dated March 10, 1994.

————. "Libraries, the Library of Congress, and the Information Age." *Daedalus* 125, no. 4 (Fall 1996):35–54.

————. "The Soviet Drama: 1. Russia's Quest for Identity." *Washington Post*, January 21, 1990.

————. "The Soviet Drama: 2. Looking to the Past." *Washington Post*, January 22, 1990.

————. "Statement of James H. Billington, the Librarian of Congress, before the Subcommittee on Legislative Branch Appropriations, Committee on Appropriations, U. S. House of Representatives." February 1, 1989.

———. "Statement of James H. Billington, the Librarian of Congress, before the Subcommittee on Legislative Branch Appropriations, Committee on Appropriations, United States Senate." March 30, 1990.

———. "Statement of James H. Billington, the Librarian of Congress, before the Joint Committee on the Library." October 4, 1988.

———. "Statement of James H. Billington, the Librarian of Congress, before the Subcommittee on Intellectual Property and Judicial Administration, House Committee on the Judiciary, 103rd Congress, First Session." March 4, 1993.

———. "Statement of James H. Billington, the Librarian of Congress, Concerning the Papers of Associate Justice Thurgood Marshall." May 26, 1993.

———. "Statement of James H. Billington, Librarian of Congress, Joint Congressional Hearing on Library and Information Services." July 11, 1991.

———. "Statement of James H. Billington, the Librarian of Congress, on S. 373, the Copyright Reform Act of 1993 before the Subcommittee on Patents, Copyrights, and Trademarks, Senate Committee on the Judiciary, 103rd Congress, 1st Session." October 19, 1993.

———. "Statement of James H. Billington, Librarian of Congress, Subcommittee on Intellectual Property and Judicial Admnistration, Committee on the Judiciary, U.S. House of Representatives." June 12, 1991.

Booraem, Hendrik V. *The Road to Respectability: James A. Garfield and His World, 1844–1852.* Lewisburg, Pa.: Bucknell University Press, 1988.

Boorstin, Daniel J. *Gresham's Law: Knowledge or Information?* Washington: Library of Congress, 1980.

———. "Libraries Are Needed to Keep Civilization in Perspective." *Phoenix Gazette,* December 10, 1979.

———. "A Nation of Readers?" *New York Times,* June 6, 1982.

———. "Poor Pay by the U.S." *New York Times,* October 27, 1981.

———. "Remarks at the Opening of the James Madison Memorial Building of the Library of Congress." Typescript dated April 24, 1980.

———. *The Republic of Letters: Librarian of Congress Daniel J. Boorstin on Books, Reading, and Libraries, 1975–1987.* Edited by John Y. Cole. Washington: Library of Congress, 1989.

———. "Statement of Daniel J. Boorstin, the Librarian of Congress, before Subcommittee on Public Buildings, Committee on Public Works and Transportation." May 8, 1984.

———. "Statement of the Librarian of Congress before the Subcommittee on Education, Arts, and Humanities, Committee on Labor and Human Resources, United States Senate," April 3, 1987.

"Boorstin as LC Librarian: Opposition Mounts." *Library Journal,* July 1975: 1,267.

Borome, Joseph A. *Charles Coffin Jewett.* Chicago: American Library Association, 1951.

Bremer, Howard F., ed. *John Adams, 1735–1826: Chronology—Documents—Bibliographical Aids.* Dobbs Ferry, N.Y.: Oceana Publications, Inc., 1967.

Brooks, David. "A Return to National Greatness: A Manifesto for a Lost Creed." *Weekly Standard,* March 3, 1997:16–21.

Carney, Eliza Newlin. "Billington's Book Wars." *National Journal,* March 21, 1992: 695–98.

Cannon, Howard W. "Opening Statement by Senator Howard W. Cannon (D-Nev.), Chairman, Committee on Rules and Administration, at Hearings on Nomination of Dr. Daniel J. Boorstin to Be Librarian of Congress." September 10, 1975.

Cole, John Y. "Ainsworth Spofford and the 'National Library.'" Ph.D. diss., George Washington University, 1971.

————. "The Center for the Book in the Library of Congress." *Quarterly Journal of the Library of Congress*, Spring 1979: 179–88.

————. "Cross-Currents: BL and LC in Historical Perspective." *Library Review*, Winter 1983: 247–58.

————. *For Congress and the Nation: A Chronological History of the Library of Congress*. Washington: Library of Congress, 1979.

————. "The International Role of the Library of Congress: A Brief History." *Alexandria* 1, no. 3 (1989): 43–51.

————. *Jefferson's Legacy: A Brief History of the Library of Congress*. Washington: Library of Congress, 1993.

————. "The Library of Congress in the Nineteenth Century: An Informal Account." *Journal of Library History* 9, no. 3 (July 1974): 222–40.

————. "A National Monument for a National Library: Ainsworth Rand Spofford and the New Library of Congress, 1871–1897." In *Records of the Columbia Historical Society of Washington, D.C. 1971–1972*, ed. Frances Coleman Rosenberger, 468–507. Washington: Columbia Historical Society, 1973.

————. "Promoting Books, Reading & Libraries: The Center for the Book in the Library of Congress, 1977–1997." Typescript dated 1998.

————. "Storehouses and Workshops: American Libraries and the Uses of Knowledge." In *The Organization of Knowledge in Modern America, 1860–1920*, ed. Alexandra Oleson and John Voss. Baltimore and London: The Johns Hopkins University Press, 1979.

————. "Studying the Library of Congress: Resources and Research Opportunities." *Libraries & Culture* 24, no. 3 (Summer 1989):357–66.

————, ed. *The Library of Congress in Perspective: A Volume Based on the Reports of the 1976 Librarian's Task Force and Advisory Groups*. New York: R. R. Bowker Co, 1978.

————, and Henry Hope Reed, eds. *The Library of Congress: The Art and Architecture of the Thomas Jefferson Building*. New York: W. W. Norton Company in association with the Library of Congress, 1997.

Collins, Kathleen. *Washingtoniana: Photographs; Collections in the Prints and Photographs Division of the Library of Congress*. Washington: Library of Congress, 1989.

Combs, Jerald A. *The Jay Treaty: Political Battleground of the Founding Fathers*. Berkeley: University of California Press, 1970.

Copyright in the Library of Congress: 125th Anniversary. Washington: Library of Congress 1995.

Curtis, James C. *Andrew Jackson and the Search for Vindication*. Boston and Toronto: Little, Brown and Co., 1970.

Dain, Phyllis, and John Y. Cole, eds. *Libraries and Scholarly Communication in the United States: The Historical Dimension*. Westport, Conn.: Greenwood Press, 1990.

Davis, Donald G., Jr. *Libraries & Culture. Proceedings of Library History Seminar VI, 19–22 March 1980*. Austin: University of Texas Press, 1981.

Davison, Kenneth E. *The Presidency of Rutherford B. Hayes.* Westport, Conn.:
    Greenwood Press, Inc., 1972.

Donald, David Herbert. *Lincoln.* New York: Simon & Schuster, 1995.

Donaldson, Scott, in collaboration with R. H. Winnick. *Archibald MacLeish: An American
    Life.* Boston: Houghton Mifflin Co., 1992.

Donohoe, Cathryn. "Librarian of Congress Turns a New Leaf." *Washington Times,*
    March 13, 1990.

Donohoe, Cathryn. "Daniel Boorstin Takes on Creation." *ASN* 23 (January 1991).

"Dr. Boorstin's Handicap." *Washington Star,* July 8, 1975: editorial.

Eaton, Margaret L. *The Autobiography of Peggy Eaton.* New York: Charles Scribner's
    Sons, 1932.

Falk, Signi Lenea. *Archibald MacLeish.* New York: Twayne Publishers, Inc., 1965.

Farney, Dennis. "Man of Ideas Daniel Boorstin Finds Joy, Problems Heading Library
    of Congress." *Wall Street Journal,* November 9, 1984.

Fineberg, Gail. "Cook Case Ruling Prompts Revision of Hiring Process." *Gazette*
    (Library of Congress), October 2, 1992.

———. "LC Celebrates Jefferson Centenary." *Gazette* (Library of Congress), April
    25, 1997.

Furer, Howard B., ed. *James A. Garfield, 1831–1881; Chester A. Arthur, 1830–1886:
    Chronology, Documents, Bibliographical Aids.* Dobbs Ferry, N.Y.: Oceana Publications,
    Inc., 1970.

Gamarekian, Barbara. "Library of Congress: Pondering the Open Doors." *New York
    Times,* January 31, 1987.

Gates, Jean Key. *Introduction to Librarianship.* 3rd edition. New York: Neal-Schuman
    Publishers, 1990.

Geer, Emily Apt. *First Lady: The Life of Lucy Webb Hayes.* Freemont, Ohio: Kent State
    University Press and the Rutherford B. Hayes Presidential Center, 1984.

Gildea, William. "Boorstin: Clearing Committee." *Washington Post,* September 17, 1975.

Goff, Frederick R. "Peter Force." *Papers of the Bibliographical Society of America* 44
    (1950):1–16.

Goode, Stephen. "Scholar and Bibliophile Reigns at the World's Greatest Library."
    Insight, January 6–13, 1997: 19–20.

Goodrum, Charles A. *Treasures of the Library of Congress.* New York: Harry N. Abrams,
    Inc., Publishers, 1991.

Hardin, James. "Folklife and Memory in Russia: An Interview with James H. Billington."
    Folklife Center News, Summer 1988.

Harper, Robert A., and Frank O. Ahnert. *Introduction to Metropolitan Washington.*
    Washington: Association of American Geographers, 1968.

Herbert Putnam, 1861–1955: A Memorial Tribute. Washington: Library of Congress, 1956.

Highsmith, Carol, and Ted Landphair. *The Library of Congress: America's Memory.* Golden,
    Colo.: Fulcrum Publishing, 1994.

Hoobler, Dorothy, and Thomas Hoobler. *Photographing History: The Career of Mathew
    Brady.* New York: G.P. Putnam's Sons, 1977.

Hunt, John Gabriel, ed. *The Essential Abraham Lincoln.* New York: Gramercy Books,
    1993.

————, ed. *The Essential Franklin Delano Roosevelt*. New York: Gramercy Books, 1995.

Jackson, Donald, ed. *Letters of the Lewis and Clark Expedition with Related Documents, 1783–1854*. 2nd edition. Volume 1. Urbana, Chicago, and London: University of Illinois Press, 1978.

Johnston, William Dawson. *History of the Library of Congress*. Volume 1, *1800–1864*. Washington: Government Printing Office, 1904.

Kaminsky, Peter. "The Nation's Library Goes Online." *Princeton Alumni Weekly*, December 20, 1995.

Komroff, Manuel. *Photographing History: Mathew Brady*. Chicago: Britannica Books, 1962.

Langdon, Dolly. "Daniel Boorstin." *People*, April 19, 1982.

Leech, Margaret, and Harry J. Brown. *The Garfield Orbit*. New York: Harper & Row, Publishers, 1978.

"Librarian of Congress." *New York Times*, July 22, 1975: editorial.

"The Librarian of Congress." *The New Yorker*, January 5, 1981:23–26.

"Librarian of Congress Selection." *Information Times* 1, no. 2 (Summer 1975).

Librarians of Congress, 1802–1974. Washington: Library of Congress, 1977.

Library of Congress Acquisitions: Manuscript Division, 1994–1995. Washington: Library of Congress, 1997.

Library of Congress Acquisitions: Rare Book and Special Collections Division, 1981–1982. Washington: Library of Congress, 1984.

McLaughlin, Jack. *Jefferson and Monticello: The Biography of a Builder*. New York: Henry Holt and Co., 1988.

MacLean, John N. "Librarian for the People." *Reader's Digest*. March 1997.

MacLeish, Archibald. *The American Story*. 2nd edition. New York: Duell, Sloan and Pearce, 1960.

————. *A Continuing Journey*. Boston: Houghton Mifflin Co., 1968.

————. *Conquistador*. Boston and New York: Houghton Mifflin Co., 1932.

————. *A Time to Speak*. Boston: Houghton Mifflin Co., 1941.

MacLeish, William H. "Remembering Archie." *Civilization*, November/December 1995:44–49.

Mearns, David C. *Lincoln Collections in the Library of Congress*. Washington: Library of Congress, 1942.

————. *The Story Up to Now: The Library of Congress, 1800–1946*. Washington: Library of Congress, 1947.

Meredith, Roy. *Mathew Brady's Portrait of an Era*. New York: W. W. Norton & Co., 1982.

Morgan, Robert J. *A Whig Embattled: The Presidency under John Tyler*. Lincoln: University of Nebraska Press, 1954.

"Nation's Library: Growing Pains." *U.S. News & World Report*, July 28, 1975.

Norris, James D., and Arthur H. Shaffer. *Politics and Patronage in the Gilded Age: The Correspondence of James A. Garfield and Charles E. Henry*. Madison: State Historical Society of Wisconsin, 1970.

Perry, George E. "Second Statement of President George E. Perry, Ethnic Employees of the Library of Congress (EELC), in Opposition to the Confirmation of Dr. Daniel J. Boorstin to be Librarian of Congress." Typescript dated September 6, 1975.

Peterson, Merrill D., ed. *Thomas Jefferson: A Reference Biography*. New York: Charles Scribner's Sons, 1986.

Polley, Robert L., ed. *The Truman Years: The Words and Times of Harry S. Truman.* Waukesha, Wisc.: Country Beautiful, 1976.

Poole, Susan D. *Chester A. Arthur: The President Who Reformed.* Reseda, Calif.: M. Bloomfield & Co, 1977.

Profiles of the Time of James Monroe, 1758–1958. Washington: Smithsonian Institution, 1959.

Randall, Henry S. *The Life of Thomas Jefferson.* Vol. 1. 1857; reprint, Freeport, N.Y.: Books for Libraries Press, 1970. Vols. 2 and 3. 1858; New York: Da Capo Press, 1972.

Randall, Willard Sterne. *Thomas Jefferson: A Life.* New York: Henry Holt and Co., 1993.

———. "Thomas Jefferson Takes a Vacation." *American Heritage,* July/August 1996: 74–85.

Raspberry, William. "Dr. Boorstin, the Library, and Affirmative Action." *Washington Post,* July 7, 1975.

Reed, J. C. "The Historical Library of Peter Force." Typescript, Rare Book and Special Collections Division.

Rider, Fremont. *Melvil Dewey.* Chicago: American Library Association, 1944.

Robbins, Michael. "'The Cosmic Significance of Trivia' and Other Concerns of Daniel Boorstin, the Nixon Administration's Resident Intellectual." *Potomac* magazine, *Washington Post,* August 12, 1973:12–14, 27–29.

Rovere, Richard H. *The American Establishment and Other Reports, Opinions, and Speculations.* New York: Harcourt, Brace & World, Inc., 1962.

Russell, Greg. *John Quincy Adams and the Public Virtues of Diplomacy.* Columbia and London: University of Missouri Press, 1995.

Rutland, Robert Allen. *The Presidency of James Madison.* Lawrence: University Press of Kansas, 1990.

Saeger, Robert II. *And Tyler Too: A Biography of John & Julia Gardiner Tyler.* New York: McGraw-Hill Book Co., Inc., 1963.

Sanford, Charles B. *Thomas Jefferson and His Library: A Study of His Literary Interests and of the Religious Attitudes Revealed by Relevant Titles in His Library.* Hamden, Conn.: Archon Books, 1977.

Sanoff, Alvin P. "'Universities Have Fallen Down on the Job' of Teaching Values: A Conversation with James Billington." *U.S. News & World Report,* October 1, 1984: 69–70.

Schrage, Michael. "Visions of Tomorrow's Libraries: Computerized Networks to Spread the Word." *Washington Post,* April 27, 1990: F3.

Schwartz, Lloyd. "Fortress of Knowledge." *Stamp Collector,* April 19, 1982.

Searcher, Victor. *Lincoln Today: An Introduction to Modern Lincolniana.* New York: Thomas Yoseloff, 1969.

Sefton, James E. *Andrew Johnson and the Uses of Constitutional Power.* Edited by Oscar Handlin. Boston: Little, Brown and Co., 1980.

Shields, Gerald R. "LJ: Viewpoint—Sorry to Bother You, Senator." *Library Journal,* August 1975.

Simpson, Brooks D. *Let Us Have Peace: Ulysses S. Grant and the Politics of War and Reconstruction, 1861–1868.* Chapel Hill and London: The University of North Carolina Press, 1991.

Sioussat, St. George Lakin. "Herbert Putnam (1861–1955)." Reprinted from *Year Book of the American Philosophical Society.* 1955.

Small, Herbert. *The Library of Congress: Its Architecture and Decoration*. Edited by Henry Hope Reed. New York: Norton, 1982.

Smith, Howard K. *Washington D.C.: The Story of Our Nation's Capital*. New York: Random House, 1967.

Socolofsky, Homer E., and Allan B. Spetter. *The Presidency of Benjamin Harrison*. Lawrence: University Press of Kansas, 1987.

Special Collections in the Library of Congress, a Selective Guide. Compiled by Annette Melville. Washington: Library of Congress, 1980.

Stein, Susan R. *The Worlds of Thomas Jefferson at Monticello*. New York: Harry N. Abrams, Inc., Publishers, 1993.

Stone, Elizabeth W. *American Library Development, 1600–1899*. New York: The H. W. Wilson Co., 1977.

Sung, Carolyn Hoover. "Peter Force: Washington Printer and Creator of the American Archives." Ph.D. diss., George Washington University, 1985.

Thomas, Bill. "King of the Stacks." *Los Angeles Times Magazine*, November 15, 1992.

Trollope, Anthony. *North America*. 2 vols. New York: St. Martin's Press, 1986.

Van Dyne, Larry. "Daniel Boorstin Remembers." *Washingtonian,* June 1982.

Virga, Vincent, and curators of the Library of Congress. *Eyes of the Nation: A Visual History of the United States.* New York: Alfred A. Knopf, 1997.

Wagenknecht, Edward, ed. *Abraham Lincoln, His Life, Work, and Character*. New York: Creative Age Press, 1947.

Washington, D.C.: A Smithsonian Book of the Nation's Capital. Washington: Smithsonian Books, 1992.

Wedgeworth, Robert, and Barbara Ringer. "The Library of Congress Advisory Committee on Copyright Registration and Deposit (ACCORD), Report of the Co-Chairs." Typescript dated September 1993.

Weeks, Linton. "Brave New Library." *Washington Post Magazine*. May 26, 1991.

———. "In a Stack of Troubles." *Washington Post*, December 27, 1995.

Welch, Richard E., Jr. *The Presidencies of Grover Cleveland*. Lawrence: University Press of Kansas, 1988.

Wiegand, Wayne A. *Irrepressible Reformer: A Biography of Melvil Dewey*. Chicago and London: American Library Association, 1996.

———, and Donald G. Davis, Jr. *Encyclopedia of Library History*. New York: Garland Publishing, Inc., 1994.

Wills, Garry. "Memories and Macaroni." *Civilization*, April / May 1997.

Winkler, Karen J. "Library of Congress Improves Services to Researchers." *Chronicle of Higher Education*, February 19, 1980: 7–8.

Index